CREATING SELVES

Dedicated to my mum
... and our network

Creating Selves
Intellectual Property and the Narration of Culture

JOHANNA GIBSON
Queen Mary, University of London, UK

ASHGATE

Published by
Ashgate Publishing Limited
Gower House
Croft Road
Aldershot
Hampshire GU11 3HR
England

Ashgate Publishing Company
Suite 420
101 Cherry Street
Burlington, VT 05401-4405
USA

Ashgate website: http://www.ashgate.com

British Library Cataloguing in Publication Data
Gibson, Johanna
Creating selves : intellectual property and the narration of culture. - (Globalization and law)
1. Intellectual property 2. Culture and globalization
I. Title
346'.048

Library of Congress Cataloging-in-Publication Data
Gibson, Johanna.
Creating selves : intellectual property and the narration of culture / by Johanna Gibson.
p. cm. -- (Globalization and law)
Includes index.
ISBN-13: 978-0-7546-4707-2 1. Intellectual property--Social aspects.
2. Creative ability. I. Title.

K1401.G535 2006
346.04'8--dc22

2006025031

ISBN 978-0-7546-4707-2

Printed and bound in Great Britain by MPG Books Ltd, Bodmin, Cornwall.

Contents

Acknowledgements

When setting out to write this book, the importance of my own network became very clear.

My friends and colleagues at Queen Mary University of London must be sincerely thanked, especially Janet Dine and Michael Blakeney, who have both shown me tremendous support and belief throughout my work. Spyros Maniatis, Adrian Sterling, Uma Suthersanen, and Graham Dutfield must also be thanked – valuable colleagues, generous both with their time and enthusiasm. Malcolm Langley, our intellectual property librarian, always ensures that whatever we are searching for he will find whenever possible. Malcolm's expertise and dedication to our intellectual property library has achieved one of the most outstanding international collections. Swee Ng, Charlotte Knights, and Sharon Watson deserve special appreciation for ensuring that the mammoth task of administering so many disorganised academics looks especially easy. And a special thanks to Guido Westkamp for his translations and discussions of German copyright law. I would like to say that any errors in the final interpretation of the German law would be purely my own, but why miss an opportunity? But Guido is indeed an incredible colleague and treasured friend.

I would also like to acknowledge Fiona Macmillan, Birkbeck College, University of London, who inspires and motivates and has an amazing capacity to render clear some of the most complicated philosophical, legal, and indeed "social" points. And I would like to thank Fiona for her creation of another significant network, that of the AHRC Birkbeck Copyright Network, an important interdisciplinary group through which I have discussed and debated many of the ideas in the progress towards this book. I am especially indebted to two indispensable members of my own network – to Sean Smith of Bristol University, for the many discussions of network theory and the sociology of networks; and to Andrés Guadamuz, University of Edinburgh, for his support and for his insight into many of the issues leading to this book. To Phillip Johnson, of the Department of Trade and Industry, I owe a special debt of thanks. He has been tireless in his enthusiasm for considering drafts and discussing and clarifying amendments in the law, in the process demonstrating a vast and proficient "inside" knowledge of the developments of the law and policy in the United Kingdom and Europe, as well as internationally. For his support, his patience, his generosity, and his expertise, I believe this book is a much richer product and was certainly a much more enjoyable experience.

I would also like to make some kind of tribute, other than the book itself, to the incredible networks beyond this text and beyond the network engaged in its writing – that of the civil society actors who have mobilised interest in intellectual property in ways that are perhaps without historical precedent. In particular, there are some very special "nodes" that have motivated my connections within this network and generated in myself and others a proliferation of ideas.

Again, I am grateful to Ashgate Publishing, especially Alison Kirk, for her enthusiasm for the project and her ongoing support throughout the process, Donna Hamer, for her tremendous efficiency and good humour, and Gemma Lowle, whose support in preparing the final product was invaluable, particularly her patience with additional footnotes of further recent developments where it was possible to include these at the last minute.

Finally, I necessarily confess that I will always be in debt (and, as always, in more ways than one!) to my mum Dawn and to my brother John. And once more, thanks to Roman the Cat, who yet again oversaw the writing process from a privileged perspective – her basket.

Johanna Gibson
London, May 2006

Introduction

> If one is to talk about individual will, then it is precisely in polyphony that a combination of several individual wills takes place, that the boundaries of the individual will can be in principle exceeded. One could put it this way: the artistic will of polyphony is a will to combine many wills, a will to the event.[1]

Why is creativity so important? Why has creativity come to mean so much to the current debates in intellectual property?

At the present time, intellectual property laws[2] and their application are the subject matter of intense and diverse international attention – in particular, the question of access to the basic tools of knowledge and learning has been mobilised among an international network of civil society organisations, academics, scientists, and other users. Indeed, the understanding of the creative process, together with concerns over access to the means for the creative process, and the products and knowledge derived from or attributed to that process, are the key concerns in today's intense intergovernmental debate, domestic government scrutiny, and (what is possibly unprecedented) public attention. Not only are there significant developments at the level of domestic and international laws, realised in the form of trends towards stronger protection for intellectual property, recognition of new subject matter for protection, and the international harmonisation of that protection, but also there is intense public interest in the concepts of creativity, of authorship, of personality, and of knowledge. Therefore, it is timely to examine these starting-points of the debates themselves, and to understand the dynamics of these exchanges with a view to a certain insight into policy and law-making in the institution of modern intellectual property.

In January 2006, the United Nations (UN) Committee on Economic, Social and Cultural Rights released a General Comment,[3] following the production of a

---

1 Bakhtin MM (1984) *Problems of Dostoevsky's Poetics*, Emerson C (ed and trans), Booth WC (intro), Minneapolis, U of Minnesota P: 21.

2 The laws of intellectual property deal with a vast array of subject matter. In addition to the major categories of copyright, patents, and trade marks, there are intellectual property rights or quasi-intellectual property rights recognised for designs, trade secrets, plant varieties, plant breeders, databases, publicity, utility models, semi-conductors, geographical indications, appellations of origin, publication, performances, recording contracts, and other related rights, broadcasts and webcasts (discussed in Chapter 3).

3 Economic and Social Council. Committee on Economic, Social and Cultural Rights. 35th Session. Geneva, 7-25 November 2005. General Comment No 17 (2005). 12 January 2006. E/C.12/GC/17.

Statement[4] on Human Rights and Intellectual Property by the Committee in 2001, concerning Article 15.1(c) of the International Covenant on Economic, Social and Cultural Rights (ICESCR).[5] Article 15 reads as follows:

> 1. The States Parties to the present Covenant recognize the right of everyone:
> (a) To take part in cultural life;
> (b) To enjoy the benefits of scientific progress and its applications;
> (c) To benefit from the protection of the moral and material interests resulting from any scientific, literary or artistic production of which he is the author.
> 2. The steps to be taken by the States Parties to the present Covenant to achieve the full realization of this right shall include those necessary for the conservation, the development and the diffusion of science and culture.
> 3. The States Parties to the present Covenant undertake to respect the freedom indispensable for scientific research and creative activity.
> 4. The States Parties to the present Covenant recognize the benefits to be derived from the encouragement and development of international contacts and co-operation in the scientific and cultural fields.

Thus, it can be seen that sub-paragraph (c) identifies the benefit (of creators) within the context of diffusion (para 2), freedom of research and creative activity (para 3) and the encouragement of international collaboration in scientific and cultural fields (para 4). The 2001 Statement commences with the recognition of what it identifies as the three key aspects of intellectual property in a knowledge economy – creation, ownership, and control – and the way these three aspects interact with human rights, positively or negatively. At this time, the Committee resolved to prepare and adopt a General Comment on the relationship between human rights and intellectual property, which was completed and adopted at the end of 2005, and published in January 2006. The General Comment identifies, as a human right, not the time-limited right of intellectual property, but rather the right to access systems that encourage creativity (of which intellectual property may be one). It establishes that it is the encouragement of creativity that is the concern of the ICESCR, and as such, the right to *access* the benefits and incentives would be characterised this way, but not the intellectual property system itself. This human right of the "right to benefit from the protection of the moral and material interests resulting from any scientific, literary or artistic production of which he or she is the author" and its relationship to intellectual property rights is set out in Paragraph 1 of the General Comment:

---

4 Economic and Social Council. Committee on Economic, Social and Cultural Rights. 27th Session. Geneva, 12-30 November 2001. Agenda Item 3. "Substantive Issues Arising in the Implementation of the International Covenant on Economic Social and Cultural Rights." Follow-up to the Day of General Discussion on Article 15.1(c), Monday, 26 November 2001. Human Rights and Intellectual Property. 14 December 2001. E/C.12/2001/15.

5 Adopted and opened for signature, ratification and accession by General Assembly resolution 2200A (XXI) of 16 December 1966.

> The right of everyone to benefit from the protection of the moral and material interests resulting from any scientific, literary or artistic production of which he or she is the author is a human right, which derives from the inherent dignity and worth of all persons. This fact distinguishes article 15, paragraph 1(c), and other human rights from most legal entitlements recognized in intellectual property systems. Human rights are fundamental, inalienable and universal entitlements belonging to individuals and, under certain circumstances, groups of individuals and communities. Human rights are fundamental as they are inherent to the human person as such, whereas intellectual property rights are first and foremost means by which States seek to provide incentives for inventiveness and creativity, encourage the dissemination of creative and innovative productions, as well as the development of cultural identities, and preserve the integrity of scientific, literary and artistic productions for the benefit of a society as a whole.

Although the General Comment identifies "the right to benefit" as a human right, while at the same time asserting that intellectual property rights are not human rights, the separation is not as clear in effect. As will be traced throughout the current work, this "right to benefit" is identified through the intellectual property system. Therefore, any "right to benefit" will be administered by the intellectual property system. Thus, although the General Comment establishes that intellectual property rights are not human rights, nevertheless, by the very fact that the intellectual property system has been established as the primary means by which to access this "benefit", intellectual property rights are in effect aligned with human rights. Therefore, the surrounding discourse on the intellectual property system is vested with the immutable language of international human rights: the logical fallacy of the "human right" of intellectual property, but one which advocates of stronger intellectual property rights have deployed with (illogical) success. Indeed, as a recent decision[6] of the European Court of Human Rights held, for human rights purposes, a trade mark is an item of property which is protected by Art 1, Protocol of the ECHR.[7]

Although intellectual property law is frequently declared, quite rightly, to be a "tool" rather than an end to be valued in itself,[8] this perhaps does not go far enough, for "tools are never 'mere' tools ready to be applied: they always modify the goals you had in mind".[9] It is thus necessary to interrogate the link between intellectual property, as the only system to administer such benefit, and the encouragement of creativity and cultural life. This work therefore analyses the construction of

6 *Anheuser-Busch Inc v Portugal*, European Court of Human Rights, Application number 73049/01, Decision of 11 October 2005.

7 See further the discussion in Burkhart G (2006) "Trade marks are 'possessions' – but applications are not (yet)", 1(4) *Journal of Intellectual Property Law and Practice* 240.

8 For instance, see the first principle of the Adelphi Charter on Creativity, Innovation and Intellectual Property, which describes the "laws regulating intellectual property" as means. 13 October 2005. Text available at http://www.adelphicharter.org/pdfs/adelphi_charter2.pdf. This is also the language of the Geneva Declaration on the Future of WIPO (the World Intellectual Property Organization), discussed again later in this chapter. The text is available at http://www.cptech.org/ip/wipo/futureofwipodeclaration.pdf.

9 Latour B (2005) *Reassembling the Social*, Oxford, Oxford UP: 143.

creativity within the cultural and legal institution of intellectual property, towards a reconsideration of the logic of benefit and the nature of creativity in contemporary life. In doing so, it addresses strategic responses to intellectual property, and suggests alternative models of encouraging, rewarding, and disseminating creative output, built upon a critical analysis of and approach to the debate and to the concept of creativity itself.

International intellectual property standards are harmonised according to Western constructions of industrialised/intellectual progress and activity.[10] Thus, it is important to examine, at least generally, the notion of creativity in an industrialised context and, to an extent, the way in which this departs from other concerns with creativity in other cultural and social contexts. It is this notion of "creativity", as valorised and utilised in the institution of intellectual property, that informs the debate and arguably sustains it in its diverse contexts. This is fundamentally because intellectual property systems have become the reference point (whether advocated, criticised, or otherwise) for diverse campaigns, including access to knowledge and technology, creative communities, scientific progress, education, entertainment, celebrity and press freedom, and more. Therefore, an examination of the concept must include an introduction to the relationship between creativity, its promotion, and the market for creative products in contemporary knowledge-based societies.

Indeed, what it is hoped will become clear in the following pages is the way in which intellectual property laws, as themselves a cultural institution, have attracted a certain expectation as the "solution" to creativity. But what it is also hoped will become clear is that intellectual property is necessarily one part of a much larger system, indeed network, of creativity and innovation. The apparent synonymity of intellectual property with innovation, as will be discussed, is a representation and thus a misrepresentation of not only the creative process but also creative use. How can this economic system that "creates" objects and regulates their transactions be responsible for both the ethical arbitration of creativity as well as the commercial? To look for the solution only within intellectual property is to re-affirm, somewhat uncritically, its position as the governing framework of all creative process.

These various strategic responses to the perceived restrictions imposed by intellectual property on the creative process are reaching international favour at this time, including Creative Commons[11] (to date concerned primarily with the dissemination of music and art, although the launch of Science Commons[12] attempts to extend the principles to other "technologies") and the free[13] and open source[14]

10 On the translation of laws, but not exceptions, see Coombe R (1996) "Left Out on the Information Highway", 75 *Oregon Law Review* 237 at 246.

11 http://creativecommons.org/. Creative Commons is dealt with in more detail in Chapter 4.

12 http://sciencecommons.org/.

13 http://www.gnu.org/. The Free Software Foundation (FSF) is considered further in Chapter 4. See further http://www.fsf.org/.

14 Considered further in Chapter 4.

software movements (concerned primarily with software development but being adapted in other contexts including biotechnology and medical technologies).

In September 2004, the Trans Atlantic Consumer Dialogue (TACD)[15] organised an international meeting of consumer groups, academics, and various stakeholders from around the world, leading to the drafting and launch of the Geneva Declaration on the Future of the World Intellectual Property Organization (WIPO)[16] with over 600 signatures.[17] At that same meeting, the Brazil/Argentina proposal on the WIPO Development Agenda was tabled, and subsequently adopted at the WIPO General Assembly.[18] With the production of the Geneva Declaration together with the international discussions within civil society on a Treaty on Access to Knowledge,[19] arising from the Geneva meeting discussions, the international legal and creative communities are witnessing a significant historical moment in the development of international intellectual property law. Indeed, the "Access to Knowledge" campaign can be read as somewhat networking these initiatives and being networked, as it were, throughout this text. The "Access to Knowledge" or A2K campaign[20] is an international coalition of civil society actors, academics, and other individuals, which, among other things, is specifically campaigning for the Treaty on Access to Knowledge.

This recent activity in civil society, linked primarily to the Geneva Declaration on the Future of WIPO, has been influential in driving the adoption of the Development Agenda by the WIPO General Assembly. This has in itself revealed critical tensions between developing countries, industry interests, and indeed the legitimacy of the institution of WIPO itself.[21] The issue of development has proved a significant catalyst in the present dealings, consolidating industry interests as the cardinal point of articulation for the increasingly emotive debate. Indeed, as the following chapters will trace, the way in which industry becomes constructed as both "creator" and the

---

15 The TACD is a forum of 65 consumer organisations from the United States and the European Union. More information is available at http://www.tacd.org/.

16 The text of the Geneva Declaration is available at http://www.cptech.org/ip/wipo/genevadeclaration.html.

17 A list of initial signatures is available at http://www.cptech.org/ip/wipo/signatures.html.

18 Proposal by Argentina and Brazil for the Establishment of a Development Agenda for WIPO. WIPO 31st General Assembly. 24 September 2004. WO/GA/31/12.

19 The treaty is discussed further below; the draft text (9 May 2005) is available at http://www.cptech.org/a2k/consolidatedtext-may9.pdf.

20 An archive of the discussions of this network is available at http://lists.essential.org/pipermail/a2k/.

21 For instance, see New W (2005) "Nations Clash on Future of WIPO Development Agenda", *IP-Watch*, 11 April. The legitimacy of WIPO has reached an important historical point, at the time of writing, and was considered fully at a recent international Consumer Conference organised by TACD in Brussels, 20-21 March 2006. Delegates included representatives of civil society and consumer organisations, academics, industry, and government representatives from throughout Europe, Australia, and the United States.

necessary prerequisite for creativity (through the economic support and otherwise) is related to the legitimation of commercial and economic entities as increasingly the key narrator. On the other hand, the issue of development is partitioned as a related but tangential issue. Given that "development" is at the same time the rhetorical impetus for increasing harmonisation and convergence in international intellectual property, the contradictions could not be more pronounced. Indeed, the relationships between discussions in WIPO, developments in traditional knowledge, and access to knowledge movements (including open source and free software, and the Creative Commons movement), require careful consideration.

Importantly, these strategic responses seen to be coming from civil society, together with developments in the laws themselves, make it very clear that the creativity relationship can no longer be bound by the traditional models of producer and consumer, or sender and receiver, of earlier communication studies. Significantly, the creativity complex is a diverse interplay and network of arguably uncertain categories of industry, creators, and users. It is thus a network of communication beyond the "creator" and beyond the "text". In other words, this network complicates the relationship of producer and consumer and recuperates the positive contribution of the user beyond that of mere appreciative spectator. This networking of creativity is manifest in counter-cultural appropriations of the dominant models (as in blogs and other examples of the "many-to-many"[22] model of creativity); however, intellectual property discourse continues to rely upon an obscuring of this network and a simplification of the traditional creator and user roles. Thus, the concept of "creativity" presents a critical nexus in the debate and a site for the negotiation of the obligations and responsibilities in knowledge creation and diversity.

Also at stake is the semantic territory of the term itself, "intellectual property". It has been argued of late that this unhelpfully broad term obscures the diversity of knowledge within its limits.[23] But indeed, this is the very nature of the problem itself and an ideological process with which the present discussion must engage directly. Therefore, it is necessary to interrogate "intellectual property" as a cultural institution in order to critique these very processes. Recently, Ron Marchant, the Chief Executive and Comptroller-General of the United Kingdom Patent Office, suggested that the Office was increasingly fulfilling tasks not anticipated in the current commercial model, including what he described as a more corporate delivery and awareness raising, looking at the institution of intellectual property overall, rather than individual categories.[24] This is an important example of the way

22 The many-to-many model concerns the notion of a matrix of users and information accessible by many other users. Further discussion of networks is undertaken in the following chapter.

23 Richard Stallman provides one of the most popular and influential examples of this argument, arguing that "intellectual property", when used in this way, is misleading. See Stallman R ([1996]2006) "Confusing Words and Phrases that are Worth Avoiding". http://www.gnu.org/philosophy/words-to-avoid.html#IntellectualProperty.

24 Marchant R (2005) Interview with Barbara Cookson. QMIPRI. London. 28 November.

in which the public face of government and policy-makers invokes "intellectual property" as a general system, and as somewhat coincident with a corporate model of creativity, potentially over-simplifying and ultimately evaluating that creativity against economic parameters alone.

Thus, when considering the cultural institution of intellectual property (whether speaking for, against, or about), it is strategic and necessary to identify that institution and describe and critique the operation of that institution. In other words, it is strategic to consider the process of that mystification, that "misleading" conduct, of the system itself. In view of the reliance upon the institution as, for example, in the business model of the UK Patent Office, the appropriation of "creativity" within a corporate model is readily apparent and open to debate. Fundamentally necessary to this debate is a more adequate consideration of the way in which the system of intellectual property is deployed in its institutional capacity in order to summarise models of innovation and indeed to stand in for the creative process itself, where creativity is assimilated within wholly economic and corporate models of innovation. The appropriation of the term and the underlying presumptions propelling its currency persist throughout the categories of intellectual property – not only copyright and patents, but also trade marks, designs, utility models, and so on. Paradoxically, to decimate the counter-discourse among the multiplicity of manifest categories is to risk maintaining the institutional legitimacy of "intellectual property". The categories themselves are created by the summarising and generalising principles of intellectual property and, on their own, are somewhat meaningless as descriptions of certain creative industries (or indeed the diversity within the categories themselves, such as the diverse industries incorporated within "patents"). It is these general principles which are being challenged in contemporary civil society debate and, it is hoped, in this work.

Indeed, to insist upon no use at all of the term "intellectual property" is to ignore the opportunity to engage precisely with the way in which the term has been adopted and has gained momentum as mimetic of creativity, as an unassailable synonym for creativity. And thus, it is potentially to overlook the way in which "creativity" has become a largely economic activity – with calculable risks and outputs, necessary returns, and individual gains. Worse, it risks contributing to the very culture of mystification that persists in the popular discourse on intellectual property laws.

Thus, the present work will attempt to engage with the "institution" of intellectual property as itself a generalising and myth-making system. In its grasp on "creativity" (offered both by the proponents and by civil society as both a justification for its expansion and a reason for its reform), the rhetoric surrounding the intellectual property system mythologises a simplified and uniform notion of the creative process that is being transcribed across technologies, systems, and behaviours. In other words, the discursive strategy is one in which the "creator" is mythologised, and the output simply commodified in terms of economic value (rather than any value specifically inherent to the object). Indeed, this is literally the case where it is seen that the price of the intellectual property is not necessarily constrained by the cost of producing the good.[25] Or, at least, the cost of production is calculated as something far greater than that particular good. For instance, prices of drugs do not necessarily reflect a value specific to the product itself, but a "value" ascribed to the industry, that is, the infrastructure of marketing, research and development, and so on, that is attributed with "creating" the product.

Attribution is significant in that "attribution", as will be seen in later discussion, is seen to be the important aspect to retain as a universal value in the international initiative of Creative Commons to provide free copyright content (music, artistic works, literature, and so on) online and elsewhere through the use of licences.[26] In this respect, Sir John Sulston has suggested that "esteem" should become recognised as a reward in the context of scientific innovation and the promotion of greater access to the tools for innovation.[27] Similarly, "attribution" is recruited by the music publishing industry, where "artists and repertoire" is also factored into the calculation of a product's value, on the basis that this income allows for the ongoing development of new artists. In particular, the institutionalism of knowledge will be understood through an increasingly networked society. The impact of the collaborative, distributed, network community is relevant not only in artistic traditions but also in the dissemination and sharing of knowledge throughout its many manifest economic categories. Collaborative traditions of knowledge creation and development operate not only in the traditionally "creative" arts, but also in sciences[28] and technology: "the actual course of work that leads to the conception and use of new technology *always* involves a group."[29] Indeed, the network itself is an example of the creative capacities of technology and was instrumental in the race for the human genome and in ensuring the public good of the knowledge being uncovered. Arguably, the very suggestion that the impact of the Internet has been overestimated is itself an indication of its success: it is so ubiquitous, so incorporated, as to be unnoticeable. Thus, it is not a phenomenon merely of the written word; it is a phenomenon of knowledge and informs much of the strategic responses currently in play, and connects the "polyphony of wills" to events we are witnessing. The

25 Most recently, there was discussion on this issue at the Launch of the Gowers Review Call for Evidence. Department of Trade and Industry. Conference Centre. 2 March 2006.

26 These licences are discussed in more detail in the discussion of Creative Commons in Chapter 4.

27 Sulston, Sir J (2005) Launch of the Adelphi Charter on Creativity, Innovation and Intellectual Property. Royal Society for the Encouragement of Arts, Manufactures and Commerce. London. 13 October.

28 On the collaborative nature of scientific culture, see Latour B and Woolgar S ([1979]1986) *Laboratory Life: The Construction of Scientific Facts*, Princeton, Princeton UP, particularly in the analysis of cycles of credit and the motivations for the pursuit of research in Chapter 5. See also Tuomi I (2002) *Networks of Innovation: Change and Meaning in the Age of the Internet*, Oxford, Oxford UP: 4.

29 Wallace AFC ([1982] 2003) *The Social Context of Innovation: Bureaucrats, Families, and Heroes in the Early Industrial Revolution, As Foreseen in Bacon's New Atlantis*, Lincoln, U of Nebraska P: 3.

network is not an end, it is a means: "Network is a concept, not a thing out there. It is a tool to help describe something, not what is being described."[30]

It is time to get out the toolbox.

30 Latour B (2005) *Reassembling the Social*, Oxford, Oxford UP: 131.

Chapter 1

Culture Wars

> [T]he artist has ceased to be the One-Alone withdrawn into him- or herself, but has also ceased to address the people, to invoke the people as a constituted force. Never has the artist been more in need of a people, while stating most firmly that the people is lacking – the people is what is most lacking.[1]

Introduction

Creativity. The "value" of creativity is currently receiving a great deal of attention from governments, civil society, and the media, driving the debates surrounding access to knowledge, access to technology, the intellectual progress of our society, and the economic development of societies around the world. As a value its fundamental significance is presumed for Europe and internationally, in the notion of the "creative economy". The value of creativity is similarly the starting point and aspirational ideal for civil society campaigns against increasing intellectual property rights and the expansion of obstacles to access for many different technologies and intellectual products. How can the one value be both outcome and casualty for increased intellectual property rights for creators? How can the one value fuel both the rhetoric for expanded rights as well as the recognition of users and increased limitations and exceptions to those rights for the benefit of users?

As a concept creativity is a fluid and uncertain territory, informed by diverse and often incompatible interpretations and conceptualisations, from economics to divination. Nevertheless, despite the uncertainty in the term, the very reliance upon "creativity" in these diverse contexts suggests the imposition of value judgements upon the subject matter at stake. For all stakeholders in the debate, the label ascribes the diverse arguments with specific and positive cultural value. In other words, "creativity" imports a sense of discrimination and judgement into the terms of the debate itself. Creativity, as the renewed basis for the codes and conventions of intellectual property, in so far as it is used by government and policy makers, specifically and implicitly instates the creator at the centre of the system: "value is always *value-for*, always tied to some valuing group".[2] Importantly, as will become clear, as the role of "creator" is increasingly assumed by the supporting industries

---

1 Deleuze G and Guattari F ([1980]1987) *A Thousand Plateaus: Capitalism and Schizophrenia*, Massumi B (trans), Minneapolis, U of Minnesota P: 346.

2 Frow J (1995) *Cultural Studies and Cultural Value*, Oxford, Clarendon P: 143.

and the "corporate author", the user is not only remedial but indeed "outside" the system,[3] and outside the language of creativity.

> It is significant that the progress of the field of restricted production towards autonomy is marked by an increasingly distinct tendency of criticism to devote itself to the task, not of producing the instruments of appropriation – the more imperatively demanded by a work the further it separates itself from the public – but of providing a "creative" interpretation for the benefit of the "creators". And so, tiny "mutual admiration societies" grew up, closed in their own esotericism, as, simultaneously, signs of a new solidarity between artist and critic emerged.[4]

Therefore, it is both critically ambiguous and yet arguably necessary to refer to the figure of the "creator" in this context, as this is the nominal source of creativity in the intellectual property system. Whether it is specified as the author, the inventor, the designer, the artist, or otherwise, the "creator" has been strategically situated as the central figure of the system. Importantly, and somewhat ironically, this allows for the fluidity of the concept itself within the economic model of creativity, incorporating not merely the identifiable individual creator, but now also the corporate entity, the supporting industry, the "creative" industries – in other words, no longer merely "owner"[5] but now also the "source" of the creative process. In this way, innovation is similarly generalised and limited to the province of the "corporate author", the "corporate creator". Thus, in the present work, an examination of the concept of the "creator" is important in order to trace the development of "creativity" as a cultural value that is summarised by intellectual property and at the same time instrumental in the generalised institutionalism of intellectual property as a system, rather than presupposing that it is a social value that is effectively identified within each category nominated within the law.

As a cultural value, the notion of "creativity" inscribes the debate with a comprehensive historical and ideological language, infusing the discourse of intellectual property systems and their critics, and lending to intellectual property a distinctly "cultural" purpose. Indeed, with respect to copyright laws, the link

---

3 Indeed, this reference to the user as being "outside" the system was made specifically at the launch of the Gowers Review into Intellectual Property (which will report to the Chancellor of the Exchequer, the Secretary of State for Trade and Industry, and the Secretary of State for Culture, Media and Sport in Autumn 2006). At this presentation, Professor Danny Quah, of the London School of Economics and Political Science, described users as standing outside the system, while he continued to rely, somewhat incomparably, upon the rhetoric of the metaphor of "balance" within the intellectual property system. Quah D (2006) Panel Presentation. Gowers Review of Intellectual Property. London. Department of Trade and Industry Conference Centre. 2 March.

4 Bourdieu P (1993) *The Field of Cultural Production: Essays on Art and Literature*, Johnson R (ed), Cambridge, Polity: 116.

5 That is, the supporting corporate interest may indeed be the right-holder, by obtaining the rights in an object of intellectual property subsequent to its creation (through licensing or assignment) and thus "own" the content and figure as a right-holder.

between author, authenticity, and cultural integrity operates most overtly and seems somewhat impalpably entrenched. Jane Ginsburg, internationally renowned expert in copyright law, asserts that copyright laws "are a component of local cultural and information policies. As such they express each sovereign nation's aspirations for its citizens' exposure to works of authorship and participation in their country's cultural patrimony."[6] Indeed, this emphasis upon the tie between the law and the culture has persisted for some time:

> [A] nation's copyright laws lie at the roots of its cultural and intellectual climate. Copyright provides the inducement for creation and dissemination of the works that shape our society and, in an imperfect and almost accidental way, represents one of the foundations upon which freedom of expression rests.[7]

What is of particular interest in the present discussion is the way in which this author-based celebration of the culture has been appropriated and incorporated by an author-based modelling of industry itself.[8]

Thus, the system itself is positioned as the necessary circumstances for creativity. Indeed, in the WIPO "publicity" for World Intellectual Property Day, the day is recognised as "an occasion to reflect on the role played by intellectual property in stimulating and safeguarding the forces of innovation and creativity".[9] Indeed, intellectual property is rendered the hallmark of creativity itself.

The counterpoint to this refrain is the increasing link between investment and creativity, whereby investment becomes vested with the authority to indicate a kind of quality of creativity and innovation. Further, as intellectual property systems expand to incorporate new technologies and diverse enterprises, "investment" becomes the organising principle by which to develop and apply new and stronger rights in contexts otherwise contrary to conventional intellectual property categories[10] – that is, investment becomes "creative".[11] One of the most commonly cited justifications for the intellectual property system is that it provides certainty for risk-takers, thus offering an incentive to create and innovate through the rewards of control over the

---

6 Ginsburg J (2000) "International Copyright: From a 'Bundle' of National Copyright Law to a Supranational Code?", 47 *Journal of the Copyright Society* 265 at 267.

7 Ringer B (1968) "The Role of the United States in International Copyright – Past, Present, and Future", 56 *Georgetown Law Journal* 1050 at 1050.

8 This is particularly acute in respect of the current controversy surrounding the proposed webcasting right, as discussed in Chapter 3.

9 WIPO Magazine (2006) January-February.

10 See further the discussion of webcasting and broadcasts in Chapter 3.

11 In this way, "piracy" and "counterfeiting" are seen as "theft" not only of intellectual property but also of creativity. For instance, in a recent letter to the *Financial Times*, Ruth Orchard, Director-General of The Anti-Counterfeiting Group (ACG), writes: "Counterfeiting steals the creativity and investment of legitimate business – consumers must be encouraged to view fakes in the same way as stolen goods, and boycott them." See Orchard R (2006) "The trade in fakes is linked to terrorism and gun-running". Letter. *Financial Times*. 27 January: 10.

product of that ingenuity.[12] This articulation of investment as the ground upon which creativity is built characterises much of intellectual property policy. Indeed, at the conclusion of the Creative Economy Conference of the United Kingdom Presidency of the European Union 2005, Lord Sainsbury of Turville, Parliamentary Under-Secretary of State for Science and Innovation, made the following statements in his speech to delegates:

> Underpinning the value of our creativity and ideas must be a robust intellectual property (IP) regime. Without a robust and fair legislative regime to protect our creators, and those who invest in creativity, we put at risk the economic basis of the Creative Economy. There are other people, of course, who are important as well as the rights' holders, but those who create and invest in creative material need effective and enforceable rights for the creative economy to flourish. Without the right IP framework Europe will miss a massive opportunity.[13]

The practical effects and surrounding arguments for the current development in stronger rights suggest that this incentive has become almost inextricable from the social and economic context, through the concept of creativity. Thus, the "risk" of creativity is perceived as being that of those making the financial investment in the process, and it is that risk which intellectual property rights are designed to mitigate.[14] However, that risk cannot be completely abrogated; rather, it is displaced onto the users or consumers who are currently experiencing more and more limited access.[15]

In addition to the construction of creativity through a financial perspective, this process also, as suggested, positions the investment-maker in the role of "creator", in that investment is held out as providing the necessary infrastructure and prerequisite circumstances for creativity. In this way, a kind of "creative accountability" is produced through the figure of the corporate entity, the "corporate author", as it were, thus authenticating creativity produced in this way while rendering suspect the quality of creativity through other means (in particular, the distributed and incremental network).

---

12 For a more detailed discussion and analysis of the justifications for intellectual property, see Drahos P (1996) *A Philosophy of Intellectual Property*, Aldershot, Dartmouth. See also the discussion in relation to trade mark law in Maniatis S (2002) "Trade Mark Rights – A Justification Based on Property", *Intellectual Property Quarterly* 123.

13 Sainsbury of Turville, Lord (2005). Speech. Creative Economy Conference. London. 7 October.

14 William Cornish discusses the efforts of authors to participate more fully in this process and to be able take on more of the risks and thus receive more of the benefit: Cornish W (2002) "The Author as Risk-Sharer", 26 *Columbia (VLA) Journal of Law and the Arts* 1.

15 This notion of risk is considered further throughout the following chapters.

In this economic system, the user is a "propertyless"[16] "peasant",[17] outside the value-making of the "creative economy".[18] Indeed, this positioning is instrumental to the economic model upon which the intellectual property system is based, whereby exchanges occur precisely due to asymmetries between identified groups and individuals. In *The Protestant Ethic and the Spirit of Capitalism*,[19] first published 1904 to 1905, Max Weber identifies this character of capitalism, and the way in which the dominant economic model identifies and arranges its subjects: "Thus, through a process of economic *selection*, the capitalism that today dominates economic life socializes and creates the economic functionaries that it needs, both owners of businesses and workers."[20]

In this work, Weber identifies a relationship or alliance between the future-directed ethic of Protestant salvation with a similar structure of advancement in the capitalist narrative. Thus, the economic narrative of progress, Weber argues, is underwritten by a guarantee of salvation:

> Protestant ascetism … created the norm on which its impact *exclusively depended*: the psychological *motivation* that arose out of the conception of work as a *calling* and as the means best suited (and in the end often as the *sole* means) for the devout to become certain of their state of salvation. Furthermore, on the other hand, in interpreting the employer's acquisition of money also as a "calling," Protestant ascetism legalized the exploitation of this particular willingness to work.[21]

Drawing upon the example of the Dutch "Dissenters" (Calvinists and Baptists) and the view that "*work and the industrious pursuit of trade*" was "*their duty to God*", Weber continues:

---

16 Weber M ([1904-5]2002) *The Protestant Ethic and the Spirit of Capitalism*, Kalberg S (trans), Oxford, Blackwell.

17 Bourdieu P (1993), *The Field of Cultural Production: Essays on Art and Literature*, Johnson R (ed), Cambridge, Polity. See further the discussion of *habitus* in the following chapter.

18 Ilkka Tuomi writes: "Classical economic theory … assumed that meaning is fully reflected in prices. Instead of grounding value to something outside the economic system, value became one aspect of the system itself. The infinite chain of means-end relations was connected by profit, which became the end of all means." The result of this is a "closed system" where "Use value is conceptually and without a residue linked to exchange value. Structurally, the economic world parallels the Newtonian closed universe, where novelty is a contradiction in terms." Thus, the user is literally outside this economic system. See Tuomi I (2002) *Networks of Innovation: Change and Meaning in the Age of the Internet*, Oxford, Oxford UP: 14.

19 Weber M ([1904-5]2002) *The Protestant Ethic and the Spirit of Capitalism*, Kalberg S (trans), Oxford, Blackwell.

20 Weber M ([1904-5]2002) *The Protestant Ethic and the Spirit of Capitalism*, Kalberg S (trans), Oxford, Blackwell: 19.

21 Weber M ([1904-5]2002) *The Protestant Ethic and the Spirit of Capitalism*, Kalberg S (trans), Oxford, Blackwell: 121.

> It is obvious how powerfully the *exclusive* striving for the kingdom of God – through fulfilment of the duty to work in a vocational calling and through strict ascetism, which church discipline naturally imposed in particular upon the propertyless classes – must have promoted the "productivity" of work in the capitalist sense of the word. For the modern worker, the view of work as a "vocational calling" became just as characteristic as the view of gain as a "vocational calling" for the modern employer.[22]

This resonates strongly with the notions of divination, of divine inspiration, attached to conceptualisations of "creativity",[23] and thus with the "morality" with which the intellectual property debate has come to be infused. Further, the "progress" and directionality of the system is re-asserted, where the narrative continues to "look for legitimacy … in a future to be accomplished".[24] The relationship between intellectual property law as an economic system, on the one hand, and calls for greater ethical accountability within the law itself, on the other, both motivates and is sustained by the very terms of the debate itself. Thus, the pre-eminence, in each sense of the word, of the system is presented in the characterisation of the creative economy. The narrative of intellectual property, as will be discussed, therefore assumes a position of ethical and moral oversight in ways that are not only improbable but also *ultra vires* for the system to brandish.

Clearly, the notions of creativity provide the necessary momentum for an examination and consideration of developments in intellectual property law, policy, and practice, in the context of the current debates. This inquiry into creativity is arguably necessary in order to unsettle the narrative of creative progress that has become somewhat dominant in these debates. Further, as a stated fundamental value of intellectual property,[25] the rhetoric of creativity informs debates surrounding new and expanding rights, including broadcasters, traditional knowledge, and celebrity or publicity rights.

But as a concept by which the debate is framed and for which the terms are set, a refiguring of creativity also promises to provide the means by which the input of the various actors (that is, including users or consumers) in a society's intellectual progress and innovation might be recognised and, indeed, rewarded. Nevertheless, the very conceptualisation of "reward" is also up for grabs in this contest.

---

22 Weber M ([1904-5]2002) *The Protestant Ethic and the Spirit of Capitalism*, Kalberg S (trans), Oxford, Blackwell: 121.

23 See further the discussion in Pope R (2005) *Creativity: Theory, History, Practice*, London, Routledge: 37-38; 137-67. Concepts of creativity are examined in more detail in the following chapter, but it is useful at this point to recognise the links between capitalist progress, creativity, and intellectual property laws in order to trace the presumption of moral pre-eminence in this way.

24 Lyotard J-F ([1986]1992) *The Postmodern Explained to Children: Correspondence 1982-1985*, Pefanis J and Thomas M (ed), Barry D et al (trans), Sydney, Power Publications: 29.

25 For instance, a most recent example is that of the publicity for World Intellectual Property Day 2006, as appears in WIPO Magazine, January-February 2006.

Narrating the Legitimacy of Intellectual Property

Intellectual property laws have become firmly institutionalised as the legitimate way in which industrialised societies recognise, validate, and celebrate innovation, originality, and, above all (at least in terms of the current rhetorical flourishes), creativity. In other words, the system itself has become mimetic of creativity in so far as it has adopted "creativity" as its purpose, its responsibility, and thus its prestige. As just mentioned, the emphasis upon "creativity" affirms, somewhat problematically, an ethical narrative for what is increasingly becoming a fundamentally economic system,[26] drawing as well upon the Weberian notion of the ethic of capitalist work. In this sense, the rhetorical strategy of "creativity" has both instated intellectual property paradigms as the means by which that creativity is recognised and transacted, as well as introduced an ethical or moral language into the transaction of knowledge through this economic system. In this way, the economic relationship is both elevated and defeated by its own "ethical" presumptions. In other words, while the system is in itself very limiting in its synonymity and simultaneity with creativity process, this also introduces an expectation of this system that must remained unfulfilled – that is, that intellectual property laws (and their administrators) can both deliver the law and arbitrate its ethical parameters. It is beyond the remit of the intellectual property law system to monitor the ethical framework, and yet this has become an expectation of the system (especially in the absence or inadequate presence of a suitably complementary framework by which to achieve this).[27]

At the same time, however, this introduces the language of "scarcity" and prestige into the intellectual property system, as though this scarcity (quality not quantity) is a sign of the quality of the systematically recognised objects.[28] But it is paradoxically the success of the system that arguably has generated the current crisis – that is,

---

26 Progressive international convergence of intellectual property laws through harmonisation of intellectual property rights based on compliance with the World Trade Organization (WTO) Agreement on Trade Related Aspects of Intellectual Property Rights (TRIPS) has occurred largely through a translation of systems into an increasingly economic rights-based model.

27 Sheldon Halpern suggests that the problem for the legitimacy of intellectual property in a digital environment is that individual ethical judgements have become necessary to maintain the efficacy of the system, given the greater ease with which an individual may breach intellectual property rights. He writes: "Individual determinations of moral and ethical conduct require a moral and ethical context. The problem for intellectual property law in general, and the law of copyright in particular, is the lack of such an underlying clear context." See Halpern SW (2003) "Copyright Law and the Challenge of Digital Technology", in Gross L et al (eds) *Image Ethics in the Digital Age*, Minneapolis, U of Minnesota P: 143 at 145.

28 The sheer quantity of information on the Internet is frequently put forward as disproportionate to the small amount of quality material, or even as an indication of its lack of quality (quality not quantity). This is similar to the kinds of criticisms made of initiatives like Wikipedia, the free online encyclopedia: http://en.wikipedia.org/wiki/Wikipedia. Wikipedia is discussed again in the following chapter.

that the global territory of intellectual property laws is experiencing a network of irruptions in response to its ethical paucity in the eyes of civil society.

Nevertheless, it has been the success of the institutionalisation of the intellectual property system that the system itself has come to operate as a narration of the creative process, whereby creativity is framed by the system's criteria and justifications for protection.[29] In other words, it is through the discourse of intellectual property laws that the creative and innovative output of society is not only made known but also measured and calibrated.[30] Further, implied in this process is a valuation of creativities, of inventiveness, as authentic and "true". Thus, the codes and conventions of the institution of intellectual property thereby are vested with the narrative authority with respect to a society's cultural output, progress, and development. In this way, intellectual property comprises a distinct language by which to classify and narrate the objects of innovation. The complexity of the creative process is obscured by the mere classification of successive innovative events, whereby innovation is identified and recognised through hindsight, through the histories provided by the system itself.[31]

The institution of intellectual property thereby narrates social innovation and creativity, and thus enjoys a sense of authorial import as both cultural repository and observatory. Creative activity that is marginal, unauthorised, and inauthentic, according to the criteria set by the overarching system, literally cannot register as creative output – it is without distinction, it is tasteless. In other words, if it cannot fulfil the core criteria then it can occupy only the periphery of "culture", the outskirts of the "official culture".[32] The authorial narration of creative output at the same time

---

29 Fiona Macmillan discusses the relationship between creativity and the rhetoric of intellectual property in Macmillan F (2002) "The Cruel ©: Copyright and Film", 24(10) *European Intellectual Property Review* 483; and Macmillan F (2003) "Copyright's Commodification of Creativity", 2 *ICFAI Journal of Intellectual Property Rights* 53.

30 For instance, the United States Patent and Trademark Office releases annual rankings of who received the most patents, which are subsequently interpreted as "innovation scores" on a global scale. Similarly, the European Innovation Scoreboard (EIS) undertakes an annual assessment of innovation performance in EU member states, following a request of the European Council of Ministers in 2000. Innovation is recognised for the purposes of the score, via the "five key dimensions of innovation performance" – innovation drivers, knowledge creation, innovation and entrepreneurship, application, and intellectual property. Innovation does not score unless it is visible through these indicators. In particular, knowledge creation is measured through investment in research and development (R & D). Further, intellectual property creation is in and of itself an end for the purposes of recording innovation. Obviously an economic model such as this requires quantifiable economic parameters, but it raises questions of innovation that cannot necessarily be measured within this model, such as the incremental innovation of traditional communities in Europe, or indeed the abundant "informal" and "unofficial" outputs of networked communities.

31 Examples include prior art searches in the examination of patentability and originality in copyright, demonstrated through evidence led during litigation.

32 The notion of the "official culture" is referred to by Mikhail Bakhtin, and is discussed in more detail in Chapter 5, where the concept of the carnival is used to articulate the complex

introduces distinctions with respect to the cultural reception of that output. Indeed, we are currently in a second wave of the "culture wars"[33] – but this war can no longer be battled upon polarities,[34] but must be one of multiplicities that may be mobilised in the network. Clearly the language of polarity continues to structure the debate and to motivate advocates of greater rights for content-holders. This can be seen in the moralising of the debate, and the engagement of the "creativity" value in government and industry language and elsewhere, suggesting a predilection for the dynamics of the wars of the 1990s.

In other words, the principle of "creativity" organises the language of proponents for more extensive intellectual property rights around an indisputable and incontestable value. Thus, the rhetorical strategy of rendering civil society homogeneous and branding its agenda as "anti-IP"[35] immediately distances and alienates that group from the unassailable and immutable human value of creativity (in so far as the institution of intellectual property has appropriated "creativity" as its objective), notwithstanding attempts to recuperate that value within civil society campaigns for access. Civil society becomes, literally, anti-social and uncivilised. In other words, the "public" is authored through the mainstreaming of creativity within intellectual property rhetoric, while civil society campaigners are constructed as the aberrant fringe-dwellers of progressive society.

Intellectual Property – a Grand Story

Creativity and innovation are thus arbitrated and validated through the intellectual property system, which can be understood to be operating as what Jean-François

---

and "surprising" relations within the network.

33 A useful collection of essays on the culture wars is available in Bolton R (ed) (1992) *Culture Wars: Documents from the Recent Controversies in the Arts*, New York, The New Press.

34 An example of the way in which polarised debate drives the "culture wars" is that of the abortion debate in the United States, which is similarly premised upon the appropriation of an indisputable value ("life") such that those seeking to advocate choice are nevertheless always already constructed as being anti-life. See the discussion in Heelas P (2002) "Work Ethics, Soft Capitalism and the 'Turn to Life'", in Du Gay P and Pryke M (eds), *Cultural Economy*, London, SAGE: 78 at 91.

35 For example, the term was used by a representative of industry to interrupt the statement made by a representative of consumer groups in "The Global Challenge" working group, during the Creative Economy Conference of the UK Presidency of the EU, staged in London, 5-7 October 2005. However, use of the term is littered throughout the discourse of the debate and has become instrumental in the sloganeering against civil society action. Similar consequences can be understood in terms of other ways in which civil society campaigns are characterised by the language, including terms such as "piracy". Use of the term "piracy" renders "access" *a priori* morally questionable and thus where campaigners advocate against increased anti-piracy measures, those campaigners are thus situated as advocating "piracy" or indeed are constructed themselves as "pirates".

Lyotard calls a "grand narrative";[36] that is, as a sustained and self-legitimating narrative of all that is innovative in an increasingly harmonised and globalised vision. The "grand narrative" is an ideological meta-narrative that purports to represent the totality of experience and "a future to be accomplished",[37] but necessarily obscures or silences certain exceptions or difference in order to present that totality. Lyotard refers to the Western model of democracy as the grand narrative of emancipation. In this tradition, the intellectual property model could be understood as the grand narrative of creativity and innovation. That is, the system identifies and presents for recognition what has been nominated as "creative", as "original" (in terms of the institutional import of the system) as implied through the fulfilment of criteria. This process is understood through the broader institutional might of intellectual property as the regulatory power of the creative economy, that which not only names but also preserves (through its narration of the value of objects and the incarnation of the market). In this process, what is created is a hierarchy of objects and creativity – a sense of distinction and taste that attaches not only to the objects but also to their use (as in the demonising of "pirates" on the Internet) creating, literally, classes of users and aristocrats of "owners". The system narrates and thus authors "culture" as singular and thus universal.

The system thereby presents critical concerns for education, learning, and innovation, not only through immediate impacts of obstacles to access of particular objects or works, but also through the operation of a process of distinguishing cultures, of establishing what is available, what is reliable, what is reviewed and thus legitimated as genuine and authentic cultural output upon which to build more. Similarly, obstacles to access somewhat censor, as it were, according to the distinction of protected materials, how the cultural repository can be accessed, used, and provide the groundwork for ongoing innovation. Nevertheless, this is not to suggest a complete dismantling of the intellectual property system, but it is to argue for a reassessment of the way in which developments are approached, policies are made, and the priorities for the system itself. Who are the critical actors in the system? Who makes investments in the system? And what kinds of investments are not being counted?

---

36 Lyotard J-F ([1979]1984) *The Postmodern Condition: A Report on Knowledge*, Bennington G and Massumi B (trans), Minneapolis, U of Minnesota P: 31-39. On the operation of intellectual property as a grand narrative and the exclusion of traditional knowledge as innovative, see Gibson J (2005) *Community Resources: Intellectual Property, International Trade and Protection of Traditional Knowledge*, Aldershot, Ashgate.

37 Lyotard J-F ([1986]1992) *The Postmodern Explained to Children: Correspondence 1982-1985*, Pefanis J and Thomas M (ed), Barry D et al (trans), Sydney, Power Publications: 29.

Recognition

Thus, despite the appropriation of the cultural value of "creativity" within strategic challenges to conventional models of "authorship" and the creative process, different kinds of creativity have nevertheless come to be evaluated within the intellectual property paradigm and according to the conventions and rules provided by that paradigm for the purposes of recognising creativity. As well as defining an apparent economic value for different categories of "properties" (through the different calculations of "risk" manifest in differing terms of protection), the power of the appropriation of "creativity" by the discourse of policy-makers and government[38] is to simplify the creative process within the intellectual property paradigm. Thus, the narrative of intellectual property objectifies the creative process in ways reminiscent of the Romantic ideals of an unassailable and indisputable creativity. Creativity outside the intellectual property paradigm is seemingly de-legitimated, unimaginable, and valueless. Indeed, it is completely "unexpected" as it were.

Hans Robert Jauss, in his work on the aesthetic of reception and the interaction between author and public, indicates the operation of genre in the production of expectations in an audience.[39] In this way, the expectations of the public somewhat constrain literary production:

> The insight that the historical essence of the work of art lies not only in its representational or expression function but also in its influence must have two consequences for a new founding of literary history … [T]he relationship of work to work must now be brought into this interaction between work and mankind, and the historical coherence of works among themselves must be seen in the interrelations of production and reception.[40]

---

38 This can be seen particularly in the language of the "Creative Economy".

39 Mikhail Bakhtin, discussed in Chapter 5, recognises the way in which genres compete and interact in what he describes as polyphony, a heteroglossia of language systems so as to produce new meaning and new forms in participating "speakers". See in particular Bakhtin MM (1986) *Speech Genres and Other Late Essays*, McGee VW (trans), Austin, U of Texas P. See further the discussion of Bakhtin in relation to networks in Chapter 5.

40 Jauss HR (1982) *Toward an Aesthetic of Reception*, T Bahti (trans), De Man P (Intro), Minneapolis, U of Minnesota P: 15. See further Jauss HR ([1982]1989) *Question and Answer: Forms of Dialogic Understanding*, Hays M (trans and ed), Minneapolis, U of Minnesota P. Compare this notion of unfulfilled expectations with more passive renditions of the consumer as a subject shaped by texts in, for example, Haineault D-L and Roy J-Y ([1984]1993) *Unconscious for Sale: Advertising Psychoanalysis and the Public*, Lockhart K and Kerslake B (trans), Minneapolis, U of Minnesota P. See also the work of Wolfgang Iser, colleague and contemporary of Jauss, where the concept of the "implied reader" is one where the reader coheres the text, and renders it complete and consistent, in the process of interpretation. See Iser W (1974) *The Implied Reader: Patterns of Communication in Prose Fiction from Bunyan to Beckett*, Baltimore, Johns Hopkins UP; Iser W (1989) *Prospecting: From Reader Response to Literary Anthropology*, Baltimore, Johns Hopkins UP, as well as the discussion in Esrock EJ (1994) *The Reader's Eye: Visual Imaging as Reader Response*, Baltimore, Johns Hopkins UP.

Arguably, what is at stake in the present dynamic between users and creators is that these expectations, somewhat prescribed by the legal framework and the conventions of creativity, are exceeding that framework. Indeed, it is the expectations of the regulatory means by which to define and narrate creativity (increasingly being debated within the discourse of the intellectual property system, its proponents, and its detractors) that are being defeated, by the very public it proposes to fulfil and satisfy.

Thus, there arises a tension between the growing reliance on intellectual property discourse as the archive of creativity, as the arbiter and measure of the creative process, and the rejection of that image of totality. Currently, unprecedented debate contributes to the process, instating the cultural institution of intellectual property, whereby intellectual property laws are increasingly being implied by industry and others as the conventions by which to understand and recognise the creative process. This is part of the process of making industry "creative".[41] Arguably, this is not something that comes from within the letter of the law itself, but is a cooperation of that system nonetheless with the industrial-creativity complex of commercial models of innovation and progress, creating a kind of "aristocracy" of "genuine" and objective intellectual property products (the "true"[42] innovation) and a "peasant" class of networked, distributed, "folk",[43] and multiple creative projects,[44] the minor "literature" of the network. The cultural institution of intellectual property thereby maintains an aristocracy of knowledge-holders and the hierarchical legitimacy of the work and institutions through which its production is recognised. Thus, the "high" cultural production[45] of the isolated artist supported by the "patronage" of industry

41 The ideological context of the concept of "creative industries" is discussed in more detail in Chapter 3, particularly in the context of the development of rights in broadcasts, webcasting and databases.

42 Zuck J (2006) "IP and the Knowledge Commons: Lobbying and Advocacy II". Panel. The Politics and Ideology of Intellectual Property. Trans Atlantic Consumer Dialogue (TACD) Conference. 20 March.

43 The term "folk" is borrowed from Mikhail Bakhtin, whose work is discussed in greater detail in Chapter 5. The word "folk" is important in the current discussion because it both communicates the collective collaboration of the network, while at the same time carries with it the negative connotations developed by the intellectual property model. Thus, it illustrates both the positive aspects of the collective as well as the operation of the system itself, which declares such productivity invalid, and indeed, the collective itself invalid as a source of such innovation. In other words, the term "folk" is in and of itself a demonstration of the way in which collaboration is dispossessed of creative significance by the system. Similar concerns led to the rejection of the term "folklore" and the adoption of the term "traditional cultural expressions", in the context of the current intergovernmental committee discussions in WIPO towards protection of the knowledge and resources of traditional and indigenous peoples.

44 Examples of "folk" creativity through digital networks include the use of web logs (blogs), online social networking (such as myspace.com), and other examples of "folk" creativity.

45 This positioning of "high culture" is not in the sense of the conventional high culture/low or popular culture divide, but in the sense of a privileged rendition of culture as recognised

is privileged over the unevaluated and proliferative dialogue and collaboration of expanding popular models of creativity.[46] In other words, that which is recognised as produced through the legitimate institutions is "authentic", as distinct from the "counterfeit" and "pirated" creativity of "uncivilised" networked "re-mix" communities and the like.[47]

Furthermore, through the authentication of creative output by virtue of the economic channels of intellectual property, together with the synonymity of the system with creativity itself, increasingly this "patronage" is presented as the necessary infrastructure for the creative process itself.[48] In this way, the "true" artist is formally identified by the "patron" (industry) through contractual obligations.[49] At

---

through the granting of intellectual property rights (the recognition of such a privileged position) as distinct from a "low" or illegible culture for which such rights are seemingly not available or are at odds with the practice itself.

46 In reference to an "organicist notion of creativity", Negus and Pickering suggest: "As a form of radical subjectivism, [artistic creativity] neglects other modes of creativity, such as the creativity sparked by dialogue and collaboration, or the creativity inherent in popular cultural traditions. Its influence over the development of the trend towards subject-centredness in modern culture, along with the accompanying ideal of authenticity, should not be underestimated." See Negus K and Pickering M (2004) *Creativity, Communication and Cultural Value*, London, SAGE: 4. The centrality of a coherent and uniform subject operates throughout scientific discourse as well. For example, Alfred Tauber identifies the same kind of "subject-centredness" in immunology, suggesting that the notion of the "self" as a discrete and composed entity is built upon conventions of identity rather than science. See Tauber A (1997) *The Immune Self: Theory or Metaphor?* Cambridge, Cambridge UP. Donna Haraway has also examined the relationship between self and non-self in immunology throughout her work, but in particular see Haraway D (1991) *Simians, Cyborgs, and Women: The Reinvention of Nature*, London, Free Association Books; and Haraway D (1992) "The Promises of Monsters: A Regenerative Politics for Inappropriate/d Others", in L Grossberg et al (eds) *Cultural Studies*, New York, Routledge: 295. Also relevant here is the work of Deleuze and Guattari on the concept of the body without organs (BwO): Deleuze G and Guattari F ([1980]1987) *A Thousand Plateaus: Capitalism and Schizophrenia*, Massumi B (trans), Minneapolis, U of Minnesota P.

47 The discussion of Pierre Bourdieu's concept of *habitus* in the following chapter is also relevant here, in that Bourdieu understands the field of production to include the interplay between the *habitus* and the wider field of production. See Bourdieu P ([1984]1993) *Sociology in Question*, Nice R (trans), London, SAGE: 141-2. See further Chapter 2.

48 An interesting example of the dynamics of a modern "patronage" and a type of industry-creativity complex is that of Charles Saatchi, a case which also demonstrates the power of the "collection" and exhibition in producing the legitimacy and success of works. In this example, the collector creates value through the very existence of the collection, and assumes the mastery and authority of the "author" of that collection (as distinct from the artist, as such). See further the very useful discussion in Negus K and Pickering M (2004) *Creativity, Communication and Cultural Value*, London, SAGE: 87-8.

49 The contractual relationship also instates the formal obligations to the "patron" and the influence of the patron as a figure of cultural authority. For example, in the case of the photographic industry, photographers are considered to be at a significant disadvantage when

the same time, however, this cultural division that is implied by the dominant models of innovation that are understood and rewarded within the intellectual property system alienates users (and thus creators) from the work itself. Thus, the role of the individual creator is displaced to the extent that the role of the supporting industries and commercial infrastructure is consolidated. Fredric Jameson's work on the way in which artistic production has become an alienated labour is instructive here:

> It used to be affirmed that art or the aesthetic in our time offered the closest accessible analogy to, constituted the most adequate symbolic experience of, a nonalienated labor otherwise unimaginable for us. This proposition in its turn derived from the preindustrial speculations of German idealist philosophy, where the experience of play offered a similar *analogon* to a condition in which the tensions between work and freedom, science and ethical imperatives, might be overcome. There are, however, good reasons why these propositions about hints, anticipations, or symbolic experiences of nonalienated labor should no longer be persuasive. For one thing, the very experience of art itself today is alienated and made "other" and inaccessible to too many people to serve as a useful vehicle for their imaginative experience.[50]

Fredric Jameson's concerns are quite meaningful in the context of contemporary debates over access to knowledge protected by intellectual property. Where intellectual property products are made increasingly exceptional, as it were, the aristocracy of "legitimate" creativity is increasingly inaccessible and unavailable to the collective networked nature of contemporary creative processes. Access is thus a privilege.[51] As Jameson might say, the access to knowledge debate must deal with the inaccessibility of intellectual property products "as a useful vehicle for their imaginative experience". In other words, access must not only be possible but it must be relevant so that the products of creative society circulate and become part of the shared imaginative experience of users and citizens. Where the law cannot keep pace with the technologies of use and collaboration, its legitimacy will be compromised and users will necessarily devise ways in which to build upon current practices in the network and in emerging technologies and their communities, despite the legal framework.

---

contracting with "industry" in this profession: "the source of 'creativity,' the locus of cultural authority, is transferred in the very first instance from the photographer to the agency." Frosh P (2003) *The Image Factory: Consumer Culture, Photography and the Visual Content Industry*, Oxford, Berg: 205.

50 Jameson F (1991) *Postmodernism, or, the Logic of Late Capitalism*, London, Verso: 146-47.

51 This resonates with the language of rights, and the concern that users are not recognised with positive rights. Rather, the interests of users are proposed to be addressed by the inclusion of limitations and exceptions to the rights of intellectual property holders; that is, merely entitlements to certain exceptional "permitted" acts. For instance, see Copyright, Designs and Patents Act (CDPA) 1988 (UK), where the language of "permitted acts" is used to describe what is granted to the user through exceptions. This clearly compromises the notion of a symmetrical balance within the system, as discussed in the following chapter.

Thus, intellectual property becomes, literally, cultural capital – it presents capital not only in the economic sense but also in the sense of power and authority (by virtue of the privileged access to knowledge). In this way, the position of industry is also reaffirmed as the core of that economic activity, as the centre of the culture complex. The supporting industries, through positive rights and through the ideological operation of the system, become identified as the legitimate producers and the source of legitimate production – what can be recognised as valuable knowledge: "Thus the direction and speed of technological innovation is inevitably affected by the institutional setting."[52] As a cultural institution, the intellectual property system vests the supporting industries with the authority to produce and "authenticate" objects of genuine creativity. The elitism of the uniform industry is thus privileged over the populism of the collaborative public networks.[53]

Networks

It is necessary to consider in more detail the dynamics and politicisation of the network structure, particularly given the pervasion of the network in the current debate, together with the increasing proliferation of networks of creativity in contemporary society. The modern network structure, generally speaking, is a phenomenon of organisation or otherwise through unanticipated links and acquaintance – contact, familiarity, proximity. That is, the network is built upon acquaintance with both individuals and knowledge. In this respect, the network de-institutionalises and de-centralises the way in which creative objects and events are developed, transformed, transmitted, exerted, consumed, and dissipated. Social networks de-institutionalise the handling of creativity. The network is at once both structural (it is connected through nodes or hubs) and structuring. The network is at once organic (in its

52 Wallace AFC ([1982] 2003) *The Social Context of Innovation: Bureaucrats, Families, and Heroes in the Early Industrial Revolution, As Foreseen in Bacon's New Atlantis*, Lincoln, U of Nebraska P: 3.

53 Negus and Pickering critique the elitism/populism dichotomy and the notion of genius in Negus K and Pickering M (2004) *Creativity, Communication and Cultural Value*, London, SAGE: 147.

rhizomatic[54] proliferation of nodes and new connections) but without an organiser.[55] The network is story, but without a single narrator.[56]

The term "node" refers to any point of connection in the network – thus, it can be through any network equipment (such as a computer or mobile phone) or indeed through any individual actor, suggesting an important prosthetic and affective relationship between the individual actor and the appliance. Thus, the link between the embodied individual and the network connector is virtually inextricable. Nodes are sometimes described in social network theory as being connected by "ties".[57] This suggests a useful metaphor for the conceptualisation of transactions in information as tools of the system rather than as the ends, the objective, of the system. This is strikingly different from the way in which knowledge is commodified as (graphic) information for the purposes of intellectual property laws (an economic world view), which seemingly operate as ways in which to halt the flow of the system and thus chart the progress of knowledge. This interruption to the flow, however, is through a conceptual shift in the way in which knowledge is generated and exchanged as a tool towards greater proliferation, rather than as an end towards fundamentally containing that proliferation for the purposes of the market. In the network, the ties merely facilitate the network; they are not the objects of the network as such. The ties are aspects of the proliferative growth into new nodes and unceasing rhizomatic

54 Rhizomes are plants which grow underground via horizontally creeping stems, proliferating (virulently) from nodes. The term is used by Deleuze and Guattari to understand the multiplicity and immanent processes of creativity in networks, together with the "underground" nature of such networks (with respect to the dominant culture) as suggested through the subterranean growth of the rhizome. The concept is traced in this work to understand the interconnections in creative flows and the way in which distributed individuals might connect and co-create in unpredictable and inventive ways. See Deleuze G and Guattari F ([1980]1987) *A Thousand Plateaus: Capitalism and Schizophrenia*, Massumi B (trans), Minneapolis, U of Minnesota P.

55 In their work on schizophrenia, Deleuze and Guattari offer the concept of the body without organs or BwO (from Antonin Artaud), which is in conflict with the constancy of the organised and discrete organism, and use this concept to understand the social body as other than the "organism". This is a particularly useful concept, as later discussion will show, with respect to networked collaboration and creative processes. See Deleuze G and Guattari F ([1980]1987) *A Thousand Plateaus: Capitalism and Schizophrenia*, Massumi B (trans), Minneapolis, U of Minnesota P. See also Deleuze G and Guattari F ([1972]1983) *Anti-Oedipus: Capitalism and Schizophrenia*, Hurley R et al (trans), Minneapolis, U of Minnesota P. See also Deleuze's earlier work on the organism in Deleuze G ([1968]1994) *Difference and Repetition*, Patton P (trans), New York, Columbia UP. This concept is discussed further in Chapter 2.

56 On the polyphony of voices (or heteroglossia and elsewhere polyglossia) and the dominance of an authorised and authorial voice in the ideological master narrative of the "official culture", see the later discussion of the work of Mikhail Bakhtin and its relevance for networks in Chapter 5.

57 Barney D (2004) *The Network Society*, Cambridge, Polity: 26.

growth (drawing upon the concept of Deleuze and Guattari).[58] Indeed, the term is useful in its conjuring of the organic concept of the rhizome, which reproduces and proliferates via nodes, making rhizomatic growth both virulent and difficult to arrest.

Thus, it is the flow of information in the network that is of critical interest to a re-conceptualisation of the priorities of intellectual property systems in the context of cultural development and diversity. Networked information flows depart from the conventional means of maintaining and distributing capital in an industrialised society, and indeed the expansion of intellectual property rights is a clear demonstration of the way in which the law attempts to capture the economy in the exchange of information, as distinct from goods and manufacture. The network is not an example of why intellectual property rights should be abandoned – and indeed, that is certainly not the argument in the present work. Rather, the network is illustrative of the way in which the law must develop in concert with the very means and practices available within society to ensure the ongoing development of knowledge and the transfer of that knowledge among and between citizens. The opportunity for dissemination of quality materials for education, research, and development by engaging novel regulatory systems, rather than attempting to limit through intellectual property these transformations in ways to deal with knowledge, is an opportunity of not only social and cultural significance, but also economic. To continue to focus on conceptualising these relations within the simplistic transactions imagined by intellectual property is to continue limiting significant economic and cultural potential. Rather than interpreting the current dynamic as a simplistic polarisation of interests and a demand for abandonment of intellectual property, the networks and their users are, rather, indicative of the way in which the law is currently out of tune with its public. The way in which the law continues to chart the limits of the network is also limiting the potential for cultural diversity and for de-centralisation of "authorship" through such networks. As Marilyn Strathern cautions, the proclamations of democratisation and sharing are somewhat simplistic. Such views suggest that these qualities are inherent to the digital network itself, rather than projects for which it can be utilised as a social tool.[59] In particular, as Strathern notes, the digital network is as vulnerable to appropriation by the dominant narrative as any other form of counter-discourse:

> No one would these days want to claim ownership of an idea or artefact on grounds of unique identity, yet there is no refuge for the social anthropologist in the idea of hybrids, networks and invented cultures either. These do not, of themselves, indicate a symmetrical, sharing morality. They are not of themselves the resistant, transgressive stands they might seem; not the revitalised assembly or parliament of things Latour so

58 See in particular Deleuze G and Guattari F ([1980]1987) *A Thousand Plateaus: Capitalism and Schizophrenia*, Massumi B (trans), Minneapolis, U of Minnesota P. The concept of the rhizome is considered in more detail in the following chapter.

59 On control in the digital environment, through technical protocols and the governance of network connections, see Galloway AR (2004) *Protocol: How Control Exists After Decentralization*, Cambridge MA, MIT P.

> freely imagines. For neither a mixed nature nor an impure character guarantees immunity from appropriation. On the contrary, the new modernities have invented new projects that forestall such imaginings. We can now all too easily imagine monopolies on hybrids, and claims of ownership over segments of network.[60]

In other words, the transcription of the law precisely creates an apparent uniqueness in commodities of information, which at the same time guarantees a certain repeatability for the purposes of transacting in ideas. Thus, the law recuperates the flight of the network and contains it within conjugated units of creativity, despite the potential that might be available in relations of networked creativity and expression. But of course, to allow a response from Latour: "Network is a concept, not a thing out there. It is a tool to help describe something, not what is being described."[61] The concern of the present work, then, is to understand how the law might better utilise this tool to describe a more creative and productive society.

Further, the "digital" network is not a phenomenon purely of the Internet,[62] nor is it necessarily all that new.[63] Rather, the network describes an interconnection of knowledge and social and political organisation more broadly in a post-industrial age.[64] Indeed, the "network" describes also the interconnections considered in the "folk" relations of Mikhail Bakhtin's carnival[65] and the co-creativity of the dialogical

---

60 Strathern M (1999) *Property, Substance and Effect: Anthropological Essays on Persons and Things*, London, The Athlone P: 135.

61 Latour B (2005) *Reassembling the Social*, Oxford, Oxford UP: 131.

62 Although, the Internet remains a key indication of the deterritorialised flow of information (as discussed in the following chapter) and social relations (for example, online social networks, web logs, electronic discussion lists, and so on). Nevertheless, the discussion of networks is not to valorise unproblematically (or evaluate at all) the productivity of the network. Indeed, this is precisely the process that is contrary to the debate over use, and it is this practice of evaluation that is nevertheless implicit and surreptitious in the application of intellectual property laws and the hierarchies of "users".

63 For instance, see Latour B ([1991]1993) *We Have Never Been Modern*, Porter C (trans), New York, Harvester Wheatsheaf.

64 Barney D (2004) *The Network Society*, Cambridge, Polity: 27. Indeed, the popular "Six Degrees of Separation from Kevin Bacon" game is in itself an example of "unoriginal" information flow, and at the same time an example of the informal network. The principle is to describe, in six steps of contact with other "nodes" (individuals) as steps, your closeness or proximity to the US actor, Kevin Bacon. This illustrates the way in which spatial metaphors nevertheless persist in a time-based network.

65 Bakhtin MM ([1968]1984) *Rabelais and His World*, Iswolsky H (trans), Bloomington, Indiana UP. Indeed, in so far as the "carnival" was facilitated and allowed by the dominant, "official" culture at certain times, the Internet and its regulation (and the way in which dominant conventions of order and regulation are presumed to apply, as discussed in Lessig L (1999) *Code and Other Laws of Cyberspace*, New York, Basic Books) suggests an important case of the "carnival" in itself. However, as will be discussed in Chapter 5, the importance of the carnival in the present discussion is the "folk" or collective underpinning the carnival and permeating, irrupting, at "other" times.

relationship.[66] It is thus possible to read the development of the technology and practices in online networks as generated in response to the need of the already established patterns of relationships in the "unofficial cultures".[67] This is not a marginalised system but a fundamental example of the way in which the intellectual property institution is time-honoured and time-bound; developments in the economic and legal models must take account of developments in use, and indeed must broaden the measurement of productivity. The intellectual property system, ideally, is based upon facilitating the flow of knowledge – its creation, its dissemination, its evolution – not repressing it.

Manuel Castells explains that, in a society for which information and knowledge (that is, intangibles) have become the key resources and repositories of capital, there will be significant challenges to fundamental social and political structures: "This new social structure is associated with the emergence of a new mode of development, informationalism, historically shaped by the restructuring of the capitalist mode of production towards the end of the twentieth century."[68] Elsewhere Scott Lash describes networks as "non-linear socio-technical assemblages" that are "[r]eplacing the classic institutions of the linear social system".[69]

However, arguably informationalism continues to be coordinated through the production models of a persistent industrialism:

> I should remind the patient reader that in the historical period of the rise of informationalism, capitalism, albeit in new, profoundly modified forms *vis-à-vis* the time of Weber's writing, is still operating as the dominant economic form. Thus, the corporate ethos of accumulation, the renewed appeal of consumerism, are driving cultural forms in the organizations of informationalism.[70]

And indeed the intellectual property system, which regulates trade in information, has persevered with an industrial model that relies upon the manifestation of ideas as physical goods, the exhaustion of information as a limited commodity, and the creation of classes of desire for the goods:

---

66 The work of Mikhail Bakhtin is considered in detail in Chapter 5.

67 On the notion of the "official culture" and "unofficial culture", see further the discussion of the work of Mikhail Bakhtin and carnival in Chapter 5, as well as earlier in this chapter in relation to the institutionalisation and legitimation of the grand narrative.

68 Castells M (2000) *The Information Age: Economy, Society and Culture. Volume I: The Rise of the Network Society*, 2nd ed, Oxford, Blackwell: 14.

69 Lash S (2002) *Critique of Information*, London, SAGE: 112.

70 Castells M (2000) *The Information Age: Economy, Society and Culture. Volume I: The Rise of the Network Society*, 2nd ed, Oxford, Blackwell: 213-14. Christopher May also writes: "while we may be living through a period in which the form and practices of our lives are changing in many ways, the understanding substance of our socioeconomic system remains largely the same", in May C (2002) *The Information Society: A Sceptical View*, Cambridge, Polity: 1.

> Although technology and technical relationships of production are organized in paradigms originating in the dominant spheres of society (for example, the production process, the military-industrial complex) they diffuse throughout the whole set of social relationships and social structures, so penetrating and modifying power and experience. These modes of development shape the entire realm of social behaviour, of course including symbolic communication. Because informationalism is based on the technology of knowledge and information, there is an especially close linkage between culture and productive forces, between spirit and matter, in the informational mode of development. It follows that we should expect the emergence of historically new forms of social interaction, social control, and social change.[71]

Informationalism nevertheless is coordinated through the production models of a persistent industrialism. However, with the increasingly networked nature of knowledge production and dissemination, this industrial model is sometimes contrary to the very processes by which productivity of knowledge is maximised. In other words, is it still practicable and indeed profitable to recognise productivity purely in the tangible good, or is it necessary to re-consider the stakeholders "inside" the system and to consider broader models of productivity to include the conduct and participation of citizens?

Ilkka Tuomi suggests that it is problematic to maintain a traditional economic model for innovation in the context of new examples (such as open source software and free software development) of proliferative and collaborative innovation occurring independently of the conventional incentives.[72] Tuomi questions the value-making of the intellectual property system in the context of new technologies and contemporary use, and maintains that innovation is an inevitably and necessarily social practice, particularly in the case of developments in technology: "The heroic individual innovator is not a good model when we try to understand the evolution and development of technology."[73] It is in this sense that the strategic central value of "creativity" is quite clear, suggesting a singular and unpaired source, as distinct from the "production" and process of the network.

Rather usefully, a significant examination into the ideological distinction drawn between the cultural value of "creativity" as something unusual and rare, in contrast to seemingly mundane and unimaginative "production", is offered by Pierre Macherey in the context of literature.

> The various "theories" of creation all ignore the process of making; they omit any account of production. One can create undiminished, so, paradoxically, creation is the release of what is already there; or, one is witness of a sudden apparition, and then creation is an irruption, an epiphany, a mystery. In both instances any possible explanation of the change

71 Castells M (2000) *The Information Age: Economy, Society and Culture. Volume I: The Rise of the Network Society*, 2nd ed, Oxford, Blackwell: 17-18.

72 Tuomi I (2002) *Networks of Innovation: Change and Meaning in the Age of the Internet*, Oxford, Oxford UP: 2-4.

73 Tuomi I (2002) *Networks of Innovation: Change and Meaning in the Age of the Internet*, Oxford, Oxford UP: 6.

> has been done away with; in the former, nothing has happened; and in the latter what has happened is inexplicable. All speculation over man the creator is intended to eliminate a real knowledge: the "creative process" is, precisely, not a process, a labour; it is a religious formula to be found on funeral moments.[74]

Although sometimes interpreted as an unhelpful dichotomy,[75] it is perhaps more useful to consider the way in which Macherey is identifying the predominant characterising of creativity as divining, a mythologising of the "source" of creative products – whether that be the author, artist, or other "legitimate" or "genuine creator". This is particularly acute in the present context, and plays out in the ubiquity of "creativity" as a shared and yet disputed value within government policy-making as well as civil society debate. In positing the notion of "production", Macherey arguably is not simply opposing "creativity" but rather is identifying the "root" of creativity – to produce. Indeed, it is this productivity (the flow of innovation) that is at stake in the current campaigns over access to knowledge. Importantly, Macherey's discussion highlights what is now significant in intellectual property debates – namely the way in which the concept of "creativity", as deployed within intellectual property narratives, is simplified as an "event" or product emanating from a single source (of activity, insight, talent, genius or otherwise) as distinct from a process that is indiscrete, collaborative, intertextual, and incremental. It is this process that plays out in contemporary networked structures of creativity and innovation, and which re-invigorates the work of Macherey in the present context.

This concept of "production" shares much with the notion of reading innovation in a social context. Importantly, the concept of "literary production" potentially re-introduces the relationships between creators/producers and readers/users/consumers in the industrial and economic context for innovation in the present day. Significantly, this concept is relevant to the institutionalism of intellectual property and the impact on production. In a network society, users are inextricable from the context for production.

Network Economies

While the intellectual property system may continue to be articulated upon conventional economic models of industrial capitalism and trade in "goods", nevertheless, the network is considered to motivate and necessitate new patterns and models in capitalist modes of production.[76] The economic principle of "increasing

74 Macherey P ([1966]1978) *A Theory of Literary Production*, Wall G (trans), London, Routledge: 68.

75 See, for instance, Pope R (2005) *Creativity: Theory, History, Practice*, London, Routledge: 7. Pope criticises Macherey as merely polarising creativity and production.

76 Boltanski L and Chiapello E ([1999]2005) *The New Spirit of Capitalism*, Elliott G (trans), New York, WW Norton & Co. Manuel Castells also identifies a shift in production, despite the continuing operation of capitalism as the dominant economic model: "[T]he state and the affirmation of national/cultural collective identity have been shown to muster decisive

returns" or "increasing returns to scale" is useful in understanding the productivity of networks.[77] This model departs from the usual "increasing economies of scale" in that it maintains that average productivity can be increased with output. Therefore, the whole is greater than the sum of its parts, as it were, in that a more than proportional increase in output can be achieved by increasing all inputs in a productive process. Kevin Kelly describes this as "the logic of the Net", arguing that it is "contrary to classical economic theories of wealth based on equilibratory tradeoff … In network economics, more brings more. This is why giving things away so often works, and why the cypherpunks want to pass out their tools gratis … you can seed the 'more' at the start by giving the tools away."[78] Yochai Benkler's work on the wealth of networks is similarly concerned with the way in which the transformation of the means and channels of production must necessarily transform markets themselves.[79] Importantly, Benkler links this transformation to civil society mobilisation and motivation for systematic change. Contrary to the scarcity (and indeed slowness) built into the intellectual property system, the network economy relies upon the instantaneity of access and the simultaneity of proliferative growth: "The key here is that wealth comes not from scarcity, as in conventional economics, but from abundance."[80]

It is thus through networks that the grand narrative of the intellectual property system is seemingly challenged. Through such networks, distributed cooperation

---

force in the arena of global competition. Families, in their complexity, continue to thrive and reproduce by the means of economic competition, accumulation, and heritage. But while all these elements seem to account, together, for the cultural sustainment of renewed capitalist competition, they do not seem to be specific enough to distinguish the new agent of such capitalist competition: the network enterprise." See Castells M (2000) *The Information Age: Economy, Society and Culture. Volume I: The Rise of the Network Society*, 2nd ed, Oxford, Blackwell: 214.

77 Intelligent Television is currently engaged in work concerned with new business models in open content. In "The Economics of Open Content", a research project funded by the William and Flora Hewlett Foundation, work is concerned with devising new models for the distribution of open content and open educational content in video and film media. Further work on "The Open Production Initiative", supported by Library and Archives Canada and the Joint Information Systems Committee (JISC), is developing new models of open production in association with cultural and educational institutions. The Andrew W Mellon Foundation and Ithaka are supporting a further project, "Marketing Culture in the Digital Age", which released a preliminary report, August 2005. See Kaufman PB (2005) *Marketing Culture in the Digital Age: A Report on New Business Collaborations Between Libraries, Museums, Archives and Commercial Companies*. Report. Intelligent Television. 25 August.

78 Kelly K (1994) *Out of Control: The New Biology of Machines*, London, Fourth Estate: 210.

79 Benkler Y (2006) *The Wealth of Networks: How Social Production Transforms Markets and Freedom*, New Haven, Yale UP.

80 Urry J (2003) *Global Complexity*, Cambridge, Polity: 53. For further discussion of this characteristic of the network, see Waldrop M (1994) *Complexity*, London, Penguin.

produces the simultaneity of collaborative creative events, and the interruptions of little narratives (*petit récit*),[81] leading ultimately to what is arguably the current process of the de-legitimation of the intellectual property system. In these irruptions of creativity, the legitimacy of this grand narrative is countered by an intrusive civil society, more and more challenged by the many publics that narrative would otherwise organise. The proliferation of civil society actors and the strategic political interventions made have been described elsewhere as "the shift (or the contribution to the shift) that free trade has produced in the arts and notions of citizenship and public culture, particularly the relationship of the state to civil society".[82] The boundaries that are drawn to calibrate and contain the field of creativity are threatened by the unanticipated and unpredictable emergence of new technologies sought to be contained within the codes of intellectual property, as well as the multiplication of creative activity and dissemination of information by contenders in the modern network. Despite the imperial dominance of the narrative, "new territories are born".[83] Similarly, Gilles Deleuze and Félix Guattari describe the minor literature[84] that is transformative, intervening in the narrative of the major literature (such as intellectual property), confronting its codes and conventions. To the extent of the many intrusions of public interest in the discourse on access to knowledge and the overreaching of intellectual property,[85] the challenges to the system itself, and the

---

81 Lyotard J-F ([1979]1984) *The Postmodern Condition: A Report on Knowledge*, Bennington G and Massumi B (trans), Minneapolis, U of Minnesota P: 60.

82 Yúdice G (2003) *The Expediency of Culture: Uses of Culture in the Global Era*, Durham, Duke UP: 215.

83 Lyotard J-F ([1979]1984) *The Postmodern Condition: A Report on Knowledge*, Bennington G and Massumi B (trans), Minneapolis, U of Minnesota P: 39. The impact of territory and belonging in the contemporary experience of the distributed creative network is discussed further in the following chapter.

84 The term "minor literature" refers to those seemingly marginalised narratives that nevertheless disrupt and transform the dominant narrative, or "major literature". In other words, the apparently distributed and unauthorised minor literatures of the collaborative network are disruptive to the mythology of the major literature of intellectual property models of creative process. Deleuze G and Guattari F ([1975]1986) *Kafka: Toward a Minor Literature*, Polan D (trans), Minneapolis, U of Minnesota P; Deleuze G and Guattari F ([1980]1987) *A Thousand Plateaus: Capitalism and Schizophrenia*, Massumi B (trans), Minneapolis, U of Minnesota P.

85 A sense of overreaching in intellectual property laws is particularly acute in bilateral agreements between states. In particular, the United States has come under criticism for its expansive negotiation of bilateral free trade agreements (FTA). In some of these agreements, terms of trade have been negotiated that bind states to obligations in excess of what is required under the WTO TRIPS Agreement as well as potentially contracting out of flexibilities currently available under TRIPS. By virtue of Article 4 of the TRIPS Agreement ("Most-Favoured Nation Treatment"), those countries agreeing to TRIPS-plus standards through bilateral agreements must similarly grant the increased rights to intellectual property not only to the other contracting party (the United States) but also to every other member state of the WTO. In other words, certain interests of the United States in trade are transformed effectively into international laws. Further, these laws are increasingly "international" in

flight[86] of users to networked access and dissemination, the legitimacy of intellectual property laws is in question. It seems that there is a genuine "crisis" in intellectual property – a legitimation crisis.[87]

As in the story "The Aleph" by Jorge Luis Borges, any attempt to account for a total and universal knowledge is forever and necessarily defeated: "What my eyes saw was simultaneous: what I shall transcribe is successive, because language is successive. Nevertheless, I shall cull something of it all."[88] What must be left out to achieve the Aleph's total picture? What is it that is culled by the current international framework of incentives and rewards for creativity? Who are the actors in the network of creativity?

Actors – the Modern Users?

> Instead of simply transporting effects without transforming them, each of the points in the text may become a bifurcation, an event, or the origin of a new translation. As soon as actors are treated not as intermediaries but as mediators, they render the movement of the social visible to the reader. Thus, through many textual inventions, the social may become again a circulating entity that is no longer composed of the stale assemblage of what passed earlier as being part of society.[89]

A radical re-thinking of the productivity of the knowledge society, and the stakeholders in the creative economy, must re-position the user "inside" the system.[90]

---

scope by virtue of the policy of negotiating such agreements with states throughout the world. This is problematic in that such agreements are negotiated between contracting states rather than in an international forum, and yet in effect the expansion of interests is international.

86 Explored further in the following chapter, Deleuze and Guattari use the concept of "lines of flight" to describe the way in which a totalising system can never contain all its elements. The network community arguably is an example of the lines of flight of users and the way in which these activities introduce instability and de-legitimate the dominant system. See Deleuze G and Guattari F ([1980]1987) *A Thousand Plateaus: Capitalism and Schizophrenia*, Massumi B (trans), Minneapolis, U of Minnesota P.

87 The term "legitimation crisis" was coined by Jürgen Habermas in his work on the public sphere and the public debate of political issues. In this work, Habermas considers the accountability of government and the problem of legitimacy in contemporary capitalist society. See Habermas J ([1973]1975) *Legitimation Crisis*, McCarthy T (trans), Boston, Beacon P. In the context of intellectual property, arguably in an increasingly closed economic system, that accountability is being sought from industry and commercial interests that are increasingly being positioned as the administrators of the system. Challenges to the dominant economic model thereby unsettle and de-stabilise the system. Such challenges might be understood in examples including file-sharing, web logs, and others.

88 Borges JL (1967) "The Aleph", in *Jorge Luis Borges: A Personal Anthology*, Kerrigan A (ed), New York, Grove: 138 at 150.

89 Latour B (2005) *Reassembling the Social*, Oxford, Oxford UP: 128.

90 Hans Joas, in his work on "integrated creativity", suggests that the study of collective action (such as the civil society action that is networked and mobilised in the current debate)

Indeed, Actor-Network-Theory (ANT) provides a method by which to describe the kind of relationality identified in the previous discussion and will provide, as this discussion progresses, an important tool by which to articulate the actions of users in the valuation and transaction of knowledge. In his consideration of what would make a successful text in his own area of inquiry, the methodology that is ANT, Bruno Latour suggests that a good account is one which, in itself, "*traces* the network".[91] Thus, a text which multiplies actors as mediators ("Mediators transform, translate, distort, and modify the meaning or the elements they are supposed to carry"[92]) must be valued over one for which actors merely work as intermediaries (an actor that "transports meaning or force without transformation: defining its inputs is enough to define its outputs"[93]). Such a text would indeed provide a superior account of the user in the intellectual property framework and it is in this way that ANT (as a tool for providing the network rather than a "network" in itself) is significant in that it materialises the actions of users, rather than alienating users as simply effects on (or indeed effects of) the market. The multiplication of mediators and the contribution to social practice is, for Bruno Latour, the mark of a *good* text and presents a strategic way of reading and recognising the participation and contribution of users within the contemporary knowledge network: "A text … is thus a test on how many actors the writer is able to treat as mediators and how far he or she is able to achieve the social."[94]

Thus, ANT describes a methodology, a tool, rather than the network itself. This is significant in the case of re-reading the user in intellectual property law, in that users (or consumers) are necessarily enrolled in the network of any text in their reading and reception and utilisation of the text. In the context of ANT, creative relationships may be read more fully as the material interactions and circumstances between users and producers, rather than fixing creativity within a product. The work (the product) is "completed" precisely because of the interactions in the network. In this way, ANT provides a means by which to describe the agency of users (as actors within the network) within the system – indeed, the actions and interests of users are necessarily accountable (and participatory) within the network. Both in describing the consequences of the current system (whereby the very dispossession of users becomes evidence of their indispensability) as well as a suggested network of co-actors, ANT is thus a critical tool. As Latour explains: "With Actor-Network you may describe something that doesn't at all look like a network."[95]

Drawing upon these distinctions, it is perhaps both strategic and pragmatic to recuperate the user, or consumer, within a network economy of knowledge

---

is critical to an understanding of the relationship between emerging social systems and individual actors: Joas H ([1992]1996) *The Creativity of Action*, Gaines J and Keast P (trans), Cambridge, Polity: 199.

91 Latour B (2005) *Reassembling the Social*, Oxford, Oxford UP: 128.

92 Latour B (2005) *Reassembling the Social*, Oxford, Oxford UP: 39.

93 Latour B (2005) *Reassembling the Social*, Oxford, Oxford UP: 39.

94 Latour B (2005) *Reassembling the Social*, Oxford, Oxford UP: 128-29.

95 Latour B (2005) *Reassembling the Social*, Oxford, Oxford UP: 142.

development and dissemination. That is, the transactions in which value is created within the network might be marked by different incentives and rewards from those operable merely through limiting the transactions themselves. Thus, value would be built not upon creating a scarcity of knowledge transfer, but rather through an understanding of how to conceptualise and commodify value on the basis of generating greater and greater numbers of connections. Limits upon transactions would come not necessarily from intellectual property laws, but rather from the ethical frameworks governing such transactions – frameworks which, as discussed, are necessarily not available within the intellectual property system itself. It is now necessary, as it were, to go outside the system: "For the first time in history, the basic unit of economic organization is not a subject, be it individual (such as the entrepreneur, or the entrepreneurial family) or collective (such as the capitalist class, the corporation, the state). As I have tried to show, *the unit is the network*."[96]

Insight is drawn from the network itself, and the way in which it maintains territory and identity despite the apparent dissipation of individual subjectivity. Arguably, however, individuals derive a sense of worth and belonging from the collective subjectivity of the network, which may indeed be understood as the ethical framework for the network and thus for the transactions in knowledge as well. For instance, external governance of the intellectual property system would necessarily be maintained by responsibilities to cultural diversity, traditional knowledge holders and customary law, and other considerations with respect to questions outside transactions in objects. Indeed, this kind of governance is not counter to the network, but built into the network in ways that are absent from the intellectual property system, a system which, as discussed, problematically and necessarily reduces all relations to a presumably symmetrical exchange of economically driven objects.

In doing so, the value created would be in recognition of a greater activity or participation on the part of the user in such a way as to address the improbability of the question of "balance" between users and creators, as they are currently figured within the law. But at the core of the current "culture wars" is the disillusionment with the very nature of this "contract" itself. The very efficacy of this notion of "balance" depends upon an assumption that the creativity relationship is somehow symmetrical, but indeed such symmetry cannot be assumed. Indeed, the rhetoric of proponents of stronger intellectual property rights depends upon the presumption that this dualistic model of creativity is appropriate and that this symmetry between producers and consumers is workable and can be achieved by the application of intellectual property laws. The "balance" between users and creators that is implied, but arguably not fulfilled, is thus, by definition, a dishonourable breaking of a "promise":

> The notion of "damage" should be placed within this second circle, which is that of *contracts*. For life in society is not based only on its conflicts but also on the giving of

96 Castells M (2000) *The Information Age: Economy, Society and Culture. Volume I: The Rise of the Network Society*, 2nd ed, Oxford, Blackwell: 214.

> our word, on exchanges of words. And conflicts arise precisely when someone's word is broken, when one party believes that the other has not kept the commitment made. Here we find ourselves in the vast domain of the mutual obligations that bind us to one another.[97]

In fact, even more troubling is the way in which this rhetoric of "balance" can be appropriated in order to oppose the roles of producers and consumers, thus maintaining the displacement of users from the creative process and devaluing any contributions made other than through the legitimated and "patronised" producer.

Indeed, more accurately perhaps, it might be suggested that the user is in fact "not" figured in the bargain at all, in so far as there is no recognition of positive entitlement through the various categories of intellectual property, just exceptions and limitations for certain "use". Thus, the user persists merely as a trace of the creator's recognition within the current intellectual property paradigm. On the other hand, understanding knowledge development and transmission through the network, the user's contribution becomes more relevant and meaningful as a genuine actor within the system.

But before it is possible to come to terms with the interests of all actors enrolled in the network, it is necessary to examine further the articulation of those interests throughout the system and throughout its interpellation of players. In particular, the characterisation of creativity might indeed be critical. Thus, in order to consider the efficacy of the network as a meaningful characterisation of innovation in contemporary intellectual property systems, it is to the conceptualisation of creativity within these systems that the discussion now turns.

97 Ricoeur P ([1995]1998) *Critique and Conviction: Conversations with François Azouvi and Marc de Launay*, Blamey K (trans), Cambridge, Polity: 119.

Chapter 2

Creativity

> Creativity is already taken care of in the disposition of a person's acknowledged sources in diverse others.[1]

Introduction

It is useful to consider a broad historical narrative of creativity for the purposes of understanding the assumptions made with regard to this elusive concept in the context of current international intellectual property debate. The investigation of the predominant conceptualisations of creativity in the context of an ever expanding international system of intellectual property, regularly broadened and strengthened to take account of new areas of technology and indeed creativity, will set the context for later considerations of challenges and negotiations of the access and dissemination of knowledge. In particular, an examination of creativity may indeed provide an insight into the way in which the notion may be applicable and relevant in understanding genuine recognition of users as producers within modern intellectual property systems and the economic models applied to innovative activity.

In this chapter, a more detailed examination of the international construction of a preferred concept of creativity through the institution of intellectual property will be undertaken, towards identifying the assumptions and motivations supporting that construction and its ongoing legitimation as an unassailable and seemingly indefinable cultural value. Indeed, in a shift from the language of the "knowledge economy" to the modern "creative economy",[2] policy-makers are perhaps identifying the commercial value in the creative process (the risk of investment), a value far exceeding that inherent in the creative product (as good) alone when it comes to its eventual tangible production. This value is maintained through a variety of mechanisms by which the scarcity in an otherwise inexhaustible product – knowledge – might be facilitated by the "commercialisation" of the creative process and the value that is sustained by intellectual property frameworks. Increasingly, therefore, intellectual property rights have been expanded to acknowledge the interests of "supporting industries", that is, the commercial network and infrastructure through

---

1 Strathern M (1999) *Property, Substance and Effect: Anthropological Essays on Persons and Things*, London, The Athlone P: 134 (on Melanesian systems of ownership).

2 That is, in that the language has now progressed from that of the "knowledge economy" to that of the "creative economy", what the rhetoric is demonstrating is an assumption of oversight not merely of the objects but of the process and cultural value itself.

which knowledge is commodified and exchanged. In other words, the "risk" of the creative process is built into the value of the product. In this way, it may be argued that the burden of this risk is being placed on the public, the user, the individual, as stronger intellectual property rights are perceived as minimising the commercial risk for supporting industries.

Thus, "creativity" has emerged as a central value within the international and diverse debates surrounding intellectual property rights. Not only is it critical to the proponents of greater access to knowledge, cited as a fundamental concern and responsibility of WIPO, but also it has been appropriated, as it were, by proponents of stronger intellectual property rights and greater returns for commercial interests in creating and exploiting those rights. The discussion in the current chapter will therefore draw upon current developments in international intellectual property law in the context of finding "creativity" and "originality".

Possessing Creativity

In the way in which the value of "creativity" has become part of the basic language of intellectual property law, a certain mystification of the process itself is occurring. In other words, the complexity of the "creative process", and indeed the networks of creative connections, the development of "creative understanding",[3] is simplified in order to be articulated through the conventional transactions recognised within the system. Thus, the intellectual property narrative of innovation relies on this mystification to obscure the collaborative and incremental processes of creativity, of intellectual activity and, indeed, to render creative products objective and asocial. This is the mystification of creative process, the simplification of the creative process – thus achieving a kind of stable and coherent "author" function. At the same time, the "author" limits proliferative flights of meaning; indeed, "The author is the principle of thrift in the proliferation of meaning".[4]

By virtue of this mystification, the concept of creativity has become firmly established in the rhetoric of advocates for stronger intellectual property rights, as well as in the arguments of those seeking to roll back intellectual property protection and to strengthen exceptions and limitations. In other words, the concept of creativity is fundamental not only as a value with which intellectual property is seen to be in possible conflict, but also as a means by which intellectual property can be established as the arbiter of that very same value. An important preoccupation of the system that is traced throughout the present discussion is the way in which "creativity" and

3 This term comes from the work of Mikhail Bakhtin and is derived from the notion of a "dialogue" or dialogical relationship as the basis for achieving greater understanding and indeed co-creativity with the author. This is discussed further in Chapter 5, but see also Bakhtin MM (1986) *Speech Genres and Other Late Essays*, McGee VW (trans), Austin, U of Texas P.

4 Foucault M (1979) "What is an Author?", in Harari JV (ed) *Textual Strategies: Perspectives in Post-Structuralist Criticism*, Ithaca, Cornell UP: 141 at 159.

"innovation" are taken to demonstrate a self-conscious departure from tradition in order to meet the threshold for "inventiveness", "originality", and "newness". It is in the articulation of the relationship between tradition and innovation, as will be seen in later chapters, that one of the most critical interrogations of the present system can be made. Indeed, it is the incremental innovations upon tradition, perhaps the most fundamental source of innovation, that are being obscured within this model.

This dynamic between tradition and innovation recalls Pierre Macherey's concerns with the relationship between creativity and production, considered in the previous chapter: "The various 'theories' of creation all ignore the process of making; they omit any account of production … All speculation over man the creator is intended to eliminate a real knowledge: the 'creative process' is, precisely, not a process, a labour; it is a religious formula to be found on funeral moments." Macherey is identifying the predominant characterising of creativity as divining, a mythologising of the "source" of creative products – whether that be the author, artist, or other "genuine creator". In positing the notion of "production", Macherey arguably is not simply opposing "creativity" but rather is identifying the "root" of creativity – to produce. This is significant in the context of the mythology of creativity underpinning the rhetorical arguments for stronger rights, which appear to rely very much on the maintenance of the opposition between creativity and production.[5] Importantly, Macherey's discussion highlights what is now significant in intellectual property debates – namely the way in which the concept of "creativity", as deployed within intellectual property narratives, is simplified as an "event" or product, emanating from a single source (of activity, insight, talent, genius or otherwise)[6] as distinct from a process that is indiscrete (and indiscreet[7]), collaborative, intertextual, and incremental.[8]

In the validation of certain forms, locations, and processes for production, the framework of the intellectual property system is similarly reliant upon the value

5 For instance, Jonathan Zuck has recently stated that a many-to-many society is not desirable precisely for the reason that we would then become "a society of producers rather than innovators". Similarly, in the context of discussions in this chapter concerning the "economics of creativity", he described the need to protect the "risk of innovation" which he quantified in terms of investment in "true innovation". Zuck maintained that the critical question for intellectual property policy was "whether we can create an environment conducive to investment in order to put in the money and time necessary for 'true' invention". See Zuck J (2006) "IP and the Knowledge Commons: Lobbying and Advocacy II". Panel. The Politics and Ideology of Intellectual Property. Trans Atlantic Consumer Dialogue (TACD) Conference. 20 March.

6 Seemingly collaborative models within intellectual property laws (including joint authorship and joint inventors) nevertheless still operate upon a singularity of the source in that the "event" of creation is time-bound and discrete.

7 This is used in the sense of the carnivalesque (Mikhail Bakhtin), as discussed later in Chapter 5.

8 Compare the criticism of Macherey for polarising creativity and production, in Pope R (2005) *Creativity: Theory, History, Practice*, London, Routledge: 7.

of "authenticity" and, as such, a process of institutionalisation of the "original".[9] Indeed, the history of teaching in artistic method suggests the way in which the act of copying re-affirms the primacy and "creativity" of the privileged original.[10] This culture of learning (*do as I do*) inscribes the "official culture", the validated form.[11] Thus, in determining the "value" of creativity, the system is similarly bestowing an authenticity upon the works thus recognised. In particular, authenticity emerges as a kind of "branding" of intellectual products, betraying a more commercial approach to the questions of creativity raised by this concept. The impression of authenticity relies strongly upon the narrative of creative process and, thus, the articulation of a stable "creator", the "genuine creator". Indeed, this creator is authenticated not only from the perspective of the process of creativity, but also from that of the perspective of the authenticity of the role and identity of the particular creator – what Bourdieu might identify as the "post"[12] of the creator or artist, discussed again later in this chapter. Thus, authenticity is derived through the supporting and legitimated infrastructure of exhibitions, collections, curation, and industry – a kind of "authoring" of the process itself through the legitimating (economic) narrative: "The uniqueness of a work of art is inseparable from its being imbedded in the fabric of tradition … In other words, the unique value of the 'authentic' work of art has its basis in ritual, the location of its original use value."[13] It is the nature of this "production" that can be traced in the work of Macherey (literature) and Bourdieu (art) and for which it is possible to extend to understand the infrastructure and institutionalising of creativity and innovation more broadly.

Further, in adopting the value of creativity, intellectual property is increasingly vested with the import of recognising not mere originality, but genuine and authentic "works". Thus, in identifying intellectual property rights in new and emerging technologies and productions, the system is always already vesting those outputs

9 See the concept of "aura" in Walter Benjamin's essay, "The Work of Art in the Age of Mechanical Reproduction", in Benjamin W ([1955]1970) *Illuminations*, Arendt H (ed and intro), Zohn H (trans), London, Fontana: 211 at 214. "Aura" is considered later in this chapter.

10 Hilary Schwartz describes a process of indoctrination in the education of artists, as preserved in the "Museums of Copies". Schwartz H (1996) *The Culture of the Copy: Striking Likenesses, Unreasonable Facsimiles*, New York, Zone.

11 See Deleuze G ([1968]1994) *Difference and Repetition*, Patton P (trans), New York: Columbia UP: 22. The relationship between *do as I do* as distinct from *do with me* is pursued further in the context of learning in a dynamic system of creativity in users and creators in Chapter 5.

12 Bourdieu describes the artist's "post" as "often existing prior to him and outlives him (entailing obligations, such as 'the artist's life,' attributes, traditions, modes of expression, etc)". Bourdieu P ([1984]1993) *Sociology in Question*, Nice R (trans), London, SAGE: 141. See also the discussion of artistic professions in Lotringer S and Virilio P (2005) *The Accident of Art*, Taormina M (trans), New York, Semiotext(e).

13 Benjamin W ([1955]1970) *Illuminations*, Arendt H (ed and intro), Zohn H (trans), London, Fontana: 217.

with creativity, by virtue of their recognition within the system. Indeed, at a recent meeting in Cambridge on rights in personality and publicity, one delegate questioned the extension of intellectual property rights to celebrity, expressing disbelief at a system in which "a person becomes a work of art".[14] As expressed in this delegate's outrage, it would seem that the intellectual property system has become synonymous with "good production" and indeed "high art", as considered in the previous chapter. The grand narrative, the meta-narrative, of the cultural institution of intellectual property is that of a kind of meta-creativity. That which is not created within the legitimated processes identified by the system will not be registered as creative, but as mere "folk" production. In this same process, by virtue of the way in which the economic infrastructure and supporting industries for creativity have come to be presented as the "prerequisite" for creativity, not only are those industries constructed as creative, but also creativity becomes something which can be manufactured. It follows that creativity is increasingly constructed upon socio-economic foundations, supported by the narrative of the ongoing "progress" and "direction" in linear economic models of creative output in contemporary societies.[15] The language and system of intellectual property thereby imposes a monocultural model on creativity, by establishing a narrative, a "myth" of modern creativity and process that identifies not only certain products but also certain ways and relations by which to make those products: "If we want to move ahead quickly while remaining precise, nothing is as concise as a myth."[16]

By way of contrast, network or "folk" production (like that imagined in the Creative Commons system) does not rely upon the narration of past events, but rather, is an ongoing and dynamic creative process. In the context of the current discussion, the network model has the potential to re-appropriate the creative process, and the mythology attached to the concept of creativity, as narrated within the intellectual property model. Thus, contemporary networks, as considered in the previous chapter, offer the opportunity for a re-invigorated "account of production"[17] and thus of the user.

Naming Creativity, Identifying Creativity

The significant power of the narration of intellectual property is derived from its capacity to "name" creativity. That is, the system identifies and provides a creative act in the differentiation of the creative process (as an otherwise continuous "flow", as considered later in this chapter) through naming – titles, trade marks, patent

14 Cambridge Centre for Intellectual Property and Information Law. University of Cambridge. Faculty of Law. 11 February 2006.

15 As discussed in the previous chapter.

16 Latour B (2004) *Politics of Nature: How to Bring the Sciences into Democracy*, Porter C (trans), Cambridge MA, Harvard UP: 10.

17 Macherey P ([1966]1978) *A Theory of Literary Production*, Wall G (trans), London, Routledge: 68.

titles, and so on are instrumental in the naming and identification of a "creative" act. This taxonomical rendering of the creative process is significant, not only from a practical point of view in the administration of the system and the "right to benefit", but also in a seeming ability to divide up all creative output by virtue of the prior definitions offered by the system. In this way, the intellectual property system is the ultimate authorial voice in identifying the apparent totality of creativity offered by a society. In the polarisation of "high" (intellectual property) and "low" (distributed "folk" production of the network, such as Creative Commons and other initiatives) not only is the latter de-valued, but also in many cases it is deemed not creative, even parasitic (in its "copies") of the genuine product.[18] Indeed, at a meeting of industry representatives and academics on the system of Creative Commons, one industry representative commented: "Creative Commons seems to be providing a big advantage to people who want a short-cut to creativity and be cast in the role of creator at the expense of genuine songwriters."[19] Another industry representative described the economic stability of industry as providing the necessary framework for creativity, such that the genuine artist can "give up their day job".[20] Thus, creativity occurring outside this situation of "authenticity" is invalid.

It appears, thus, that this mystification of the creative process owes much to the Romantic notion of the creator and the presumption that creativity emerges from a single spiritual source – the author, the artist, the inventor, the creator. Indeed, this romanticising of the "role" of the creator (and the creator's "post"[21]) is complicit in the ongoing distinction of intellectual property's "high" creativity from the "low", "peasant", "folk" output from the "non-genuine" creator,[22] or worse, the "pirate".[23]

Drawing upon this figure of the genuine creator, representatives of industry have variously been able to suggest its role as the prerequisite for creativity, the

---

18 Such impressions of Creative Commons were expressed by delegates at the Creative Economy Conference of the UK Presidency of the EU, in the stream, "Licensing Fit and Fair". Individuals accessing the system were described in ways oppositional to the implied "genuine creator" supported by the patronage of a formal contract with industry (publishing, recording, and so on).

19 Queen Mary, University of London. Charterhouse Square. 27 January 2005.

20 However, this polarisation of "genuine songwriters" and those who must "keep their day job", as it were, is not necessarily supported by the evidence. See for instance, on music artists' earnings, Kretschmer M (2005) "Artists' earnings and copyright: A review of British and German music industry data in the context of digital technologies", *First Monday,* volume 10, number 1 (January).

21 Bourdieu describes the artist's "post" as "often existing prior to him and outlives him (entailing obligations, such as 'the artist's life,' attributes, traditions, modes of expression, etc)". Bourdieu P ([1984]1993) *Sociology in Question*, Nice R (trans), London, SAGE: 141.

22 Note the earlier discussion of this divide in relation to the example of Creative Commons.

23 Note the discussion of language in Chapter 1.

economic circumstances for creativity.[24] In other words, the economic framework is presented as indeed essential and thus prior to creativity, and so is necessarily the circumstances to release the inherent and innate genius of the "genuine creator". In this way, the language and mystique of the "genuine creator", the innate genius, together with the ongoing adherence to creativity, in fact reinforces the dominance of the economic model of progress (and patronage) through the very branding of the system with these terms. This charisma of the figure of "genius" operates as a kind of personality – that is, it invests intellectual property systems with the personality, the "self", that legitimates the system as social and beyond question. Strategies branded as "anti-IP"[25] are therefore situated as anti-social in that they displace and distribute the power of the intellectual property hero. Creative Commons, for instance, opens the "publicity" of creativity to anyone in ways that defy and confound the classic model. A creator could be just anybody.

The "risk" of creativity, as discussed in the previous chapter, is thereby monitored in terms of the investment of the supporting industry in "genius". Without adequate protection of the industry (indeed, a type of "right to benefit" from that investment), it is suggested that this risk would pose a potential obstacle to ongoing creativity. Thus, the expansion of rights to "protect" an industry is legitimated as the protection, rather, of the "right to benefit" of the creator. With the strengthening of rights in various forms of intellectual property, and the expansion of rights to incorporate new and unanticipated developments within industries (for example, the proposed protection for webcasting),[26] the framework for law-making appears to be increasingly concerned with the risk of industry, rather than the personal risk of the "creator". Further, with greater rights, that risk is not dissipated but rather it is displaced onto the user, for whom access is inevitably compromised.

Newness and Novelty

> *Mélange*, hotchpotch, a bit of this and a bit of that is *how newness enters the world.*[27]

---

24 Such references have been made at several industry consultations and meetings, including the Creative Economy Conference of the UK Presidency of the EU, "Licensing Fit and Fair", 5-7 October 2005, where industry representatives suggested that composers attempting to use Creative Commons are "vulnerable". Elsewhere, it has been suggested that "it is not a question of creativity *per se*, but the cost of providing the framework for creativity" (Creative Commons Research Group, Queen Mary University of London, 27 January 2005).

25 See further the discussion in the previous chapter.

26 WIPO Standing Committee on Copyright and Related Rights. Draft Basic Proposal for the WIPO Treaty on the Protection of Broadcasting Organizations Including a Non-Mandatory Appendix on the Protection in Relation to Webcasting. 14th Session. Geneva, 1-5 May 2006. SCCR/14/2. See also the discussion in Chapter 3.

27 Rushdie S (1991) *Imaginary Homelands*, London, Penguin P: 394.

The mystification of the creative process cooperates with the direction and progress[28] narrated by the intellectual property system. This progress is seemingly undeniable, whereby the "conventions" of intellectual property (the criteria for protection, that is recognition, within any of the categories of intellectual property) at the same time allow (and constrain) what can be recognised as new. In other words, intellectual property in itself provides a tradition of creativity, albeit a very recent one, and a narrative of creative process. This same assumption of "progress" attaches to the exportation of intellectual property systems to developing and least developed countries, whereby its very presence is seen to be compatible with (indeed inextricable from) economic development, despite adequate evidence (and arguably despite evidence to the contrary).[29]

However, newness (and thus innovation) is itself a cultural value – necessarily situated, contingent, and local. It is recognised by virtue of its comparability to what is known and valued within a narrative of innovation according to its recognition within the conventions of that narrative. This cultural contingency of newness or novelty is especially significant in the context of protection of traditional knowledge and traditional cultural expressions, particularly where such knowledge is ossified as "ancient" and "historical", prepared as an anthropological artefact, and its newness obscured by the parameters of the dominant intellectual property model of recognition.[30] This is necessarily a contingent value, and indeed a located value. In other words, that "recognition" both establishes the sense of self, of self-recognition, for those whose knowledge and values are identified within the system, and dislocates that knowledge (and knowledge-holders) that is without position, without territory, within the system. The "self" is inevitably territorial ("my place in the world"), and at stake in the creative economy is the very territory of knowledge, the empire[31] of

28 Further discussion of this notion of direction and "progress" can be found in Chapter 1.

29 For instance, see Graham Dutfield's discussion of the development of technologies in the United States and the resistance to the implementation of comprehensive patent protection until a concurrent benefit in being an exporter of technology began to apply: Dutfield G (2003) *Intellectual Property Rights and the Life Science Industries: A Twentieth Century History*, Aldershot, Ashgate.

30 For a full consideration of traditional knowledge and the conflict with intellectual property models of knowledge recognition and diversity, see Gibson J (2005) *Community Resources: Intellectual Property, International Trade and Protection of Traditional Knowledge*, Aldershot, Ashgate.

31 The use of "empire" comes from the work of Michael Hardt and Antonio Negri to indicate the way in which intellectual property, albeit a territorial system, is increasingly suggesting a transnational framework for transactions in knowledge, that is, one without necessarily referring to nation-states as such. See Hardt M and Negri A (2000) *Empire*, Cambridge MA, Harvard UP. Hardt and Negri describe empire in the context of a capitalist globalisation, through which, arguably, the forces for expansion of intellectual property systems might be recognised. Of increasing relevance in this respect is the growing reliance of the United States upon bilateral free trade agreements (particularly with developing countries), which may exceed restrictions and overcome flexibilities that currently apply

an increasingly internationally harmonised cultural system: "Can this becoming, this emergence, be called Art? That would make the territory a result of art. The artist: the first person to set out a boundary stone, or to make a mark. Property, collective or individual, is derived from that, even when it is in the service of war and oppression. Property is fundamentally artistic because art is fundamentally *poster*, *placard*."[32] Indeed, one might argue that what is at stake in the institution of intellectual property is not the artist, but the territory.[33]

Thus, when it comes to territory, the question of recognition (and self-recognition) resonates strongly with the concept of genre and the construction of expectations in an indiscriminate "public". In other words, the "public" is "overcoded" and presented with seemingly indisputable limits within which to recognise creativity and thus oneself.[34] However, genre also introduces the capacity for strategic readings and departures from those expectations.[35] This is important particularly in those industries where genre identifies not only categories of works, but also collectives or interpretive communities. The notion of interpretive community comes from Stanley Fish.[36] The concept refers to the sharing of codes or conventions within the

---

under international agreements (including TRIPS) and yet "internationalise" the bargain thus made.

32 Deleuze G and Guattari F ([1980]1987) *A Thousand Plateaus: Capitalism and Schizophrenia*, Massumi B (trans), Minneapolis, U of Minnesota P: 316.

33 As Rosemary Coombe has suggested, "Those who control intellectual properties must always cope with the presence of others in the cultural spaces they attempt to colonize." See Coombe R (1998) *The Cultural Life of Intellectual Properties: Authorship, Appropriation, and the Law*, Durham, Duke UP: 129.

34 Self-recognition and identity is also an aspect of critical inquiry in feminist theory, particularly in the work of Judith Butler with respect to the social self, gender, and identity. Butler's theory of the social self as an object upon which discursive strategies legitimate the recognition only of particular identities lends particular insight into the discursive legitimation of certain creative activity through the intellectual property paradigm. See, in particular, Butler J (1990) *Gender Trouble: Feminism and the Subversion of Identity*, New York, Routledge; Butler J (1993) *Bodies that Matter: On the Discursive Limits of "Sex"*, New York, Routledge; and Butler J (2000) *Antigone's Claim: Kinship Between Life and Death*, New York, Columbia UP.

35 For instance, the work of Henry Jenkins on fan culture and his appropriation of Michel de Certeau's concept of "reading as poaching" to describe the strategic re-reading and re-presentation of texts is informative on this issue. See Jenkins H (1992) *Textual Poachers: Television Fans and Participatory Culture*, New York, Routledge; and also Jenkins H (1988) "Star Trek Rerun, Reread, Rewritten: Fan Writing as Textual Poaching", 5 *Critical Studies in Mass Communications* 85. See also De Certeau M (1984) *The Practice of Everyday Life*, Rendall S (trans), Berkeley, U of California P. The concept of "textual poaching" is particularly relevant in the context of user appropriation and revision of texts (particularly in the case of trade marks and branding) such that the user is inextricable from the value created in the brand (see the later discussion in Chapter 4).

36 Fish S (1980) *Is There a Text in This Class? The Authority of Interpretive Communities*, London, Harvard UP.

community in order to engage "interpretive strategies" in reading the text, whereby meaning is thus generated in collusion with the reader rather than prior to that interpretation. Fish explains this in later work:

> What was required was an explanation that could account for both agreement and disagreement, and that explanation was found in the idea of an interpretive community, not so much a group of individuals who shared a point of view, but a point of view or way of organizing experience that shared individuals in the sense that its assumed distinctions, categories of understanding, and stipulations of relevance and irrelevance were the content of the consciousness of community members who were therefore no longer individuals, but, insofar as they were embedded in the community's enterprise, community property.[37]

This definition is somewhat useful in deciphering the political activity of the dissonant "public", that unlike the notion of a generalised "public" as the apposite of the creator, this definition does not require consensus on meaning within that public, as might otherwise be the consideration in a kind of deliberative democratic approach to user interests. When interrogating the politicisation of user groups and the construction of user interests within civil society discourse, the organisation of that group with the notion of a nominal consensus is implied or even advised.[38] However, the imposition of that consensus paradoxically re-instates the dualistic normative narrative of the world view posited by proponents of economic models of creativity – that is, an antagonistic relationship between creators/producers and users/consumers. On the question of a democratic consensus, Chantal Mouffe explains:

> One of the shortcomings of the deliberative approach is that, by postulating the availability of a public sphere where power would have been eliminated and where a rational consensus could be realized, this model of democratic politics is unable to acknowledge the dimension of antagonism that the pluralism of values entails and its ineradicable character. This is why it is bound to miss the specificity of the political which it can only envisage as a specific domain of morality.[39]

Arguably, it is necessary to interrogate the nature of the "public" in which such consensus is contrived. In so far as the singular public, both for governments and

---

37 Fish S (1989) *Doing What Comes Naturally: Change, Rhetoric, and the Practice of Theory in Literary and Legal Studies*, Oxford, Clarendon P: 141.

38 For instance, speaking at the International Consumer Conference, "The Politics and Ideology of Intellectual Property", Rufus Pollock of the Open Rights Group insisted upon the need for greater organisation, coordination and consensus among consumer groups; indeed, he explicitly polarised the interests as those of rights-holders and those of users. This is arguably a misconception of the debate and a problematic reassertion of a nominal user in ways cooperative with the dominant institution of intellectual property, and completely contrary to the stated objectives.

39 Mouffe C (2000) *The Democratic Paradox*, London, Verso: 98-99.

for civil society, is a "fictional entity",[40] it remains a central protagonist of the debate, seemingly no matter the rhetorician. However, the "public" that is defined in intellectual property policy arguably does not match the "public" that is represented and indicated by civil society, and the term is ultimately deceiving and disabling when it comes to recognising the diversity in the debate, and in the issues themselves. Indeed, the very notion of the "public" as it is generated both by policy-makers and by civil society as a potentially homogeneous group (especially with respect to the notion of uniform "organisation") defeats the very diversity of user access and expectation that is suggested by civil society actors. Aside from the pluralities of "publics", the term "counterpublic" suggests a useful departure from the highly politicised and evaluative category of the "public":

> A counterpublic, against the background of the public sphere, enables a horizon of opinion and exchange; its exchanges remain distinct from authority and can have a critical relation to power; its extent is in principle indefinite, because it is not based on a precise demography but mediated by print, theatre, diffuse networks of talk, commerce, and the like.[41]

Thus, the concept of the counterpublic is strategic in its emphasis on the actions and customs of the public, rather than its identity. Indeed, the network is instrumentally a counterpublic in its very resistance to the process of nominating an identifiable public. For civil society organisations, necessarily the stake is access, no matter the publics.

The "territory" of the user network, therefore, is particularly significant from a political perspective, especially when considering the political and ideological nature of the international discussions concerning access to knowledge. Recalling the concerns of Mouffe with respect to the misplaced emphasis on unanimity and consensus, it is useful to consider why consensus is so desirable, and the way in which civil society can resist the regionalising of the debate and maximise the impact of the network.[42] In other words, not unlike the concepts of Deleuze and Guattari, as will be discussed, Mouffe also rejects an imposed organic unity of society, a homogeneous conceptualisation of the user. Thus, the democratic objective will not necessarily be consensus on the issues but a consensus on a political good as practice in order to challenge and de-institutionalise the centrality of the dominant discourse (intellectual property). The recognition of creativity and newness is therefore bound not only by the territorial limits of shared meaning (language, culture, and community), but also by the "territorial" restrictions imposed by the proprietary system of recognising valuable creative events. Thus, access to knowledge becomes a campaign for territory, for the domain of self-recognition in the creative process.

---

40 Warner M (2005) *Publics and Counterpublics*, New York, Zone: 12.

41 Warner M (2005) *Publics and Counterpublics*, New York, Zone: 56-57.

42 See also Urry J (2000) *Sociology Beyond Societies: Mobilities for the Twenty-First Century*, London, Routledge: particularly 36-37. See also the discussion in Urry J (2003) *Global Complexity*, Cambridge, Polity.

The notion of "newness" and originality thus appears to be critical to the understanding of a genuine creativity, whereby incremental and derivative creativity is criticised as unoriginal and the intellectual property system is vested with the responsibility and capability of identifying the "true" innovation.[43] How, then, does the language of intellectual property locate creativity and originality in newer forms – such as databases, broadcasts, and webcasting?

Investment and Renewal

> The simulacrum, the simulation of a packet of noodles, has become the true concept; and the one who packages the product, commodity, or work of art has become the philosopher, conceptual persona, or artist.[44]

By definition, newness is transient, compromised by its use, and can and must be lost in order to maintain the narrative of progress.[45] However, in current controversies over the perceived opportunity for rights in perpetuity through renewal,[46] how is newness renewed?

Arguably, the work, the expression, maintains its newness, as it were. It continues to be "original" and singular in a chronology of "newness" that is maintained (and recorded in the case of rights by registration, as in designs, trade marks, and patents, for example) by the narrative of intellectual property. That expression is always new – it is not imitated or repeated, it is territory that is secured by that piece of property, that piece of intellectual property. Thus, within the language of intellectual property, newness is no longer transient. Or at least, newness has been extended and continues to be extended for the life of the monopoly granted. In the case of copyright and the debate over extension of term, newness is enduring for longer and longer. In this way, the "value" of the work, both economically and culturally, is increasing. To benefit from the "newness" of intellectual property, that "newness" must be artificially maintained by the intellectual property system in ways not incompatible with broader notions of novelty within the cultural economy.[47]

---

43 Zuck J (2006) "IP and the Knowledge Commons: Lobbying and Advocacy II". Panel. The Politics and Ideology of Intellectual Property. Trans Atlantic Consumer Dialogue (TACD) Conference. 20 March.

44 Deleuze G and Guattari F ([1991]1994) *What is Philosophy?* Tomlinson H and Burchell G (trans), London, Verso: 10.

45 This is illustrated by the system itself, in principles such as "prior art" and "novelty" in patent law.

46 For instance, see the discussion in Landes WM and Posner RA (2003) "Indefinitely Renewable Copyright", 70 *University of Chicago Law Review* 471.

47 For instance, see the discussion in Negus K and Pickering M (2004) *Creativity, Communication and Cultural Value*, London, SAGE: 10. As discussed in the previous chapter, the "creative economy" suggests an equally closed system. Ilkka Tuomi suggests that, in the closed system offered by an economic world view, "novelty is a contradiction in terms". See

Thus, the continuous "time" of innovation is reduced to the structural economic space of external measurements, an analog of the digital and continuous innovation in time: *time is money*. Henri Bergson, in his extensive examination of the nature of time, change, and its measurement, argues that time and duration are continuous and immeasurable, and yet they are rendered perceptible through the spatialisation or calibration of time, the rendering of time through a spatial metaphor.[48] As Bergson explains, space becomes a symbol of time.[49] Expressions and their duration become a symbol of change and innovation:

> If I draw my finger across a sheet of paper without looking at it, the motion I perform is, perceived from within, a continuity of consciousness, something of my own flow, in a word, duration. If I now open my eyes, I see that my finger is tracing on the sheet of paper a line that is preserved, where all is juxtaposition and no longer succession; this is the unfolded, which is the record of motion, and which will be its symbol as well.[50]

Similarly, in another attempt to point to the passage of time, Yve-Alain Bois suggests: "Moreover, you are never sure of having seen clearly, of having put your finger on it (there are so many points)."[51] Through the points, the objects, arguably, as a system for measuring innovation, the model of intellectual property can be understood as spatialising time (literally, through the imposition of terms of protection, defining the duration of newness). But at once this compromises perception, at once missing many points: "But by invading the series of our psychic states, by introducing space

---

Tuomi I (2002) *Networks of Innovation: Change and Meaning in the Age of the Internet*, Oxford, Oxford UP: 14.

48 See Bergson H ([1888]2001) *Time and Free Will: An Essay on the Immediate Data of Consciousness*, Pogson FL (trans), 3rd ed (1913), Mineola NY, Dover; and the later consideration of Einstein's theory of time as in fact a theory of space, of measurement, in Bergson H ([1922]1999) *Duration and Simultaneity: Bergson and the Einsteinian Universe*, Lewis M and Durie R (trans), Manchester, Clinamen P. F David Peat also considers the inanimate transformations in time described in general relativity and quantum theory, in Peat FD (2000) *The Blackwinged Night: Creativity in Nature and Mind*, Cambridge MA, Perseus: 148-150. Bergson's understanding of the continuity and immeasurability of time informs Deleuze and Guattari's concepts of connected flow and smooth space, that is, space that is not calibrated or "striated" by regulatory systems of measurement. This is discussed further below, but in particular see Deleuze G and Guattari F ([1980]1987) *A Thousand Plateaus: Capitalism and Schizophrenia*, Massumi B (trans), Minneapolis, U of Minnesota P.

49 Manuel Castells identifies a similar construction of time in order to spatialise flows in a virtual network: "Space shapes time in our society, thus reversing an historical trend: flows induce timeless time, places are time-bounded." See Castells M (2000) *The Information Age: Economy, Society and Culture. Volume I: The Rise of the Network Society*, 2nd ed, Oxford, Blackwell: 495.

50 Bergson H ([1922]1999) *Duration and Simultaneity: Bergson and the Einsteinian Universe*, Lewis M and Durie R (trans), Manchester, Clinamen P: 34.

51 Bois Y-A (1997) "Very Slow", in Bois Y-A and Krauss R *Formless: A User's Guide*, New York, Zone: 198.

into our perception of duration, it corrupts at its very source our feeling of outer and inner change, of movement, and of freedom."[52] The intellectual property system "marks time", slowing the instantaneity of network creativity so that it becomes perceptible and manageable in the transactions thus regulated.

All at once, however, this spatial metaphor is seemingly out of step with the creativity and collaborative impact of networks and new technologies. Indeed, where networks seemingly traverse traditional boundaries of the nation-state and governed space, the question of time becomes critical: "The loss of material space leads to the government of nothing but time."[53] Time is the territory at stake in intellectual property – the time of innovation, of change, of newness. The appropriation of territory thereby demarcates and directs the traditions, the domain, and the kinship of competing discourse. In this way, what is presented as the measurement of innovation is perhaps a mere creation, a semblance, of innovation: "By assuming that we merely measure, predict, or harness this world of situations, individuals, and forces, we mask the fact that we create it."[54]

Indeed it is the governance of time that alienates the holders of traditional knowledge from the model of protection offered by intellectual property system. It is these compromises that make the assimilation of traditional knowledge within intellectual property frameworks problematic.[55] The traditional incremental (and continuous) innovation in traditional and indigenous societies is not easily calibrated within intellectual property logic. The mutual cooperation defies the conventional marks of the beginning and end of discrete knowledge objects. Similarly, the governance of objects through the intellectual property model attempts to appropriate the territory of cyberspace through time – literally through the regulation of network exchanges and relationships, through network traditions and diversity. Possibly suggesting a different relationship to time from that understood in traditional and indigenous communities, and yet perhaps not, the network similarly confronts the narration of time that is offered by simple linear models of innovation. Attempts to over-regulate in the face of the increasing disjunction between the conventional economic model of innovation in intellectual property systems and the instantaneous, immeasurable, and "priceless" innovation of the Internet, are ever more about the ambition to govern and territorialise virtual space. This regulation obscures the

---

52 Bergson H ([1888]2001) *Time and Free Will: An Essay on the Immediate Data of Consciousness*, Pogson FL (trans), 3rd ed (1913), Mineola NY, Dover: 74.

53 Virilio P ([1977]1986) *Speed and Politics: An Essay on Dromology*, Polizzotti M (trans), New York, Semiotext(e): 141. Deleuze and Guattari also consider the rapidity of "smooth space", which is used here to understand the network in the discussion below, but see Deleuze G and Guattari F ([1980]1987) *A Thousand Plateaus: Capitalism and Schizophrenia*, Massumi B (trans), Minneapolis, U of Minnesota P: 371.

54 Wagner R (1981) *The Invention of Culture*, Rev ed, Chicago, U of Chicago P: 71.

55 For further discussion on this conceptualisation of traditional knowledge as proprietary objects within intellectual property models, as distinct from resources of cultural diversity and community, see Gibson J (2005) *Community Resources: Intellectual Property, International Trade and Protection of Traditional Knowledge*, Aldershot, Ashgate.

innovation and the authenticity of networks. What is the speed of innovation? What are the markers of duration that are so necessary to intellectual property and yet so illogical in the case of contemporary networks or traditional societies?

Arguably, the governance of time is possible through the imposition of economic quanta of innovation. The intellectual property system relies upon the artificial construction of scarcity in what are otherwise inexhaustible "public goods"[56] (information and ideas) through the measurement of ideas (as otherwise continuous and immeasurable) via spatial metaphors of the objects of intellectual property. In other words, this scarcity creates the market for intellectual property.[57] Such markets are perceived to be vulnerable to increasing threats from challenges to the dominant economic models for innovation, thus motivating the broadening of intellectual property protection in order to incorporate those challenges within its boundaries.

Paradoxically, or obviously, the very means by which the system creates scarcity and thus value in its objects (through the application of time-limited monopolies) and an enduring "newness", is also that which calculates a certain "obsolescence" for those objects, at least as far as the commercial market is concerned. This obsolescence drives the system, that is, it is the contrived catalyst for subsequent innovation within this economic model. However, with increasing lobbying for extensions of term in copyright,[58] the use of technical protection measures,[59] and

---

56 The construction of information as a global public good (in other words, it is non-rivalrous, non-excludable, non-crowdable) is found throughout the current debate over open access models (derived from open source software development) for scientific publishing, scientific research, and biotechnology. See the discussion of information as a public good, and the relationship to intellectual property laws, in Vaver D (1997) *Intellectual Property Law: Copyright, Patents, Trademarks*, Toronto, Irwin Law: 3-6.

57 Plant A (1934) "The Economic Theory Concerning Patents for Invention", 1 *Economica* 30. See also Gibson J (2005) *Community Resources: Intellectual Property, International Trade and Protection of Traditional Knowledge*, Aldershot, Ashgate: 83-84. In the current tension between increasing rights and progressively alienated users, James Boyle has suggested that we are currently experiencing a different kind of scarcity, the "scarcity of imagination": Boyle J (2005) Launch of the Adelphi Charter on Creativity, Innovation and Intellectual Property. Royal Society for the Encouragement of Arts, Manufactures and Commerce (RSA). London. 13 October.

58 Increased lobbying followed, in particular the passing of the Copyright Term Extension Act 1998 (Sonny Bono Copyright Act) in the United States. Also relevant on this point was the extensive material presented to the Supreme Court in an unsuccessful challenge of the constitutionality of this Act in *Eldred v Ashcroft,* 537 US 186 (2003).

59 The use of technical protection measures (TPM) effectively facilitates the regulation of the "object" itself after it has been lawfully acquired. In other words, copy-protection software in CDs and DVDs and other mechanisms may be deployed (and may not be declared to the user at the time of purchase). Obviously, while labelling should be mandatory in these circumstances, more importantly this practice compromises the original "bargain" ostensibly struck between users and producers in the performance of the intellectual property system itself. This practice is sometimes also referred to as digital rights management (DRM), although this is not strictly correct, in that DRM can be merely self-identification on a website.

other erosion of the territory of users, this obsolescence in the rights themselves (as a driver of production) is being undermined: "The imperative of built-in obsolescence – whether informing the manufacture of toothbrushes, training shoes, cameras or cars – has become vital according to the growth criteria by which modern economies are judged to function correctly."[60] Why, then, is there so much interest in extending term and thus defeating the system's built-in obsolescence (as an effective commercial and economic system)? And from what policy basis does extension of term apparently derive its support? Are the supporting industries, the "patrons" of intellectual property, enjoying a "renewed" aristocracy as the arbiters of cultural progress and knowledge? Is this a renewed Romanticism? Are the current intellectual property debates a sign of a neo-Romantic time? However, this time, the markets themselves have been assimilated with the distinction of the "work". The system itself thus creates the privilege and precious distinction of the creative or innovative event as an increasingly rare occurrence and scarce commodity. Creativity is priceless.

Manifest Innovation

Despite the diversity of knowledge and technologies, as well as the apparent diversity in the categories of intellectual property themselves, the system as a whole generally relies upon a persistent adherence to the "presence" or "expression" of the work. Patents make invention (really an idea) a kind of expression, a finished and discrete work, through the mimicry of copyright in the specification of the patent.[61] Similarly, designs are registered in the United Kingdom either through the filing of a specimen or a representation (drawing).[62] Thus, both administratively and ideologically, as it

---

This distinction is set out in the WIPO Copyright Treaty (WCT) (Arts 11 and 12) and the WIPO Performances and Phonograms Treaty (WPPT) (and similarly in Articles 18 and 19), and elsewhere. On the human rights implications of TPM, see Westkamp G (forthcoming) "Information Access, *Lex Digitalis* and Fundamental Rights in Modern Copyright Law", in Macmillan F (ed) *New Directions in Copyright: Volume IV*, Cheltenham, Edward Elgar.

60 Negus K and Pickering M (2004) *Creativity, Communication and Cultural Value*, London, SAGE: 11.

61 In the United Kingdom, the law of patents is found in the Patents Act 1977 (UK) as amended and the Patents Rules 1995. The Patents Rules are currently being re-drafted. An informal consultation paper has been released by the Patent Office (UK): Modernisation and Consolidation of the Patent Rules: An Informal Consultation. Of particular interest here is that until 1716, a patent was identified simply by a title, by the power of the law to name something, literally, as inventive. The monopoly defined by the title could thus be very broad. See Roughton A et al (eds) (2005) *The Modern Law of Patents*, London, LexisNexis: 120.

62 The Registered Designs Act 1949 (UK) does not expressly require the production of a specimen, but it is provided for as an option in the Rules made under the Act. Design law in the UK was in the process of being substantially amended at the time of writing. These amendments have now been made by the Regulatory Reform (Registered Designs) Order 2006 (SI 2006/1974) and the Registered Designs Rules 2006 (SI 2006/1975), which come into force 1 October 2006. Although these Instruments have made substantial changes to

were, the intellectual property system is manifest innovation writ large. At the same time, this necessarily obscures peripheral process. That is, the creative process that is made manifest, that is "expressed" through the intellectual property system (such as through the procedural requirements of patents that render invention finished), mystifies and disguises the becoming of collaborative and networked creative communities.

Roland Barthes' work on myth adds much to the reading of the mythology of the intellectual property system, in so far as the intellectual property system has become instated as the signifier of creativity, the code for reading the creative output of an increasingly harmonised (by virtue of the law itself) "international" knowledge community (as Bergson might suggest, the symbol of innovation). The challenge to this mythology is the nature of that output itself. As Barthes famously suggests in "The Photographic Message", the totality of the photographic image, the seemingly perfect reproduction of reality (the denotation), is perhaps compromised by the social interpretation (connotation) of that image: "*it is a message without a code*; from which proposition an important corollary must immediately be drawn: the photographic message is a continuous message."[63] Thus, it is at the level of the social interpretation of the message (the connotative activity of users and consumers) that the myth-making of the dominant discourse and ideology of the intellectual property system may be dismembered: "Denotation, or the appearance of denotation, is powerless to alter political opinions: no photograph has ever convinced or refuted anyone (but the photograph can 'confirm') insofar as political consciousness is perhaps non-existent outside the *logos*: politics is what allows *all* languages."[64] The polyphony of languages is noise which is background in intellectual property, but "preserved along with the music"[65] in the knowledge flows of the network.

---

the prosecution of applications and maintenance of registered designs, and have abolished substantive examination, the new laws actually enhance the requirements for representations, as some form of representation is now always required for publication. Previously, the publication of designs was not a statutory requirement. See Consultation on the Modernisation of the UK System of Registration of Designs (closed 7 October 2005).

63 Barthes R (1977) "The Photographic Message", in *Image Music Text*, Heath S (trans), London, Fontana: 15 at 17. Note also the concept of "unlimited semiosis" in Eco U (1976) *A Theory of Semiotics*, Bloomington, Indiana UP; and Eco U (1989) *The Open Work*, A Cancogni (trans), London, Hutchinson Radius.

64 Barthes R (1977) "The Photographic Message", in *Image Music Text*, Heath S (trans), London, Fontana: 15 at 30.

65 Monod J ([1970]1972) *Chance and Necessity: An Essay on the Natural Philosophy of Modern Biology*, Wainhouse A (trans), London, Collins: 113. Here Monod is describing the creation (as distinct from revelation) in evolution. That is, evolutionary process is not a process of revealing expected evolutionary "events", but rather, is a system of "the unrestricted liberty of creation, thanks to the replicative structure of DNA" (113). Like Monod's account of DNA, the replicative structure of the organic network can be similarly described as "that registry of chance, that tone-deaf conservatory where the noise is preserved along with the music" (113). In other words, the network does not evaluate, judge, and select; rather, it is the tool by which connections of proliferative creativity are possible.

Creative Flows

The current challenges of digital technologies and networked communities to conventional models of the creative work that are offered by copyright (and mimicked in the "copyright-like" manifestations of patents, trade marks, designs, and so on) are not without critical precedent. Indeed, in the context of media and cultural studies, television presented a type of "work" that could not be finished and stored in ways analogical to, for instance, the printed work. In his study on television, Raymond Williams[66] describes the production and experience of the audience as contrary to that associated with books, as cultural artefacts or objects. In other words, these were necessarily incompatible cultural experiences, and yet, from a legal point of view, subjected to the same kinds of frameworks that were contrived for the printed work. In describing the phenomenon of television, Williams uses the term "flow" to refer to the continuity of the experience.[67] As others have explained with respect to television (but perhaps equally pertinent in the context of current developments in technologies of communication): "There is no way to separate a technical advance from the ultimate uses and deployments imagined for it."[68] For some, the concept of the flow raises concerns that "all of this demands a fundamental shift in our textual ontology, away from the 'text itself' (not to mention the 'things themselves') and toward a conception of the textual system as an illimitable matrix crossing at variable speeds through all cultural, political and social dimensions".[69] In other words, the technology of television together with the concept of the "flow" is troubling for the figure of the core work or subject matter of intellectual property. The continuity of this experience is reminiscent of the "continuity of consciousness, something of my own flow" which Bergson describes with respect to the immeasurability of expression, "in a word, duration".[70]

Walter Benjamin recognises a similar liberation (indeed "flow") in his work on the loss of the work of art's "aura" in an age of communication technologies

66 Williams R (1974) *Television: Technology and Cultural Form*, London, Fontana.

67 See Dienst R (1994) *Still Life in Real Time: Theory After Television*, Durham, Duke UP, where Dienst suggests that Williams tries to produce television "as a cultural construct comprising nothing less than a new structure of visibility": 12. The experience of watching is traced through an interesting history of television in Spigel L (1992) *Make Room for TV: Television and the Family Ideal in Postwar America*, Chicago, Chicago UP, where Spigel notes that in the early history of television, networks reinforced the "aesthetic of 'presence'" for audiences, through live broadcasts. Arguably, a similar phenomenon is being revived in the proliferation of reality television programming today, where the link between the "artist" or celebrity and the consumer is seemingly heightened and the distance between radically reduced.

68 Dienst R (1994) *Still Life in Real Time: Theory After Television*, Durham, Duke UP: 6.

69 Dienst R (1994) *Still Life in Real Time: Theory After Television*, Durham, Duke UP: 137.

70 Bergson H ([1922]1999) *Duration and Simultaneity: Bergson and the Einsteinian Universe*, Lewis M and Durie R (trans), Manchester, Clinamen P: 34.

including photography and cinema, suggesting that the technologies of reproduction interfere with the authenticity of the original by interfering with the need for its presence, described as a prerequisite for authenticity.[71]

> One might subsume the eliminated element in the term "aura" and go on to say: that which withers in the age of mechanical reproduction is the aura of the work of art. This is a symptomatic process whose significance points beyond the realm of art. One might generalize by saying: the technique of reproduction detaches the reproduced object from the domain of tradition. By making many reproductions it substitutes a plurality of copies for a unique existence.[72]

Benjamin considers the challenges to traditional conventions of perception, posed by the new technologies of representation and reproduction, and suggests a consequence of alienation from both the creator and the created, but at the same time a political mobilisation through the continuity of the work. Indeed, the alienation from the location of the art reasserts the locale, the territory, of the user: "And in permitting the reproduction to meet the beholder or listener in his own particular situation, it reactivates the object reproduced."[73] Thus, the object becomes, as it were, unfinished, continuous, infinite.[74] Arguably, what communication technologies present are significant challenges to the "code" with which creative output is perceived and understood, not only the legal coding (of the intellectual property system) but also the suitable location (as in the authentic work of art) represented by the infrastructure (of the supporting industries) and the institutional legitimation (such as through the processes of exhibition,[75] academic and research institutions,

---

71 "The Work of Art in the Age of Mechanical Reproduction", in Benjamin W ([1955]1970) *Illuminations*, Arendt H (ed and intro), Zohn H (trans), London, Fontana: 211 at 214. An interesting manifestation of the tension with new technologies can be seen in the emergence of site-specific art in the 1960s and an insistence on the location of the art within its context as part of the manifestation of the art itself, as distinct from the commodification and infinite reproducibility of art as commercial object. Examples include the use of installations, performance art, and others. For a useful history of site-specific art as well as a critique of current challenges to the notion of physical place, see Kwon M (2002) *One Place After Another: Site-Specific Art and Locational Identity*, Cambridge MA, MIT.

72 "The Work of Art in the Age of Mechanical Reproduction", in Benjamin W ([1955]1970) *Illuminations*, Arendt H (ed and intro), Zohn H (trans), London, Fontana: 211 at 215.

73 "The Work of Art in the Age of Mechanical Reproduction", in Benjamin W ([1955]1970) *Illuminations*, Arendt H (ed and intro), Zohn H (trans), London, Fontana: 211 at 215.

74 See also Heidegger's work on distance in cinema in "The Thing", in Heidegger M (1971) *Poetry, Language, Thought*, Hofstadter A (trans), New York, Harper & Row, where Heidegger suggests a similar alienation of the audience, but arguably without the level of recuperation of the spectator's activity that is seen in Benjamin's work.

75 On the power of the very decision to collect and exhibit, see the discussion of the Charles Saatchi "authoring" of artists in Negus K and Pickering M (2004) *Creativity, Communication and Cultural Value*, London, SAGE: 87-88. The authors make the link

and so on) of the objects themselves. Thus, while intellectual property laws might be understood as overcoding the original with respect to time and place (the duration of the work, the quantification or "placement" of time), the "cinematic" networks of creativity confront this system.

In other words, the continuity identified in early work on cinema, television, and other communication technologies is becoming prolific, as it were, in the continuous creativity that can be identified in network paradigms. This is played out in the working concept of the "many-to-many"[76] paradigm. The term "many-to-many" is used to describe the communication activities in many online paradigms, including web logs (blogs), Wiki, file sharing and so on. Wikipedia,[77] "the free encyclopedia that anyone can edit",[78] itself defines the "many-to-many" paradigm as one in which people both contribute and receive information[79] – that is, individuals both produce and consume, create and use. Wikipedia is a multi-lingual free-content online encyclopedia, with all entries available for anyone to edit. Wikipedia is an important example of the tension between the distributed collaborative networked creative process and the authored, uniform economic model of the creative process. Wikipedia reports the controversy that the project has attracted and, in particular, criticisms of the content as unreliable, inconsistent, or mere opinion. On the other hand, the established, authoritative centres of encyclopedic knowledge illustrate these assumptions about "legitimate" sites for knowledge creation and the illegitimacy of the network. This kind of reasoning can be traced not only in the opposition to online materials but also in the criticism of free and open source software (described as unreliable as distinct from the accountability assumed by the uniform corporate "author", such as Microsoft).[80]

It appears that not only is an increasing emphasis on the economic model (and the corporate/industry author) attempting to counter the network flow and the "many-to-many" (as distinct from "author" or "creator" based) model of creativity and of intellectual property rights, but also, the increasing significance of network creativity is motivating greater and greater reliance by industry on the old models

---

between knowledge and power, and indeed the power to identify works and purchase whole collections for exhibition, thus vesting such objects with institutional validation as "works of art" through the very (externalised) action of collecting.

76 For a particularly insightful analysis of the "many-to-many" model in the context of economic models of the "few-to-many", see Aigrain P (2006) "Capabilities in the Information Era". Presentation. TACD Conference. The Politics and Ideology of Intellectual Property. Brussels. 20 March.

77 Wikipedia, "The Free Encyclopedia", is a non-commercial online encyclopedia, founded by Jimmy Wales and Larry Sanger, and owned by the Wikimedia Foundation. For more information see http://en.wikipedia.org/wiki/Main_Page. See also its "self-definition" at http://en.wikipedia.org/wiki/Wikipedia.

78 The slogan of Wikipedia. See http://en.wikipedia.org/wiki/Wikipedia.

79 http://en.wikipedia.org/wiki/Many-to-many.

80 The case of free and open source software development, and the rise of the corporate author, is discussed further in Chapter 4, "Negotiating Self".

in what might be described as an attempt to obscure this creative activity. That is, an economic model of creativity and of the system itself casts uniformity upon new technologies and their use through the definition provided by the summarising concept of "investment". In other words, while the text may be displaced, the uniformity of the economic model of intellectual property operates to recuperate the core subject matter (economic risk) in new technologies, counter to the network of use and of users that might be facilitated by those technologies. Increasingly, the subject matter of protection (in effect) is the market and the supporting infrastructure. How the "balance" in the already asymmetrical relationship between creators and users can be recuperated is an increasingly complicated, even illogical, question under these circumstances.

The concept of flow in the work of Gilles Deleuze and Félix Guattari offers resonances with Williams' notion of televisual flow as well as important developments in the context of Internet computing technologies and paradigms. Deleuze and Guattari introduce, in this context, the desire for communication and the inevitable but somewhat problematic stability introduced by intellectual property for the purposes of reconciling new technologies. That is, the law overcodes the connections of networks of users and their creativity, and conjugates or calibrates their flow, reterritorialising the new creativities of the network society and containing them within the dominance of the intellectual property system and its associated discourse of creativity, the territory of the debate:

> A social field is always animated by all kinds of movements of decoding and deterritorialization affecting "masses" and operating at different speeds and paces. These are not contradictions but escapes ... But at the same time, and inseparably, there occur overcodings and reterritorializations. The Crusades were overcoded by the pope and assigned territorial objectives. The Holy Land, the Peace of God, a new type of abbey, new figures of money, new modes of exploitation of the peasant through leasehold and the wage system (or revivals of slavery), urban reterritorializations, etc., form a complex system. At this point, we must introduce a distinction between the two notions of *connection* and *conjugation* of flows. "Connection" indicates the way in which decoded and deterritorialized flows boost one another, accelerate their shared escape, and augment or stoke their quanta; the "conjugation" of these same flows, on the other hand, indicates their relative stoppage, like a point of accumulation that plugs or seals the lines of flight, performs a general reterritorialization, and brings the flows under the dominance of a single flow capable of overcoding them.[81]

At the same time, however, Deleuze and Guattari explain that it is "precisely the most deterritorialized flow, under the first aspect, that always brings about the accumulation or conjunction of the processes, determines the overcoding, and serves as the basis for reterritorialization under the second aspect".[82] Merely countering the

81 Deleuze G and Guattari F ([1980]1987) *A Thousand Plateaus: Capitalism and Schizophrenia*, Massumi B (trans), Minneapolis, U of Minnesota P: 220.

82 Deleuze G and Guattari F ([1980]1987) *A Thousand Plateaus: Capitalism and Schizophrenia*, Massumi B (trans), Minneapolis, U of Minnesota P: 220-21.

dominant discourse will re-establish it, reterritorialise the connection of flows. What is necessary is an examination of the very discourse of intellectual property systems and the rhetoric of proponents for stronger systems, such that the limits within the system itself might be understood and critiqued.

In this context, Deleuze and Guattari's concept of the body without organs, or BwO,[83] becomes much clearer. When considering the connection flow of the network community and the collaborative creativity arising from such communities, the problematic concern for an intellectual property system is the inability to summarise and identify the "creator", indeed, the organism. Deleuze and Guattari explain: "[T]he BwO is not at all the opposite of the organs. The organs are not its enemies. The enemy is the organism. The BwO is opposed not to the organs but to that organization of the organs called the organism."[84] This concept is very appealing when trying to understand network organisation and network actors, and is rather illustrative of the challenge of the network to conventional proprietary organisation of knowledge and its creation. The network is a connected and yet unconjugated flow. While hubs may be developed, these are without location and without permanent authority – they are designs of the network, not the designers as such. In this way, the network resists the coherence of the organism that is applied to the traditional narrative of creativity and innovation:

> The BwO is not opposed to the organs; rather, the BwO and its "true organs," which must be composed and positioned, are opposed to the organism, the organic organization of the organs ... The organism is not at all the body, the BwO; rather, it is a stratum on the BwO, in other words, a phenomenon of accumulation, coagulation, and sedimentation that, in order to extract useful labor from the BwO, imposes upon it forms, functions, bonds, dominant and hierarchized organizations, organized transcendences. The strata are bonds, pincers.[85]

In the context of networks, this phenomenon of connection is explained using rhizomatic models of the matrix of communication and creativity, as distinct from the traditional model of the hierarchical tree of knowledge.[86] The organisation of knowledge and creativity in new technologies and collaborative user groups is usefully informed by the concept of the rhizome (which usefully introduces the concept of "nodes" both in the biological as well as the network sense), not least due to the departure from the organistic model underlying intellectual property discourse.

83 Introduced in the previous chapter.

84 Deleuze G and Guattari F ([1980]1987) *A Thousand Plateaus: Capitalism and Schizophrenia*, Massumi B (trans), Minneapolis, U of Minnesota P: 158.

85 Deleuze G and Guattari F ([1980]1987) *A Thousand Plateaus: Capitalism and Schizophrenia*, Massumi B (trans), Minneapolis, U of Minnesota P: 158-59.

86 Deleuze G and Guattari F ([1980]1987) *A Thousand Plateaus: Capitalism and Schizophrenia*, Massumi B (trans), Minneapolis, U of Minnesota P. See also Ansell-Pearson K (1999) *Germinal Life: The Difference and Repetition of Deleuze*, London, Routledge; De Landa M (2000) *A Thousand Years of Nonlinear History*, New York, Zone; and De Landa M (2002) *Intensive Science and Virtual Philosophy*, New York, Continuum.

It is here that the reterritorialisation of the network, by the legal discourse, can be most usefully resisted in that the rhizome eludes the dualistic (and hierarchical) modelling within intellectual property discourse – creators and consumers, originals and copies, invention and imitation, and so on. Thus, through unanticipated, unexpected, and unpredictable connections, genuine creativity is embodied and habituated in the collaborative network. In this sense, the overcoding and isolation of the creative event within increasingly restrictive intellectual property rights closes the system. On the other hand, the connection offered by the network will "open a cosmos"[87] to a proliferation of creators. In representing creativity, a reliance on the intellectual property model will fail; but in approximating creativity through the infinite connections of the virtual network, the social dynamics of the creative relationship are actualised.[88] This recalls the earlier consideration of the anxiety over the departure from a text-based model of core identities in communication: "The world has become chaos, but the book remains the image of the world: radicle-chaosmos rather than root-cosmos. A strange mystification: a book all the more total for being fragmented ... A system of this kind could be called a rhizome."[89]

Indeed, elsewhere Deleuze and Guattari very appealingly explain the concept through this very reasoning of the book metaphor. That is, what is witnessed is a fragmentation of the book as the "root", the core, to the multiplicity of the rhizome – creativity goes, literally, "underground":[90]

> The same applies to the book and the world: contrary to a deeply rooted belief, the book is not an image of the world. It forms a rhizome with the world, there is an aparallel evolution of the book and the world; the book assures the deterritorialization of the world, but the world effects a reterritorialization of the book, which in turn deterritorializes itself in the world (if it is capable, if it can).[91]

A similar fragmentation of any coherent picture is also offered by Borges in his story, "The Aleph".[92] Here the ability of the Aleph to represent the totality of the world simultaneously and at once is rendered illogical by its inability to represent itself – representing everything and nothing. Intriguingly, the Aleph itself is beyond

---

87 Deleuze G and Guattari F ([1980]1987) *A Thousand Plateaus: Capitalism and Schizophrenia*, Massumi B (trans), Minneapolis, U of Minnesota P: 345.

88 Deleuze G and Guattari F ([1980]1987) *A Thousand Plateaus: Capitalism and Schizophrenia*, Massumi B (trans), Minneapolis, U of Minnesota P: 422-23.

89 Deleuze G and Guattari F ([1980]1987) *A Thousand Plateaus: Capitalism and Schizophrenia*, Massumi B (trans), Minneapolis, U of Minnesota P: 6.

90 Later, in Chapter 5, this notion of the earthliness can be traced in the concept of the carnivalesque in the work of Mikhail Bakhtin, and the indissoluble link to the earth: see Bakhtin MM ([1968]1984) *Rabelais and His World*, Iswolsky H (trans), Bloomington, Indiana UP: 252.

91 Deleuze G and Guattari F ([1980]1987) *A Thousand Plateaus: Capitalism and Schizophrenia*, Massumi B (trans), Minneapolis, U of Minnesota P: 11.

92 Borges JL (1967) "The Aleph", in *Jorge Luis Borges: A Personal Anthology*, Kerrigan A (ed), New York, Grove: 138.

representation: "Perhaps the gods would not be against my finding an equivalent image, but then this report would be contaminated with literature, with falsehood. For the rest, the central problem is unsolvable: the enumeration, even if only partial, of an infinite complex."[93] In describing what he saw, Borges is literally without shared language other than the prescription and narration provided at once for him by the Aleph:

> I saw the Aleph from all points; I saw the earth in the Aleph and in the earth the Aleph once more and the earth in the Aleph; I saw my face and my viscera: I saw your face and felt vertigo and cried because my eyes had seen that conjectural and secret object whose name men usurp but which no man has gazed on: the inconceivable universe.[94]

The meta-narrative of the Aleph is a failure for at once it must select not only its subject matter but also its perspective. The universe is inconceivable not only in its totality, but also in terms of that which cannot come within the conjugation of "that conjectural and secret object" of the Aleph. Thus, "the book is not an image of the world":

> A rhizome ceaselessly establishes connections between semiotic chains, organizations of power, and circumstances relative to the arts, sciences, and social struggles. A semiotic chain is like a tuber agglomerating very diverse acts, not only linguistic, but also perceptive, mimetic, gestural, and cognitive: there is no language in itself, nor are there any linguistic universals, only a throng of dialects, patois, slangs, and specialized languages. There is no ideal speaker-listener, any more than there is a homogeneous linguistic community.[95]

Rhizomatic models, like bindweed, are also particularly difficult to eradicate from the garden. It is indeed in this sense that the "viral" metaphor, somewhat disparaged within particular communities,[96] is usefully recovered in that the virus, according to Deleuze and Guattari, is a particularly significant example of a rhizomatic connection that resists the reterritorialisation of the hierarchical evolutionary model. This is arguably in much the same way that networked communities of users/creators resist the author-oriented narrative of intellectual property metaphors of creative process, the arborescent model of the tree of knowledge:

> More generally, evolutionary schemas may be forced to abandon the old model of the tree and descent. Under certain conditions, a virus can connect to germ cells and transmit itself as the cellular gene of a complex species; moreover, it can take flight, move into the cells of an entirely different species, but not without bringing with it "genetic information"

---

93 Borges JL (1967) "The Aleph", in *Jorge Luis Borges: A Personal Anthology*, Kerrigan A (ed), New York, Grove: 138 at 149-50.

94 Borges JL (1967) "The Aleph", in *Jorge Luis Borges: A Personal Anthology*, Kerrigan A (ed), New York, Grove: 138 at 151.

95 Deleuze G and Guattari F ([1980]1987) *A Thousand Plateaus: Capitalism and Schizophrenia*, Massumi B (trans), Minneapolis, U of Minnesota P: 7.

96 For instance, see Jones P (2003) "The GPL is a License, Not a Contract", *LWN.net*, 3 December.

from the first host ... Evolutionary schemas would no longer follow models of arborescent descent going from the least to the most differentiated, but instead a rhizome operating immediately in the heterogeneous and jumping from one already differentiated line to another. Once again, there is *aparallel evolution*, of the baboon and the cat; it is obvious that they are not models or copies of each other (a becoming-baboon in the cat does not mean that the cat "plays" baboon). We form a rhizome with our viruses, or rather our viruses cause us to form a rhizome with other animals.[97]

This concept of flow resonates with that used by Manuel Castells precisely in the process of characterising the territories and terrain of the network society and its creativity. The information flow described by Castells at once confounds the location at the creator and yet points to the space and domain of creativity.[98] In interview with Martin Ince, Castells explains:

> The most difficult concept to grasp of my whole theory is the space of flows. Yet, it is fundamental. I have tried again and again to explain it, to illustrate it, because I believe it is the most direct expression of the technological transformation of our existence. But it is difficult, because it is counter-intuitive. Space is always a mental construction. Not only a cultural construction, but a materially mental construction, because we must place ourselves somewhere. But the space of our lives, of our direct experience, is not the space of the economy, not the space of information, not the space of science, not the space of art – all realms of activity that ultimately frame and influence our lives.[99]

Thus, the "author" of networked information cannot be identified, as such, other than through the practice of the network. Castells explains that the network society evades the need for consensus as a uniform "public", a consensus that is otherwise imposed on the "user" or "public" by its rendition within the intellectual property system:

> The understanding of our world requires the simultaneous analysis of the network society, and of its conflictive challenges. The historical law that where there is domination there is resistance continues to apply. But it requires an analytical effort to identify who the challengers are of the processes of domination enacted by the immaterial, yet powerful, flows of the network society.[100]

---

97 Deleuze G and Guattari F ([1980]1987) *A Thousand Plateaus: Capitalism and Schizophrenia*, Massumi B (trans), Minneapolis, U of Minnesota P: 10.

98 Compare the work of Martin Heidegger on distance and nearness in communications technologies (including cinema, radio and television) in the essay "Das ding", translated as "The Thing", in Heidegger M (1971) *Poetry, Language, Thought*, Hofstadter A (trans), New York, Harper & Row.

99 Castells M and Ince M (2003) *Conversations with Manuel Castells*, Cambridge, Polity: 55-56.

100 Castells M (2000) *The Information Age: Economy, Society and Culture. Volume III: End of Millennium.* 2nd ed. Oxford, Blackwell: 382. See also the discussion of "information flows" in Castells M (2000) *The Information Age: Economy, Society and Culture. Volume I: The Rise of the Network Society*, 2nd ed, Oxford, Blackwell; and Castells M (1997) *The*

Just as Chantal Mouffe rejects this artificial consensus and indeed Barthes too notes the heteroglossia of politics ("politics is what allows *all* languages"[101]), so too is the strength of that heterogeneity to be seen in Castells' concept of flow. This is the "dialogic" and chaotic space of the network that resists narration and yet builds the territory and belonging of the networked community: "It redefines distance but does not cancel geography."[102] In other words, the space of flows is manifest beyond the physicality of place.[103] Networks of connected users thus enjoy a personal proximity in the territory of their shared knowledge and practices, despite (or perhaps because of) the dislocation otherwise in place:

> Throughout history in most human practice, simultaneity depended on vicinity, on territorial proximity. Now, what happens when we can do things together in real time, but from very distant locations? There is simultaneity, but the spatial arrangement that allows it is a different one. It is based on telecommunications, computer systems, and the places from where this interaction takes place. This is the space of flows: not just the electronic/telecommunications circuits, but the network of places that are connected around one common, simultaneous social practice via these electronic circuits and their ancillary systems.[104]

This territorial proximity, this "belonging", achieved through the practical experience of the network, provides some insight into the relationship between the modern network "peasant" class of creativity, and the aristocracy of "patronised" creativity within the conventional industrial models supported by the intellectual property framework. Pierre Bourdieu's notion of the (bodily) *habitus*, as shared practice and custom, can be understood also in terms of the way that custom incarnates the territory and sensation of belonging for users. A re-reading of the *habitus* is useful in understanding the creativity of the network as distinct from individual and situated creators, as well as the continuity of the creative practice. The network has shared customs and practices, but it is a *habitus* of choice.

Information Age: Economy, Society and Culture. Volume II: The Power of Identity, Oxford, Blackwell.

101 Barthes R (1977) "The Photographic Message", in *Image Music Text*, Heath S (trans), London, Fontana: 15 at 30.

102 Castells M (2002) *The Internet Galaxy: Reflections on the Internet, Business, and Society*, Oxford, Oxford UP: 207. See also Urry J (2000) *Sociology Beyond Societies: Mobilities for the Twenty-First Century*, London, Routledge: Chapter 6. See also the expression of race, belonging and identity in the case of online artistic communities in Bailey C (1996) "Virtual Skin: Articulating Race in Cyberspace", in Moser MA and MacLeod D (eds) *Immersed in Technology: Art and Virtual Environments*, Cambridge MA, MIT P: 29.

103 For a discussion of this tension between space and place in post-colonial indigenous communities, see Gibson J (2005) *Community Resources: Intellectual Property, International Trade and Protection of Traditional Knowledge*, Aldershot, Ashgate.

104 Castells M and Ince M (2003) *Conversations with Manuel Castells*, Cambridge, Polity: 56.

Bourdieu's work on distinction and class is particularly relevant here, in that the virtual domain, the incarnated "space" of network flows, can nevertheless be understood as promulgated through the *habitus*, from which the improvisations of the collaborative network can derive.[105] In this way, the creative process is inextricable from the production and institutional context in which it takes place, is recognised, and is valued: "What is called 'creation' is the encounter between a socially constituted *habitus* and a particular position that is already instituted or *possible* in the division of the labour of cultural production."[106] The concept is thus useful for greater insight into the context of "production" and the growing attribution of the ideology of "creativity" to industry, as discussed in the previous chapter and illustrated by Bourdieu's consideration of artistic production: "the sociology of cultural products must take as its object the whole set of relationships … *between the artist and other artists*, and beyond them, the whole set of agents engaged in the production of the work, or, at least, of the *social value* of the work (critics, gallery directors, patrons, etc)."[107]

At the same time, while explaining the way in which the institution of industry might be positioned as "creative" in the current rhetoric advocating more

105 In the context of television and female fan communities, what has been described in the work of Camille Bacon-Smith arguably can be understood in terms of the *habitus* as a collective subjectivity upon which individual innovation is possible, not necessarily through challenging the traditions of the community, but rather through innovating on those traditions: Bacon-Smith C (1992) *Enterprising Women: Television Fandom and the Creation of Popular Myth*, Philadelphia, U of Pennsylvania P. In a discussion of *habitus*, John Frow explains: "The point of this is not to establish the truism that different classes adopt different lifestyles, but to explore the process by which differences in cultural preference become socially functional", in Frow J (1995) *Cultural Studies and Cultural Value*, Oxford, Clarendon P: 29. Similarly, the collective subjectivity recognised in indigenous communalism derives not from an antagonistic relationship to custom and tradition, but rather, a responsibility to its narration and an innovation upon that narration: see Gibson J (2005) *Community Resources: Intellectual Property, International Trade and Protection of Traditional Knowledge*, Aldershot, Ashgate. Similarly, the online modification of games is central to maintaining the value of the "source" game for the gaming community. As Rosemary Coombe explains, in this kind of fan community, the members reject the item as personal property but nevertheless act as loyal fans: "a potential unrealized or betrayed by those who 'own' the intellectual property rights in it." See Coombe R (1998) *The Cultural Life of Intellectual Properties: Authorship, Appopriation, and the Law*, Durham, Duke UP: 125. This antagonism between fans and intellectual property holders has reached an extreme point where content owners are litigating against individual end-users accessing illegitimate music and film downloads; that is, they are suing the "fans". On these issues see the work of the United States civil society organisation, the Electronic Frontiers Foundation (EFF), on music use and this type of end-user litigation: "But suing fans doesn't pay artists." Materials are available at http://www.eff.org/share/.

106 Bourdieu P ([1984]1993) *Sociology in Question*, Nice R (trans), London, SAGE: 141.

107 Bourdieu P ([1984]1993) *Sociology in Question*, Nice R (trans), London, SAGE: 140.

expansive rights, this understanding of production also indicates the indispensable interconnections between artists. Thus, the interplay between *habitus* and what Bourdieu describes as the artist's "post"[108] – that is, the institutionally legitimated "role" into which the artist is placed by the field of production – is an important process of the artist's belonging, collaboration, and generative production. Indeed, it is the important "creative process". Arguably, *habitus* is not necessarily the limit but rather the means of embodying *habitat*:

> [*Habitus*] is an embodied class (including biological properties that are socially shaped, such as sex or age) and, in all cases of inter- or intra-generational mobility, it is distinguished (in its effects) from class as objectified at a given moment (in the form of property, titles etc), inasmuch as it perpetuates a different state of the material conditions of existence – those which produced it and which in this case differ to some extent from the conditions of its operation.[109]

Bourdieu has been interpreted as suggesting that the *habitus* is somewhat obscured and unavailable for intervention.[110] Indeed, in this respect, the customs and practices of *habitus* suggest the mystification of the overcoding of creative life that is perhaps at play in the intellectual property regime. However, the nature of *habitus* is far more complex than that of restrictive and binding custom and, in this respect, an immensely useful tool in deciphering the organisation of communities while also understanding individual autonomy within these groups. *Habitus* is incorporated into the body, it is intrinsic to the organism of community, of the network: "all the principles are 'embodied,' turned into postures, dispositions of the body. Values are postures, gestures, ways of standing, walking, speaking. The strength of the ethos is that it is a morality made flesh."[111] *Habitus* thus provides a way in which to understand the inscription of tradition (as innovation) in the contemporary network.[112] Indeed, *habitus*, rather than restraining and fixed, may be distinguished quite markedly from habit, the latter being "repetitive, mechanical, automatic, reproductive rather than productive".[113] As Bourdieu explains, it is the very generative and productive nature of *habitus* that he seeks to represent: "I wanted to insist on the idea that the *habitus*

---

108 Bourdieu describes the artist's "post" as "often existing prior to him and outlives him (entailing obligations, such as 'the artist's life,' attributes, traditions, modes of expression, etc)". Bourdieu P ([1984]1993) *Sociology in Question*, Nice R (trans), London, SAGE: 141.

109 Bourdieu P ([1979]1986) *Distinction: A Social Critique of the Judgement of Taste*, Nice R (trans), London, Routledge: 437.

110 Similarly, consider also the work of Judith Butler on the way in which the social body is discursively constructed by legitimated institutions and narratives. For instance, see Butler J (1990) *Gender Trouble: Feminism and the Subversion of Identity*, New York, Routledge.

111 Bourdieu P ([1984]1993) *Sociology in Question*, Nice R (trans), London, SAGE: 86.

112 As Bourdieu explains: "the term constantly reminds us that it refers to something historical." See Bourdieu P ([1984]1993) *Sociology in Question*, Nice R (trans), London, SAGE: 86. This aspect of *habitus* is explored further in Chapter 5, where the concept of tradition as innovation, and use as transformative, is considered in the work of Paul Ricoeur.

113 Bourdieu P ([1984]1993) *Sociology in Question*, Nice R (trans), London, SAGE: 87.

is something powerfully generative … It's a kind of transforming machine."[114] This resonates with the generative polyphony suggested by networked relations and connections of creativity: "So the *habitus* is the principle of a real autonomy with respect to the immediate determinations of the 'situation'."[115]

Michel de Certeau similarly reads *habitus* more strategically, and recognises the very innovation that arises from an individual's engagement and gaming with shared social practices and custom: "Innumerable ways of playing and foiling the other's game (*jouer/déjouer le jeu de l'autre*), that is, the space instituted by others, characterize the subtle, stubborn, resistant activity of groups which, since they lack their own space, have to get along in a network of already established forces and representations."[116] Thus, the game of distinction, of attributing "taste" to a hierarchy of users, may be strategically confounded by the network: "it depends both on the deal (having a good hand) and on the way one plays the cards (being a good cardplayer) … in short, an ability to maneuver within the different conditions in which the initial capital is committed."[117]

What is offered by the current debates in access to knowledge and the legitimacy (or illegitimacy) of intellectual property is an opportunity to understand the way in which the highly coded and yet infinitely proliferative network community can reveal the selection of actions in the *habitus*, the freedom that is possible in habit. Fundamentally what is at stake is the continuous space of the network flows, as distinct from the regulated and limited place of the originary and authentic expression legitimated within the legal and regulatory frameworks. Michel de Certeau provides a useful clarification of place and space in Bourdieu, in what he calls "*an economy of the proper place (une économie du lieu propre)*".[118] He explains the two forms of this economy: "on the one hand, the maximization of the capital (material and symbolic wealth) that constitutes the essence of *patrimony*; on the other, the development of the *body*, both individual and collective, that generates duration (through its fertility) and space (through its movements)."[119] Thus, the regulated place of capital, in which the intellectual property system cooperates and fulfils, suggests the patri-lineal narrative of creative process as historical, comprehensible, and representable.

---

114 Bourdieu P ([1984]1993) *Sociology in Question*, Nice R (trans), London, SAGE: 87.

115 Bourdieu P ([1984]1993) *Sociology in Question*, Nice R (trans), London, SAGE: 87.

116 De Certeau M (1984) *The Practice of Everyday Life*, Rendall S (trans), Berkeley, U of California P: 18. Discussed further in Chapter 5, Paul Ricoeur's method achieves something similar in his work on tradition, suggesting that: "The labor of imagination is not born from nothing. It is bound in one way or another to the tradition's paradigms. But the range of solutions is vast." See Ricoeur P (1984) *Time and Narrative: Volume 1*, McLaughlin K and Pellauer D (trans), Chicago, U of Chicago P: 69; and see further the discussion in Chapter 5.

117 De Certeau M (1984) *The Practice of Everyday Life*, Rendall S (trans), Berkeley, U of California P: 53.

118 De Certeau M (1984) *The Practice of Everyday Life*, Rendall S (trans), Berkeley, U of California P: 55.

119 De Certeau M (1984) *The Practice of Everyday Life*, Rendall S (trans), Berkeley, U of California P: 55.

On the other hand, the continuous and enduring space of the body, the *habitus*, is comparable to the concept of the "flow" and to the smooth and unmarked space[120] of the continuous and connected network, the habitat, the "dwelling".[121] On the one hand the limited and situated notion of property, on the other hand the connected and continuous notion of territory in "heirs",[122] or what might be referred to as the kinship of the flow. As Bourdieu explains:

> Constructing the notion of habitus as a system of acquired dispositions functioning on the practical level as categories of perception and assessment or as classificatory principles as well as being the organizing principles of action meant constituting the social agent in his true role as the practical operator of the construction of objects.[123]

Thus, the *habitus* allows for connected flow, as it were. In *Outline of a Theory of Practice*, originally published in 1972 as *Esquisse d'une théorie de la pratique, precede de trois études d'ethnologie kabyle*, Bourdieu appears to describe most elegantly, in his explanation of *habitus*, the contemporary network community:

> The structures constitutive of a particular type of environment (e.g. the material conditions of existence characteristic of a class condition) produce *habitus*, systems of durable, transposable *dispositions*, structured structures predisposed to function as structuring structures, that is, as principles of the generation and structuring of practices and representations which can be objectively "regulated" and "regular" without in any way being the product of obedience to rules, objectively adapted to their goals without presupposing a conscious aiming at ends or an express mastery of the operations necessary to attain them and, being all this, collectively orchestrated without being the product of the orchestrating action of a conductor.[124]

This provides further insight into the activity and role of the "hub" or "node" of a network – such "individuals" are collective and orchestrated but cannot sustain themselves as such. Rather, they sustain the network. The network is conducted, but has no conductors. By way of contrast, the intellectual property system necessarily isolates and suspends creativity at a moment, interrupting the continuous flow of creativity in the network, and the open-endedness of creativity.

---

120 On the concept of connected "smooth space" as distinct from the conjugated "striated space" of the State apparatus, see Deleuze G and Guattari F ([1980]1987) *A Thousand Plateaus: Capitalism and Schizophrenia*, Massumi B (trans), Minneapolis, U of Minnesota P: Chapter 14, "1440: The Smooth and the Striated".

121 De Certeau M (1984) *The Practice of Everyday Life*, Rendall S (trans), Berkeley, U of California P: 55.

122 De Certeau M (1984) *The Practice of Everyday Life*, Rendall S (trans), Berkeley, U of California P: 55.

123 Bourdieu P (1990) *In Other Words: Essays Towards a Reflexive Sociology*, Adamson M (trans), Stanford, Stanford UP: 13.

124 Bourdieu P ([1972]1977) *Outline of a Theory of Practice*, Nice R (trans) Cambridge, Cambridge UP: 72.

Cultural Flows

Culture is a deeply compromised idea I cannot yet do without.[125]

As an indisputably positive value, the rhetorical turn of creativity imports cultural distinction, as it were, into the intellectual property system. That is, it provides a purpose, a target, at which proponents of stronger rights may suggest they are aiming. But fundamentally, the notion of "culture" as an overarching value is equally perplexing in that it too presents an otherwise fluid and unstable concept that the intellectual property system has come to embody. Nevertheless, there is suggested, through the very use of the term "culture", the possibility to re-insert the public, the user, into the debate, "inside" the system, even if somewhat alienated from the "aristocracy" of the authentic and legitimate creator. Indeed, even the very process of demarcating culture alerts one to the process by which culture, as with innovation, is marked and traversed by the system that purports to recognise and nurture it. To see culture, as it were, is to define its limits within a continuity of shared meaning. Thus, an examination of the way in which "culture" both asserts the system and undermines it will situate the markers of intellectual property systems firmly within the terrain of shared meanings. Thus, "culture" provides the contextual and societal motivation for the central importance given to creativity in contemporary debates and government policy. And, inevitably, this conceptual framework of "culture" introduces cultural diversity as itself a catalyst for creativity and a "resource" (both to utilise and to display) in the knowledge society.

Thus, if the "authenticity" of creation is the necessary indication of culture and, as discussed, intellectual property laws have become increasingly empowered with the role of arbitrating creativity, of authenticating legitimate and genuine creation, then the relationship between this system and the question of "culture" is seemingly critical. These are indeed the culture wars – a contest not for culture, but between cultures. Indeed, the case of traditional knowledge has shown the way in which, in an effort to encapsulate it within the logic of intellectual property, the diversity of knowledge systems and community identities is somewhat (necessarily) summarised and rendered circumspect.

The law itself marks and characterises phenomenal cultural expressions within its language. All senses have come within its definitions, or at least, have been presented for its arbitration – seeing, hearing, touching, tasting, and performing – sensations that have increasingly broken free of the intellectual property system and yet have been recovered through an expansion of rights to incorporate the "totality" of cultural experience and to present that totality as a graphical expression of intellectual property. For instance, in the European law of trade marks, anything can be registered as a trade mark as long as that "sensation" (smell, taste, hearing, and possibly even touch) can

---

125 Clifford J (1988) *The Predicament of Culture: Twentieth-Century Ethnograph, Literature, and Art*, Cambridge MA, Harvard UP: 10.

be graphically represented, and thus recognised.[126] Similarly, as discussed earlier, the invention (arguably the idea) that is the subject matter of a patent must be graphically represented through the specification. Registered designs are also expressed through graphical representations. Furthermore, the reaching of intellectual property models around webcasting and broadcasts, and the intractable adherence to conventional models of marketing music, betray these persistent assumptions towards "broader and more extended legislation, as well as new definitions of property in order to apply old laws to new things".[127] The intellectual property system is an archaically graphic system[128] and fiercely modernist in this respect.[129] The visual alone is to be trusted as presenting the "truth" of innovation, as illuminating the authenticity of the object. "The primacy of the visual … not only tends to create a certain type of human identity or subjectivity but also tends to valorise the individual as writer/author/subject."[130]

Increasingly, this emphasis on the graphic is nevertheless being tested in the digital context. This is occurring not only in the case of attempts to engender new types of rights (as in webcasting and broadcasts) but also in the application of older forms of intellectual property, including copyright. An exemplary case comes from German copyright law,[131] where a draft law, if enacted, will limit the electronic delivery of content by libraries (this being possible only where the publisher offers such a service).[132] Para 52a of the current law provides for limitations in relation

---

126 Article 2 of the Trade Marks Directive 89/104/EC. This visualising of the creative in the sensation can be seen in other jurisdictions as well.

127 Seeger A (2004) "The Selective Protection of Musical Ideas: The 'Creations' and the Dispossessed", in Verdery K and Humphrey C (eds), *Property in Question: Value Transformation in the Global Economy*, Oxford, Berg: 69 at 79.

128 Certain rights may seem to qualify this, although even performers' rights have a graphical quality.

129 On the privileging of the "visual" throughout philosophy, see Barry A (1995) "Reporting and Visualising", in Jenks C (ed) *Visual Culture*, London, Routledge: 42. See also the collection of essays on "ocularcentricity" in Levin DM (ed) (1993) *Modernity and the Hegemony of Vision*, Berkeley, U of California P. Note also the relationship between the graphic and surveillance, as a kind of record of creativity. Intriguing here is Virilio's notion of "omnivoyance" as "Western Europe's totalitarian ambition" in Virilio P (1994) *The Vision Machine*, London, BFI: 33. That is, an ambition to see all, to represent all through vision, and one which can also be seen in Borges' critique: Borges JL (1967) "The Aleph", in *Jorge Luis Borges: A Personal Anthology*, Kerrigan A (ed), New York, Grove: 138.

130 Wright S (2001) *International Human Rights, Decolonisation and Globalisation: Becoming Human*, London, Routledge: 127.

131 *Urheberrechtsgesetz* or *Gesetz über Urheberrecht und verwandte Schutzrechte* (Law on Copyright and Neighbouring Rights, as amended in 2004).

132 The final government draft is currently before Parliament, for which libraries have been asked to submit a self-declaration (not yet available). The proposed law (in German) is available at http://www.kopien-brauchen-originale.de/media/archive/139.pdf. The draft amendment, as prepared by the Ministry of Justice, is available at http://www.bmj.bund.de/media/archive/1122.pdf (26 January 2006).

to making works publicly available for the purposes of education and research;[133] but a new provision, para 52b, relates to a different situation, that of research or private study. Para 52b relates to the public display of works, and limits electronic reading of works to spaces exclusively within libraries, museums, or archives.[134] The *Aktionsbündnis Urheberrecht für Bildung und Wissenschaft* (Alliance for Copyright in Education and Science) has brought together scientists, academics, and various organisations concerned for the consequences of this law for research and education. In so doing it has obtained signatures from six prominent scientific organisations,[135] 260 professional bodies and institutions, as well as 3500 individuals,[136] on a Declaration rejecting the erosion of limitations and privileges for education and science that is proposed in the draft bill. The Göttingen Declaration on Copyright for Education and Research (5 July 2004)[137] states that: "In a digitised and networked information society, access to global information for the purposes of education and science must be guaranteed at all times from any place",[138] and explicitly declares support for the comments of German President Horst Köhler: "In my opinion, Germany is proceeding too slowly along the road to the science society. Germany must become a country of ideas!"[139] This proposed German law resonates with the concept of the work's "aura", suggested by Walter Benjamin[140] and discussed earlier, where the authenticity of the work demands interaction with it in its original (institutional) context. The "quality" attributed by the system seems to rely upon the ideology of the tangible graphical representation.[141]

---

133 Under para 52a, it is permissible to make small parts of works and works of a small size publicly available for the purpose of education and research. The number of persons must be limited and pre-defined: para 52a (1) No. 1.

134 Under the new para 52b, any work can be made publicly available exclusively on the premises of publicly accessible libraries, museums or archives for purposes of research or private study. Further, the author is remunerated, indicating that this is not a genuine general limitation. Rather, it is a statutory licence to make the material available.

135 Fraunhofer-Gesellschaft, Helmholtz-Gesellschaft, Conference of University Rectors, Max-Planck-Society, Gottfried Wilhelm Leibniz-Gesellschaft, Science Council/ Wissenschaftsrat.

136 Alliance for Action. "Digitisation and Online Accessibility" and "Preservation of Digital Content": View from the Alliance for Action "Copyright for Education and Science". Online Consultation.

137 The text of the Göttingen Declaration on Copyright for Education and Research (5 July 2004) is available at http://www.urheberrechtsbuendnis.de/GE-en.pdf.

138 The Göttingen Declaration on Copyright for Education and Research (5 July 2004). Preliminary Remarks.

139 Quoted in The Göttingen Declaration on Copyright for Education and Research (5 July 2004). Goals.

140 "The Work of Art in the Age of Mechanical Reproduction", in Benjamin W ([1955]1970) *Illuminations*, Arendt H (ed and intro), Zohn H (trans), London, Fontana: 211 at 214.

141 A similar tension between authenticity and electronic media can be seen in art institutions themselves, particularly in terms of conventional institutional "authorship" and

The intellectual property system, therefore, appears to be incompatible with new technologies of legitimate dissemination, so much so that the law, in this particular case, seeks to render such transmissions illegitimate in themselves. More generally then, the adherence to the graphic, the "aura" of the object, appears to be persistent. First, the graphic is not only a pragmatic decision of the system, but also a way in which to structure innovation according to discrete events of invention and originality. Secondly, in the reduction to the graphic, the greater expanses of an idea are perhaps being contained within a more limited and indifferent representation which comes to represent the idea;[142] and in doing so, the greater reaches of imagination are potentially curtailed in the broad claim of the image. It is no longer an imitation of the idea; rather, the system renders it the idea itself. This is the significance of the grand narrative: "A perfect imitation is no longer an imitation."[143] That is, the system itself has come to represent the ideas it attempts to trace. Thus, expanding rights will, as James Boyle has said, lead to a "scarcity of the imagination".[144] It is necessary to understand the limits of representation, in a broader sense, in order to exemplify the assumptions of the intellectual property system's definition of individual moments of valuable innovation and illumination. This is not to overturn the practice of the system, but rather, it is to overcome (and re-affirm) the limits of the system. In a digital context, where the central turn of the graphic raises some ambiguity, the dogmatism of the expression is undermined. However, what has been witnessed is an attempt to build upon the basic principles of the intellectual property system in order to render graphic the connections in the network, as it were. To this end, the organising principle is increasingly that of investment, such that webcasting and other new opportunities can be caught within the "net", as it were. Culture is indeed a contested territory.

---

containment of meaning within an exhibition or collection, and thus the accompanying "authority" or power. The use of online documentation and "exhibition" presents benefits to the art institution (in terms of cost, contemporary image, and presence in a globalised context), but for some commentators there are associated risks: "The greatest danger of art institutions embracing Internet art is that in doing so they will change it to fit their purposes." See Stallabrass J (2003) *Internet Art: The Online Clash of Culture and Commerce*, London, Tate: 119.

142 Interestingly on this point, the theme for World Intellectual Property Day 2006 – *It Starts with an Idea* – is the "celebration of ideas". According to WIPO Magazine: "Ideas, inspiration, ingenuity – these are the seeds from which innovations and creations grow." See WIPO Magazine (2006) January-February.

143 Derrida J ([1972]1981) *Dissemination*, Johnson B (trans), Chicago, U of Chicago P: 139.

144 Boyle, J (2005) Launch of the Adelphi Charter on Creativity, Innovation and Intellectual Property. Royal Society for the Encouragement of Arts, Manufactures and Commerce. London. 13 October.

Marking Creativity, Recognising Culture

> Recognition is defined by the harmonious exercise of the different faculties in relation to the different representations (sensible, intellectual, memorial, etc) of a single object. The model of recognition therefore implies a further presupposition, namely that of an underlying agreement among the faculties themselves. Typically, this accord is grounded in the unity of the thinking subject.[145]

> The true picture of the past flits by. The past can be seized only as an image which flashes up at the instant when it can be recognized and is never seen again … For every image of the past that is not recognized by the present as one of its own concerns threatens to disappear irretrievably.[146]

And indeed, for every image, for every expression that is not recognised by the present, the fate of obscurity is assured. As a system providing apparent consensus on the moment and the limits of the creative object, the intellectual property system orients the creative object in cultural space. But the questions arise as to what is this sense of culture, and how has the system itself expanded to deal with new forms and new mechanisms of expressing culture, not by way of renewed diversity in the system, but by way of assimilating difference and diversity within the monocultural experience of linear models of innovation. At the same time, aberrant and indecipherable expressions of culture are marginalised in what amounts to a demarcation of legitimate culture (a kind of "high culture" of "works of art", as it were, identified through the intellectual property system) and illegitimate (outside the economic exchange) cultural forms. When it comes to the question of "culture" and "taste", the process of the valuation of the *habitus* by the dominant interests can be registered in the hierarchical values being played out in contemporary intellectual property disputes: "It is a question not of differences in themselves but of the ability of the dominant class to impose the value given to these differences: to impose a recognition of the distinction between 'good' taste and 'vulgar' taste, between legitimate and illegitimate styles."[147] In other words, the *habitus* is not a system of rigid and inescapable bonds of custom, rather the interest in the *habitus* is the very way in which it generates a collective subjectivity that is subsequently identified and ranked.[148] In the case of the creativity of networks, a networked "public" is thus

---

145 Patton P (1996) "Introduction", in Patton P (ed) *Deleuze: A Critical Reader*, Oxford, Blackwell: 1 at 7.

146 "Theses on the Philosophy of History", in Benjamin W ([1955]1970) *Illuminations*, Arendt H (ed and intro), Zohn H (trans), London, Fontana: 245 at 247.

147 Frow J (1995) *Cultural Studies and Cultural Value*, Oxford, Clarendon P: 29.

148 As Chris Jenks explains: "The possessors of the dominant-group habitus are the inheritors of cultural capital, their forms of reality and cognition are always appropriate." See Jenks C (2005) *Culture*, 2nd ed, London, Routledge: 130-31. However, where Jenks suggests that *habitus* is somehow prescriptive, it is perhaps more appropriate and indeed more useful to consider and understand *habitus* as the phenomenon of the attribution of ranking and taste by the dominant group.

identified and de-valued (as "pirates", as inauthentic producers) while the creative products are themselves rendered illegitimate. Thus, the "value" of the network is produced not only by its narration through intellectual property laws, but also through the industries legitimated by the intellectual property system:

> Given that works of art exist as symbolic objects only if they are known and recognized, that is, socially instituted as works of art and received by spectators capable of knowing and recognizing them as such, the sociology of art and literature has to take as its object not only the material production but also the symbolic production of the work, i.e. the production of the value of the work or, which amounts to the same thing, of belief in the value of the work. It therefore has to consider as contributing to production not only the direct producers of the work in its materiality (artist, writer, etc.) but also the producers of the meaning and value of the work – critics, publishers, gallery directors and the whole set of agents whose combined efforts produce consumers capable of knowing and recognizing the work of art as such.[149]

It is this sense of culture that preoccupies this work, and indeed, the sameness that is implied by recognition. In other words, those cultural objects fulfilling the criteria for recognition under the intellectual property system fulfil merely one cultural terrain, but nevertheless, the institutionalism of intellectual property suggests a hierarchical privilege for such expressions, in the economic world view of knowledge. Recalling the rhetoric of the "creative economy", there is a sense that expressions which cannot be reconciled within this economy, for which the transactions are regulated by intellectual property laws, are thus inauthentic. It is not "authentic creation".

As suggested at the end of the previous chapter, culture can be understood not by its indices of creativity (as suggested in the "creative economy") but as itself a continuous flow and connection between participants. In the hierarchising of cultural artefacts, the same processes of marking time through the intellectual property system become clear. As John Frow has identified in the practice of grouping "cultures", the taxonomical organisation of culture is at once limiting: "it is precisely this assumption of a set of uniform criteria, or of a uniform hierarchy of criteria, that has played the major organizing role in the most authoritative and entrenched practices of reading – with the inevitable effect of repressing the difference and the specificity of other practices, casting them as naïve or exotic or perverse."[150] Again, it is this calibration or conjugation of the cultural terrain that obscures cultural diversity – traditional knowledge and cultural expressions, collaborative and incremental innovation, the culture of the network, are all examples of the very limited cultural rhythm that is suggested by the broken melody of the dominant "cultural" institution.

---

149 Bourdieu P (1993) *The Field of Cultural Production: Essays on Art and Literature*, Johnson R (ed), Cambridge, Polity: 37. Hal Foster describes a similar process in his work on presentational political art, where he identifies the "rhetoricity" of such works in rendering social practices as "iconic ideals", as for instance in representations of the industrial worker: Foster H (1985) *Recodings: Art, Spectacle, Cultural Politics*, Seattle, Bay P: 155.

150 Frow J (1995) *Cultural Studies and Cultural Value*, Oxford, Clarendon P: 132.

At its very least, the term "culture" suggests process and growth, not only in the sense of the canonised arts, but also in the sense of cultivation.[151] But used in this singular way, the plurality of "cultures" is somewhat obscured and obscure. In the sense of its status in the current debate, and in government policy,[152] a singular and substantial value of "culture" persists, as indeed does a singular "creativity". Equally strategic is the concept of the singular "public", a concept of practical application and yet impossible to decipher: "it seems that in order to address a public, one must forget or ignore the fictional nature of the entity one addresses."[153] And indeed, it is in this sense that the ideological ranking of the *habitus* becomes clear, whereby the "public" can be rendered uniform and de-valued all at once. In the same way, while nevertheless suggesting a process, the use of creativity and culture in the institutional context reaffirms values of seemingly superior political and moral legitimacy, values which are elsewhere multiplied and "de-conceptualised".[154]

In the economy of intellectual property, therefore, the user is "propertyless", the "peasant" class. It is this dispossession of the user that will be traced in the following chapter.

---

151 Williams R (1981) *Culture*, London, Fontana: 10.

152 For instance, in the United Kingdom it is the Department of Culture, Media and Sport – not the Department of Cultures, Media and Sport. This is repeated throughout similar government departments or ministries throughout the world. It would appear that the concept of culture is not in decline as a singular value.

153 Warner M (2005) *Publics and Counterpublics*, New York, Zone: 12. Nevertheless, as considered in earlier discussion, the singularity of the "public" remains appealing not only for policy-makers but also for civil society: "The idea of a public is motivating, not simply instrumental. It is constitutive of a social imaginary" (12).

154 Arjun Appadurai approaches this question in another way, by preferring the adjectival meaning rather than the noun: "Resisting ideas of culture that tempt us to think of actual social groups as cultures, I have also resisted the noun form *culture* and suggested an adjectival approach to culture, which stresses its contextual, heuristic, and comparative dimensions and orients us to the idea of culture as difference, especially difference in the realm of group identity." See Appadurai A (1996) *Modernity at Large: Cultural Dimensions of Globalization*, Minneapolis, U of Minnesota P: 13.

Chapter 3

Creating Self

We create the self out of the world of action, and the world of action out of the self.[1]

> The proposition that the writer or artist is a creator belongs to a humanist ideology. In this ideology man is released from his function in an order external to himself, restored to his so-called powers. Circumscribed only by the resources of his own nature, he becomes the maker of his own laws. He creates. What does he create? Man. Humanist thought (everything by man, everything for man) is circular, tautological, dedicated entirely to the repetition of a single image. "Man makes man" (in this sense Aristotle is the theoretician of humanism): by a continual unbroken investigation he releases from within himself what is already there; creativity is self-multiplication.[2]

Introduction

Creation is self-multiplication, creativity is creating self.

Indeed, the very basis of "creation" is itself the story – it is through the narration of self that "property" of selfhood is achieved. The critical concern, however, is the authority of that narration. From where is that authority sourced, and in what way is the dominant narrative of intellectual property limiting "selves" in the network?

It is instructive to consider the relationship between possessory models of creativity (as established in the intellectual property systems), expression of self, and the construction of individualistic, competitive identities within the dominant narrative of economic progress and creative process. In particular, the way in which the "self-organising" system of the intellectual property institution impacts upon access to collaborative and collective expression is pivotal to a re-thinking of the "presence" of the user within this economy.

As introduced in the preceding chapters, intellectual property presents a distinct language by which to recuperate and reconcile creative events within the logic of the economic model of creativity. As a language it imposes a linguistic order and certainty upon those events. It is critical, therefore, to understand the way in which this linguistic certainty comes to nominate and identify the "self" through

1 Wagner R (1981) *The Invention of Culture*, Rev ed, Chicago, U of Chicago P: 79.

2 Macherey P ([1966]1978) *A Theory of Literary Production*, Wall G (trans), London, Routledge: 66.

conventional narratives of creativity that are offered within the current commercial models.

In this way, the tension between the "mystifying" process in intellectual property and the cacophony of the collaborative dialogue offered through strategies of negotiating that language becomes more distinct – indeed, sensible. Thus, towards an understanding of the creation not of self, but of the collective subjectivity of selves, pursued throughout this text, it is necessary to characterise the notion of "self" that is undersigned by the intellectual property narrative. In other words, the "self" is illusory other than through the certainty offered in the arbitration and adjudication of creative events, the conjugation of creative progress – the intellectual propertisation of creativity.

The Creative Self, the Propertied Self

> *Public memorials* are national property, or more precisely – like works of art in general without regard to their *use* [*Benutzung*] – it is their indwelling soul of remembrance and honour which gives them their validity as living and self-sufficient ends; but if this soul abandons them, they are then in this respect ownerless as far as the nation is concerned and become contingent private possessions.[3]

For Hegel, the opportunity for the creation of contingent private possessions from public memorials indicates, paradoxically, a loss of value. In many ways, Hegel's consideration of selfhood (almost 200 years old) is decidedly relevant in the context of the contemporary network. The "freedom" of property that is presumed in the rhetoric of intellectual property advocates might indeed be rejected in that such enclosure of knowledge represents an institutional failure to allow for the arbitrariness (and freedom) and self-respect of the network. Indeed, "Non-property, the non-ownership of things, or a common ownership of goods, is just a little self-contradictory."[4] As Hegel suggests, it is the recognition conferred by property which renders it "the *existence* [*Dasein*] of personality".[5]

The language of property appears to be critical to the articulation of the intellectual property system, not only in the introduction of impressions of "exhaustion" and competition, but also in the rhetoric of "ownership", and the trespass upon the personal identity of that dominion, that is engaged by advocates for stronger rights. This rhetoric ties the individual subjectivity (derived through property) to the kind of economic narrative of self-worth[6] recognised earlier and identified in

---

3 Hegel GWF ([1821]1991) *Elements of the Philosophy of Right*, Wood AW (ed), Nisbet HB (trans), Cambridge, Cambridge UP: 94.

4 Hegel GWF ([1807]1977) *Phenomenology of Spirit*, Miller AV (trans), Oxford, Oxford UP: 258.

5 Hegel GWF ([1821]1991) *Elements of the Philosophy of Right*, Wood AW (ed), Nisbet HB (trans), Cambridge, Cambridge UP: 81.

6 This link between individual subjectivity/selfhood and economic concerns is considered again later in this chapter, in the context of celebrity and personality rights, and in

Weber's characterisation of the ethic of capitalism.[7] Similarly, the polarity of users and creators (discussed throughout this work) rests upon the presumption of these categories as fixed and immutable identities, rather than the fluid and inconstant relations any one individual can experience.

The way in which the individual competitive and ambitious self is realised within intellectual property models of creativity is critical to understanding the way in which the application of the laws to characterise transactions of knowledge between individuals creates "classes" of users. In particular, the process by which possessory models of creativity are maintained and justified is of special interest in so far as users, within this system of manifest self-possession, are "propertyless" – literally, dispossessed. The user is *a priori* disenfranchised. A detailed consideration of the creative "self" is necessary towards an understanding of the ongoing success of proprietary-like models of creativity, together with a re-examination of the mythology of the "genuine" creators.

Becoming clear is the way in which creativity is apparently fixed and situated within the work – identified, recorded, and "safeguarded" by the intellectual property system.[8] The quality and "direction" (in terms of progress and the narrative of improvement) provided by the presumption of "creativity", as the value warranted by the intellectual property system, are intrinsic to the system's complicity with conventional notions of the "self". Indeed, in Western capitalist ideology, notions of individual self-expression are articulated as fundamental values of "freedom". Further, the individual control (or indeed "ownership", both culturally as well as legally through intellectual property) over one's expression is bolstered by the access to the resources to display that "self".[9] Thus, knowledge indeed is power; in addition, access to knowledge is inextricable from the self-possession of expression. Denial of that access literally dispossesses citizens.

As greater limits are placed upon the availability and dissemination of knowledge, and opportunities for access are abrogated and increasingly contrived, users are deprived. Not only are users economically deprived by a seemingly growing imbalance in the intellectual property system, but also they are culturally deprived through the specificity of situations in which access is possible. Significantly, ongoing resistance

---

the context of locating creativity within certain new forms, such as broadcasts.

7 Weber M ([1904-5]2002) *The Protestant Ethic and the Spirit of Capitalism*, Kalberg S (trans), Oxford, Blackwell.

8 WIPO Magazine (2006) January-February.

9 This can also be seen in the context of current discussions towards protection of the traditional knowledge and resources of indigenous and traditional communities, where the discussion is frequently framed as a battle of self-determination that is contingent upon dominion over resources. For instance, see Simpson T (1997) *Indigenous Heritage and Self-Determination: The Cultural and Intellectual Property Rights of Indigenous Peoples*, Copenhagen, IWGIA. This is distinct from the indigenous philosophies of communalism in which resources are intrinsic to the operation of community itself. See Gibson J (2005) *Community Resources: Intellectual Property, International Trade and Protection of Traditional Knowledge*, Aldershot, Ashgate: 44.

of intellectual property laws to the culture of the network means that users, participants and actors in that network, are also disconnected and dissociated from each other, expropriated. Thus, the ideology of the system subsumes notions of self-esteem and self-worth and articulates these through self-possession in property. Arguably, this model is incompatible with the potential of collective subjectivities through networked collaborations and communications, and through continuous knowledge flows and relations between actors, including users, in networked creativity. On the contrary, the intellectual property system is distinctive in its reliance upon the fixed presence of a propertied self and the inanimate and "timeless" objects suspended in the slowness (and institutions) of the system.

It is also critical at this point to negotiate the fact (and indeed instrumental to the arguments made here) that creators are also articulated as users and can be similarly expropriated from the network available to them. Thus, although a creator may access the means for selfhood in a particular opportunity and expression, at the same time that creator can experience elsewhere the disinheritance from one's knowledge through the operation of limits in other situations. The polarisation of users and creators must be resisted, especially in the context of the seemingly intractable and immutable opposition that is perpetuated by the language of the law itself, in the very "territory" of users themselves, the public domain.

Public Domain, Public Execution

What is critical in distilling the terms of the debate is an examination of the way in which references to the public domain operate in the construction of the users (including the particular issues of construction of traditional peoples as any other users with respect to their "public" traditional knowledge[10]) as a passive audience, as consumers, and indeed as somehow opposite to the business of creativity.[11] The very nature of the Western concept of the public domain is such that intellectual property ownership is prior to the debate. Users are somewhat diminished as coming after intellectual property and, to a certain extent, "created" by intellectual property in so far as they arise as an audience of the knowledge products within the creative economy of intellectual property. This process of distance and disengagement from the creative enterprise is critical to the construction of the passive and anonymous user or consumer of the personality of the creator. Active users are thus not conceivable and any "creativity" in that use is not recognisable within the paradigm. Intellectual property rights-holders, by the same process, are constructed as the initial or primary

10 This concern is discussed in more detail later in this chapter.

11 Alastair Hannay makes similar comments on the notion of the political public, where he argues that the public merely has "a watching brief" in modern political debate. Hannay A (2005) *On the Public*, London, Routledge: 67. In modern intellectual property law debates, Hannay's concept is useful in understanding the way in which NGOs are able to participate formally within the debate and the extent to which that participation (and representation) is recognised.

public invested in participation in the debate.[12] Arguably, intellectual property rights are somewhat conceived as a prerequisite for participation, a requirement of the "political" participation in the debate in that they indicate an "investment" in the civilised organisation of the public.[13] The public domain is becoming increasingly privatised in an extension of the private sphere of intellectual properties. In other words, the disenfranchised "propertyless" user is literally outside the sphere of participation.

The public domain, as it operates within an increasingly globalised system of intellectual property protection, imagines a "global" public, as it were. That is, the "public" about which the institution of intellectual property is articulated is a kind of culturally and socially universalised, uniform, international public. The individual self-possessed "owner" is thus constituted against the anonymous and homogeneous public, with the increasingly economic rendition of the private "owner".[14] This is a considerably strategic aspect of the rhetoric of intellectual property in that the public domain and this "universal public" assimilates the publics of various cultures as a singular and fixed "public". Traditional communities are assimilated in a similar and notably problematic process. In the context of traditional knowledge, free access to that knowledge through its situation within the public domain may simply constitute an imposition of regularity and universality through a standardising of cultural diversity. The overarching cultural institution of intellectual property facilitates this universal "culture" while at the same obscuring comparable concepts of the "public domain", as in place within diverse traditional or tribal communities. In other words, the simplification of this "global" public domain makes possible an ahistorical universalised public out of diverse cultures, individuals, and groups. It brings colonised and coloniser together in the competitive territory of the public.[15]

---

12 In practical terms this is often realised in the form of a certain authority or qualification granted to rights-holders within the debates, whereby the arguments of publishers are sometimes interpreted as more credible and informed and the interests of consumers in those debates somewhat distanced. This was a criticism made by consumer groups of recent government consultations in Europe (for instance, see the Access to Knowledge campaign archives concerning the Creative Economy Conference, UK Presidency of the EU, London 5-7 October 2005).

13 In this respect, intellectual property rights and the risks undertaken in their creation (as creators and as investors) are almost privileged with respect to the ethical position of the various interests. For instance, see the "unreasonableness" applied to positions contrary to intellectual property rights in Sell SK (1999) "Multinational corporations as agents of change: the globalization of intellectual property rights", in Cutler AC et al (eds), *Private Authority and International Affairs*, Albany, SUNY P: 174-75.

14 Note discussions on the way in which "selfhood" is extended to corporate entities such that "investment" becomes coincident with creativity.

15 For further discussion of traditional knowledge and the concept of the public domain, see Gibson J (forthcoming) "Audiences in Tradition: Traditional Knowledge and the Public Domain", in MacQueen H and Waelde C (eds) *Intellectual Property: The Many Faces of the Public Domain*, Cheltenham, Edward Elgar.

Thus, the notions of "public domain" and "public interest" as they may operate within the rhetoric of the more corporate "intellectual property" are not properly public at all in so far as individuals and communities are anonymised and alienated within that public. In other words, within the narration of the intellectual property system, the "public" is not a functioning public.[16] The users of the public domain are not a functioning public (as defined by that very system and by the rhetorical strategies of its advocates), but a public created out of the structures presented by the intellectual property framework that anticipates their identity or representation, that brings the public into view. In fact, this mythical public is extremely strategic. It is made possible by the regulation of the public domain by intellectual property laws – that is, how, what, when, and where the public may use certain intellectual property rights; how the public may use knowledge; how the public may create. Furthermore, the regulation of the public domain is considerably commercial, focused upon the questions of the market and the assessment of the value to be realised, in calculations of the duration of the monopoly to be applied. These parameters for the creation of the global public domain are indeed quite irrelevant or incomparable to those that may regulate the public domains of various communities.

Indeed, within this anonymous public the active user is somewhat compromised, subjugated to the personality of the creator. Controversially, perhaps, unlimited access to knowledge may simply reiterate this subjugation. To a certain extent, limits upon the abstraction and construction of knowledge within these polarising Western concepts of the public domain and privatised intellectual property rights unsettle the dynamics of the dominant rhetoric without necessarily reinforcing the language of limits at work in intellectual property paradigms. But the conceptualisation of access within the networked community as unlimited and unmitigated is a strategic miscalculation of the diverse ethics and philosophies of such communities. The characterisation of the "access to knowledge" campaign in this way is, in itself, a means by which to construct the coalition of civil society actors within this campaign as opposed to the primary social values recruited and appropriated by the intellectual

16 Hannay A (2005) *On the Public*, London, Routledge: 7. Hannay explains, in the context of political participation (but the comments can be extended to an interpretation of the way in which the regulation of intellectual property rights modifies and creates the creative public), that the public is not functioning in that its members are not active participants in the political process. Similarly, the "public" constructed with respect to the public domain alienates users from the creative process.

property rhetoric – that is, civil society becomes a uniformly uncivilised "rabble"[17] of anti-IP.[18]

Thus, the Western concept of the public domain, as it operates within the language of international intellectual property systems, puts the audience in its place, demarcating the territory of knowledge and the personality (the recognised "creators", the intellectual property rights-holders) of the authority over that territory. The public domain, therefore, is a kind of property of the private individuals, the private creators, who are necessarily members of the public and creators of the means (intellectual property) by which the public domain (and thus the public itself) is recognised and valued. Indeed, the debate over the protection of traditional knowledge is frequently dominated by industry representatives. Intellectual property ownership is almost a guarantee of entry into the debate, while users are almost uniformly abandoned for lack of evidence, as it were. The public, the users, are created by intellectual property, they come later than intellectual property, subsequently to it, and thus they are frequently marginalised in the creative economy of intellectual property systems. The public domain, in this way, is a spectacle; the users are merely the witnesses, spectators, audience of that spectacle.

In an important way, intellectual property laws and concepts depend upon the distance that is generated between the "public" thus created and the knowledge in the public domain, the distance between creators and users that dominates the current debates over access and protection. The "use" and access sought by the public is somewhat displaced from the personality of the public, the unaccountable witness. In other words, where the risk involved in creativity is recognised and evaluated in terms of commercial parameters (such as the calculation of the appropriate duration of monopoly in order to make the financial return necessary to encourage and support that risk), the public is therefore unaccountable with respect to that risk. In this way, the participation of the public (the user) is "de-valued" (as mere witness, spectator) in the creative economy. Intellectual property recognises, identifies, and regulates the creativity and originality of the knowledge. The public, as audience, necessarily cannot participate in that performance but is, rather, constituted by it; the public is a consumer of that performance, a topic of the commercially constructed public domain. This distance in turn makes the notion of the witnessing "public",

17 Hegel speaks of the dispossessed poor as being cast adrift as a rabble, unable to coordinate, estranged, and cut off from society. Unable to make links with each other, the poor are disowned, from themselves and from society. The orchestration of a "peasant" class of users in the intellectual property system, and the rendering of the public as a disorganised "rabble", is a mythology that must be resisted without compromising the diversity and freedom that is possible through the network: "In this position, where the existence of freedom becomes something wholly contingent, inner indignation is necessary. Because the individual's freedom has no existence, the recognition of universal freedom disappears. From this condition arises that shamelessness that we find in the rabble." Hegel GWF ([1821]1991) *Elements of the Philosophy of Right*, Wood AW (ed), Nisbet HB (trans), Cambridge, Cambridge UP: 453.

18 See the discussion of this in Chapter 1.

the "global" public, possible, and further indoctrinates the public as audience and as distinct from the creative process.

As suggested, increasingly the organising principle for "creativity", the groundwork of intellectual property, has become that of investment. The "risk" of creativity is one which is most frequently quantified in financial terms, such that the "quality" of creative activity has come to be recognised through an economic framework. This is traced through two recent and somewhat contested examples –webcasting and celebrity.

Broadcasts, Webcasts, and Outcasts

In the United Kingdom, the law of copyright has increasingly dissolved any practical distinction between the traditional works of copyright (literary, dramatic, musical, and artistic) and subject matter (films, sound recordings, and broadcasts) which was not a traditional work of copyright but was nevertheless protected as such. Conceptually, therefore, broadcasts have become comparable to "authored" works.[19] This is a substantial expansion of what was originally conceptualised in the Rome Act of the Berne Convention for the Protection of Literary and Artistic Works.[20] In this 1928 revision of Berne, Article 11 *bis* gave authors the exclusive right to authorise a broadcast (and thus, stop others from broadcasting) an authorial work to the public by way of broadcast. There was not a right for broadcasters under international treaties until 1961, when it was created under the International Convention for the Protection of Performers, Producers of Phonograms, and Broadcasting Organizations (Rome Convention 1961). Article 13 of the Rome Convention 1961 gives broadcasting organisations (the broadcaster) the right, among other things, to prohibit the re-broadcast of their broadcast. In other words, it creates a proprietary and authorial-like right in the broadcast and a "creator" in the broadcaster. Interestingly, considering the emphatic position of the United States in favour of the current Draft WIPO Treaty on the Protection of Broadcasting Organizations,[21] including an immovable adherence to the inclusion of protection of webcasting within this agreement, the United States is still yet to become a party to the Rome Convention.

Authors in Space

The Draft Treaty has met with much opposition, especially in respect of the proposed right in webcasting and the associated regulation of information on the Internet. The

19 See the discussion in Bently L and Sherman B (2004) *Intellectual Property Law*, 2nd ed, Oxford, Oxford UP: 32.

20 The Berne Convention for the Protection of Literary and Artistic Works.

21 WIPO Standing Committee on Copyright and Related Rights. Draft Basic Proposal for the WIPO Treaty on the Protection of Broadcasting Organizations, Including a Non-Mandatory Appendix on the Protection in Relation to Webcasting. 14th Session. Geneva, 1-5 May 2006. SCCR/14/2. 8 February.

protection in relation to webcasting was first proposed in 2004 by the United States, Kenya, and Egypt.[22] In effect, the proposals in the Appendix to the Draft Treaty extend the "author" function identified in broadcasters to webcasting. The Appendix is non-mandatory; however, this status is somewhat disrupting the passage of the Treaty and it has been suggested that this obstacle may indeed lead to a change in status.[23]

Thus, the development in broadcasts and webcasts as works, in and of themselves, is in part motivated and sustained by the language of the author (and the "genuine"). Further, these developments are an indication of the way in which the "official culture" of intellectual property attempts to traverse and contain the territory and potential of networked communication, by the imposition of the conventions and

22 WIPO Standing Committee on Copyright and Related Rights, Consolidated Text For A Treaty On The Protection Of Broadcasting Organizations, 11th Session, 7-9 June 2004, SCCR/11/3 February 29: page 20.

23 For a review of the major issues see Boyle J (2005) "More Rights are Wrong For Webcasters", *Financial Times*, 26 September. At the time of writing, the 14th Session of the Standing Committee on Copyright and Related Rights had just concluded discussions (1-6 May 2006) where it was decided that webcasting and simulcasting (simultaneous transmissions of broadcasts over the Internet) would be placed on a separate and later negotiating track, including a separate meeting in 2007. This move appears to be a decision motivated by the desire to maintain negotiations, rather than a genuine responsibility to the political debate over webcasting. Immediately prior to going to press, the 15th Session (11-13 September 2006) had just concluded, agreeing in principle to a Revised Draft Basic Proposal for the WIPO Treaty on the Protection of Broadcasting Organizations, SCCR/15/2, 31 July 2006. The Standing Committee has recommended to the General Assembly (meeting 25 September to 3 October 2006) that a Diplomatic Conference on the Treaty should be convened mid 2007. However, there is a strong possibility that this will be resisted, as some delegations, including the United States, have expressed strong reservations about proceeding with this draft. A statement on behalf of several representatives of industry in the United States (including AT&T, Dell, Intel, Sony Electronics Incorporated, and US Telecom), issued 19 September 2006, urges their government to oppose the Treaty, arguing against the "broad draft treaty language" as well as the uncertainty at the procedural level. See Request for US Government Opposition to Advancing a Diplomatic Treaty Conference on the Proposed WIPO Treaty on the Protection of Broadcasting Organizations From Certain Information Technology, Consumer Electronics and Telecommunications Industry Representatives, 19 September 2006. Further, many representatives from civil society and consumer groups (including Electronic Frontier Foundation, Consumer Project on Technology, and Public Knowledge) have also expressed concern at the negotiation procedure, suggesting that the Revised Draft was hastily concluded and the recommendation for a Diplomatic Conference issued despite inadequate consensus. A joint statement issued by industry and civil society organisations continues to raise concerns regarding the justification and scope of the Treaty, as well as uncertainty regarding limitations and exceptions, and the issue of intermediary liability. See Statement Concerning the WIPO Broadcast Treaty Provided by Certain Information Technology, Consumer Electronics and Telecommunications Industry Representatives, Public Interest Organizations, and Performers' Representatives, 5 September 2006.

logic of the economic model of creativity.[24] Indeed, the "technophobic" authoring of broadcasts and webcasts in this way inserts a humanistic (and indeed human) narrative into seemingly unaccountable stories of communication. As Manuel Castells explains: "rather than converging with the media, the Internet is asserting its specificity as a communication medium."[25] The interconnected networks of cultures at play in the Internet will be overcoded by such a right to the extent that the potential of the Internet will be subdued, and become merely coincident with conventional media models. Thus, the specificity of the Internet is lost.

At stake is not the work, but the transmission, the very links themselves between participants in the cultural life of the Internet.[26] In creating rights in webcasting, what is being recognised is precisely not a right to protect and facilitate communication in networks (indeed it could decimate them), but a right to price them. Such rights create nothing but the market in the signals themselves. Surely it is not possible to point to the coherent, the complete, the finite webcast. In this very example, the law seeks to contain and traverse the continuum, the flow of communication, the transmission. There is no work: *We are not buying, just looking.*

Divining Rights

The controversy of the protection of webcasting thus raises the very fundamental issue of evidence in the "progression" of intellectual property developments, of preparation as distinct from "divining" rights intervention:

> There was never any evidence that even broadcasters needed the right. And the capital requirements and business models of the two industries are entirely different. And the reach of the webcasts would in effect be global. And there is no evidence at all that webcasters need any kind of protection.[27]

---

24 Adrian Sterling has produced some interesting considerations of the extension of copyright (by virtue of the broadcast right and satellite transmission) into space. See Sterling JAL (2004) "Space Law". British Literary and Artistic Copyright Association (BLACA). Presentation. 11 November. See also Sterling's Draft Protocol on Space Copyright Law and Extraterritorial Exploitation of Protected Material. QMIPRI. http://www.qmipri.org/psc.html.

25 Castells M (2002) *The Internet Galaxy: Reflections on the Internet, Business, and Society*, Oxford, Oxford UP: 199.

26 Art 6 of the Draft Basic Proposal creates an exclusive right in the broadcaster to prevent re-transmission of a broadcast. Art 7 gives an exclusive right in fixation, and Art 8 creates the right to prevent any unauthorised reproduction of such fixation. These provisions would similarly apply to webcasts if the non-mandatory appendix were to be adopted, thus developing the law far beyond the obligations in the Rome Convention.

27 Boyle J (2005) "More Rights are Wrong for Webcasters", *Financial Times*, 26 September. The emphasis on requiring adequate and appropriate evidence for policy-making and legal developments is of critical importance to civil society campaigners on access to knowledge. Note also the principle in the Adelphi Charter for Creativity, Innovation and Intellectual Property, Principle 9, which calls for an automatic presumption against creating

In other words, "faith-based" policy-making and developments in stronger laws are precisely directed towards "creating" a market, of identifying ways in which to generate an imbalance so as to create a "valuable" need. Indeed, "one might say that money has been, so to speak, the steam engine, then petroleum … and so on".[28] The "faith" of the expanding intellectual property system rests in the "author", the celebrated principle of organisation and the singular source of creative "genius". However, the institutional dogma of the "author" instates industry as the source, and the economic circumstances for creativity become inextricable from the process itself. Tied as it is to the capitalist economic narrative of salvation, the "future" narrative of intellectual property is, somewhat paradoxically perhaps, secured by its traditions. This emphasis on "futures" is particularly powerful in the legitimation process of the intellectual property grand narrative. Examining his work on meta-narratives, and in so doing including the Christian narrative of salvation (and the resonances with creativity as divination[29]), Jean-François Lyotard explains that such narratives of self-legitimation are always necessarily directed at the future:

> These narratives aren't myths in the sense that fables would be (not even the Christian narrative). Of course, like myths, they have the goal of legitimating social and political institutions and practices, laws, ethics, ways of thinking. Unlike myths, however, they look for legitimacy not in an original founding act but in a future to be accomplished, that is, in an Idea to be realised.[30]

Thus, the future-oriented development of intellectual property laws, the faith-based approach to stronger and new rights, is self-legitimating by virtue of the persistent links to the aspirational (and incontestable) ideals of creativity and innovation. Indeed, the necessary interrogation for the re-thinking and re-placement of users within the system is that of the system itself, and, indeed, of creativity. As the development of publicity protection shows (as will now be discussed), creativity has become a powerful organising principle for the recognition and extension of rights, increasingly underwritten by the economic circumstances in which it is perceived to be achieved.

By the same process, the concept of "tradition" may be incorporated and recuperated by intellectual property systems in the "future-oriented" creation of markets. Indeed, many rights are being created and extended for past acts of innovation.[31] For instance, the protection offered in Europe for a recognised Protected

---

new areas of intellectual property law and extending existing rights, stating that where changes are sought, "The burden of proof must lie on the advocates of change."

28 Negri A (2004) *The Politics of Subversion: A Manifesto for the Twenty-First Century*, New ed, Cambridge, Polity: 210.

29 See in particular the discussion in Chapter 1.

30 Lyotard J-F ([1986]1992) *The Postmodern Explained to Children: Correspondence 1982-1985*, Pefanis J and Thomas M (ed), Barry D et al (trans), Sydney, Power Publications: 29.

31 Indeed, this is played out in the example of performers' property rights in the United Kingdom, introduced by the Copyright and Related Rights Regulations 1996 (UK), to

Geographical Indication (PGI) – namely the recognition and protection of established, traditional and cultural products tied to the specific and earthly uniqueness of a place – has been appropriated recently in potentially anti-competitive ways. The case of Melton Mowbray Pork Pies[32] is illustrative of this, where protection is being sought for the traditional recipe for Melton Mowbray Pork Pies. The application was made to the European Commission, on behalf of the recently formed Melton Mowbray Pork Pie Association (MMPPA), by the United Kingdom's Department for Environment, Food and Rural Affairs (DEFRA), and applies to an area of 1800 square miles. One of the major producers of pies under the name of "Melton Mowbray", Northern Foods (with 25 per cent share of the market) is outside this geographical area, but would nevertheless be prevented from ongoing production if the PGI is granted, despite being in production since the 1800s. Northern Foods appealed the decision in the United Kingdom High Court of Justice, Queen's Bench Division, Administrative Court, arguing, among other things, that the protection covers an unusually large area and that this area was defined in order to catch one of the major companies producing the recipe, Samworth Brothers (with 55 per cent share of the market, and a factory in Leicester City). The court has now asked for advice from the European Court of Justice. Thus, the existence of the intellectual property right created a unique cultural product and provides the circumstances to present the "authenticity" of that product. In other words, the commercial market, created by a right, becomes mutually constitutive of the "culture."

The case of the Melton Mowbray pie may be related to the concept of "cultural branding", whereby a brand becomes valued as part of the national culture, precisely through its circulation and exchange between users.[33] However, in the present case, the process of that value creation has been appropriated through the prior identification of the end product (by the intellectual property system), such that the contribution of users to that value creation is displaced. In other words, the protection of the category of PGI, in this particular example of its application (which is arguably in ways contrary to the original intention of the protection), has allowed the potential right-holder to identify, prior to any engagement with the user, the cultural significance of its new product.

Arguably, new intellectual property rights have little to do with the possible anticipation and encouragement of innovation, and much about identifying owners of what might retrospectively be labelled as "creative". Indeed, this is the story-telling, the narration of culture.

---

implement the Directive 92/100/EEC on Rental/Lending and Related Rights.

32 See *Northern Foods Plc v DEFRA and MMPPA* [2006] ETMR 31. The Melton Mowbray Pork Pie Association (MMPPA) information on the application for protection is available at http://www.mmppa.co.uk/protecting.html. A press statement from Matthew O'Callaghan on the referral is available at http://www.mmppa.co.uk/news.html.

33 For a discussion of cultural branding, see Hold DB (2004) *How Brands Become Icons: The Principles of Cultural Branding*, Boston, Harvard Business School P.

Creative Publicity

Your identity is your most valuable possession – protect it.[34]

Celebrity and the emerging right in publicity presents an intriguing example of the reach of "creativity" and the way in which the myth of the creator is sustained through an emphasis on the selfhood of the celebrity figure. This can be understood alongside the relationship between individual subjectivity and economic rights, traced in earlier discussions.[35] Further, the narration of "celebrity" as creative is similar to the process by which culture and creativity are defined through the application of "property" value. Indeed, celebrity is a critical example of the logic of intellectual property, whereby the "branding" of cultural value through economic value has been translated to the case of the individual celebrity subject. The celebrity becomes a creative industry in its own right, but what "creativity" is being encouraged by this investment in selfhood? Further, as will be discussed, a certain "rupture" can be deciphered in this dominant narrative, through the counter-cultural activity of "fans". This provides particular insight into the "limits" of intellectual property in the contemporary network and important understandings of the autonomy of "actors" within that network.

The Incentive to Celebrity

The identification of a publicity right (as a property interest rather than a mere interest in reputation), as distinct from a privacy right, was first made in 1977 in the decision of the Supreme Court of the United States, in the case of *Zacchini v Scripps-Howard Broadcasting Co*.[36] In this same decision, the notion of incentive was explicit. Justice White stated that the "[p]etitioner's right of publicity here rests on more than a desire to compensate the performer for the time and effort invested in the act; the protection provided an economic incentive for him to make the investment required to produce a performance of interest to the public". In other words, the right of publicity was directly related to the incentive to perform, which was interpreted as being in the public interest, drawing upon arguments very similar to those made in favour of copyright and patent laws. This appears to make it clear that the right of publicity in the United States was at least introduced and explained through, or indeed founded upon, intellectual property principles of creativity and proprietary rights.

The reasoning in this decision suggests the potential for unregulated consumption of or access to celebrity to result in the loss of celebrity value – the celebrity can become exhausted. And indeed, Landes and Posner note "the trademark and right-

---

34 *The Incredibles* (2004) Bird B (dir. and scr.). Character of Helen Parr/Elastigirl.

35 Landes WM and Posner RA (2003) *The Economic Structure of Intellectual Property Law*, Cambridge MA, Harvard UP: 37-70. See also the discussion of personality rights in Beverley-Smith H (2002) *The Commercial Appropriation of Personality*, Cambridge, Cambridge UP.

36 *Zacchini v Scripps-Howard Broadcasting Co*, 433 U.S. 562, 576 (1977).

of-publicity cases that recognize that intellectual property *can* be diminished by consumption".[37] It would seem that publicity, the very process by which celebrity is created, may be the very process by which it is depleted, the very limiting process of celebrity.[38]

In providing the incentive to perform, the construction of publicity rights in the foundational *Zacchini* decision suggests a certain insight into what might be "protected" should a celebrity successfully challenge the intrusion of the paparazzi or passer-by in capturing their "performances" in the public domain, as it were – such as the public beach.[39] In the United Kingdom, this might be understood as something similar to Part 2 of the Copyright Designs and Patents Act (UK), or the CDPA, which gives performers rights in their performances. But of particular interest to the current discussion is the fact that Part II has just been re-drafted in order to give performers moral rights in their performances in sound recordings and live performances, but not in audio-visual works. This is a significant consequence of the economic constraints within which not only users but also individual "creators" are being defined, while at the same time, supporting industries are increasingly being positioned as the critical nexus of creative output and process. The reason for the exclusion of audio-visual works is their exclusion from the WIPO Performances and Phonograms Treaty 1996, which the recent United Kingdom amendments sought to implement. This exclusion was after strenuous lobbying from the United States film industry, which sought to curtail the possible expansion of performers' rights as a "risk" to the industry itself. Given the success of this lobbying, a future international framework for publicity that would allow assignment of economic rights in publicity to studios and the like is not unthinkable. Indeed, it heralds a possible return to the historic studio system,[40] putting creativity in the hands of the producers. Thus, producers would control the "creativity" of the celebrity and the surrounding discourse, and influence the narration of the celebrity through the media. Paul MacDonald explains this process in the

37 Landes WM and Posner RA (2003) *The Economic Structure of Intellectual Property Law*, Cambridge MA, Harvard UP: 223-24.

38 Indeed, fame is a requirement before a mark is eligible for dilution protection under the United States Lanham Act. Such protection recognises that a mark is so "famous" that its value can be diminished by use (by other people) in ways other than those for which it is registered. See Schechter F (1926) "The Rational Basis of Trademark Protection", 40 *Harvard Law Review* 813.

39 For instance, see the complaint made by Anna Ford against the Daily Mail for the publication of photographs of herself, her partner, and her children, while on holiday at the beach: *Ford v Daily Mail and OK Magazine*, PCC Report 52, 15 September 2000; *R (on the Application of Ford) v Press Complaints Commission* [2002] EMLR 5. See also BBC News, "Newsreader Loses Privacy Bid", 31 July 2001, http://news.bbc.co.uk/1/hi/uk/ 1466459.stm. Compare the similar circumstances in *McGregor v Fraser*, where the court ordered an assessment of damages for breach of confidence and invasion of privacy, as well as compensation under the Data Protection Act 1998 (UK): *McGregor v Fraser* [2003] EWHC 2972.

40 For a discussion of the studio system, see the collection of essays in Staiger J (ed) (1995) *The Studio System*, New Brunswick, Rutgers UP.

early studio system, whereby "Producer control of the star discourse saw the mutual reinforcement of the professional and private identities of performers, constructing the star as a coherent and non-contradictory image",[41] and it seems strikingly relevant today. Indeed, it is precisely this point which has led to the stalling of discussions on the WIPO Audio-Visual Treaty,[42] with an intractable deadlock on this issue between France and the United States.

In the case of celebrities, would consent then be required in order to exploit the performances of the celebrity in the public domain? The individual is in the public sphere, but "celebrity", as protected, is not in the public domain. The "copying" of celebrity in these instances is not licensed by the individual – it is an "intrusion", an "infringement", upon celebrity. In other words, the right to publicity is a right to negotiate one's public – the possibility to protect privacy in a public place. This is an intriguing negotiation of the tension between "publicity" as a branch of privacy (and human rights) or rather as an emerging branch of intellectual property rights (as in the United States). In the United Kingdom, the courts have appeared to be more willing to accommodate privacy within proprietary-like actions: "English law is far more attuned to property rights than to human rights; privacy has traditionally been protected, if at all, through a collection of quasi-proprietary actions. Breach of confidence remedies have been built on the notion that confidential information is akin to property whose owner ought to be able to control its use."[43] Indeed, interpreting publicity as property allows the courts to, in this case, limit the reach of the creator by imposing limitations on the scope of the right. In this way, a proprietary right might be more useful in addressing the potentially negative impact on press freedoms, rather than through recognition of publicity as a human right to privacy.[44] As a property right, the "celebrity" may be subject to limitations and exceptions that might not be so easily applied in the context of a privacy right. It may indeed be that an assertion of some kind of quasi-intellectual property right in celebrity may overcome calls for interpretations of celebrity integrity within the discourse

---

41 MacDonald P (1998) "Reconceptualising Stardom", supplementary chapter in Dyer R ([1979]1998) *Stars*, New ed, London, BFI Publishing: 175 at 178.

42 For the basic proposals, see WIPO Standing Committee on Copyright and Related Rights (2000) Basic Proposal for the Substantive Provisions of an Instrument on the Protection of Audiovisual Performances to be Considered by the Diplomatic Conference. Geneva, 7-20 December 2000. IAVP/DC/3. See also the discussion in Lewinski, S von (2001) "The WIPO Diplomatic Conference on Audio-Visual Performances: A First Resume", 23(7) *European Intellectual Property Review* 333.

43 Robertson G and Nicol A (2002) *Media Law*, 4th ed, London, Sweet & Maxwell: 281.

44 For instance, the court was reluctant to recognise privacy as a human right in *Campbell v MGN Ltd* [2004] 2 AC 457, by virtue of the celebrity's active pursuit of publicity, deemed to compromise any expectation of privacy. However, in the United Kingdom, the courts are reluctant to recognise publicity as a property right. In *Douglas v Hello Ltd* [2005] EWCA Civ 595, the Court of Appeal held that "confidential or private information, which is capable of commercial exploitation but which is only protected by the law of confidence, does not fall to be treated as property that can be owned and transferred" (para 119).

of privacy, and indeed re-assert the relationship between fan and the production of value in the celebrity.

The Elvis Presley trade mark litigation in England in the late 1990s[45] explicitly acknowledged the role of the fan or public in the construction of celebrity, when the Court of Appeal refused to grant a general protection to Elvis as a trade mark.[46] Jennifer Davis has maintained that "the judgment appears to recognise a public sphere in which meaning is socially created and to which the public should have access" and that "it is the public which has endowed [Elvis] … with the celebrity which makes memorabilia carrying his name so popular".[47] The nature of celebrity is such that its creation is indebted to the investments of the fans. In a sense, fandom is the industrial and economic infrastructure by which the creativity of celebrity is made possible, as it were.

Areas of intellectual property protection, particularly trade marks, copyright and related rights, are increasingly being exercised in the context of increased public participation and influence by fans, not least in the face of enhanced technologies of copying, file sharing, and downloading.[48] Rather than attempting to strengthen rights and indeed technological mechanisms to prevent such active use and interaction with the protected work, perhaps these phenomena are highlighting the problematic simplicity suggested by intellectual property laws when it comes to understanding the creator/user relationship and subject/object relationship. Arguably, the phenomenon of celebrity, and the access of fans to images and reporting is relevant to an understanding of the potential for alternative business models in other areas of the "creative industries", including the music and other industries and the strategic responses in Creative Commons,[49] free software,[50] and open source[51]

45 *Elvis Presley Trade Marks* [1997] RPC 543; *Elvis Presley Trade Marks* [1999] RPC 567 (CA). See also *Elvis Presley Enterprises, Inc. v Capece*, 950 F Supp. 783, (S.D.Tex 1996).

46 *Elvis Presley Trade Marks* [1999] RPC 567 (CA).

47 Davis J (2000) "The King is Dead: Long Live the King", *Cambridge Law Journal* 33 at 36.

48 The work of the public and strategic consumption is considered in relation to trade marks and branding in the following chapter.

49 Creative Commons can be found at http://creativecommons.org. As discussed elsewhere in this work, Creative Commons aims to make copyright material freely and widely available to creators, through the use of alternative licensing models, for the purposes of further incremental developments and innovations.

50 The Free Software Foundation claims to maximise innovation in software development through the facilitation of incremental collaborative developments. Otherwise protected material is made available through general public licences (GPL), allowing the continued distribution of source code to licensees, conditional upon the disclosure of any subsequent developments upon that source code through its use. See further http://www.fsf.org/.

51 Open source development depends upon similar licensing models but allows for the commercialisation of products provided that the source code continues to be made freely available. In all three of these examples (Creative Commons, open source, and free software), copyright is the basis upon which the licences are made such that the ongoing dissemination may be regulated and "free".

software movements. These various responses to perceived restrictions to creativity, paradoxically imposed by copyright, mount critical challenges to conventional mythologies of the author and creativity. Fundamentally, what reward is in place for the public contribution to the creation of value in celebrity and indeed in areas of contemporary copyright?

The mythology of the creator, and the innate genius of the "genuine" creator, is not only a function of identifying the creativity in the work, but also, as discussed in the previous chapter, a critical mechanism by which the supporting industry (the circumstances or "economics" of creativity) becomes vested with comparable cultural value in the creativity complex: "The increasing social and legal recognition of personality is related to changes in the costs and benefits of personalized versus anonymous production of goods, both tangible and intangible."[52] The myth of "celebrity" creates the myth of exhaustibility (the possibility of diminishing the value of celebrity through its consumption) necessary to justify the restriction of access to that image. In the similar process of "branding" in trade marks, the value of the mark arguably is achieved largely through a kind of "fame" generated through successful branding.[53] It would appear to be disingenuous to deny the participation of the product's public. As Landes and Posner explain, trade mark law is increasingly about the protection of personality, the "author", of creativity: "A name-brand product has personality; the generic version of the product does not. Not only do brand names reduce consumer search costs … but famous brands are 'celebrities' in their own right, whose logos fashion-conscious people wear proudly on their clothing."[54] Thus, the "creativity" of celebrity is an amalgam of the authenticity of the star-function, in concert with the circumstances to make this happen. As Celia Lury suggests, the star-function organises the creative principle in this relationship, indicating a conventional narrative of authorship and directionality of creative process: "In many ways the star-function can be seen as a transformation of the author-function in the later stages of corporate production for a market in that the imprint of the star acts as a means of linking the signs of creative labour with the exhibition value of the works produced."[55]

The function of celebrity, therefore, is similar to that traced through the concept of "creator" in any other orientation of "intellectual property". The celebrity simplifies and codifies the process of creativity in identity, such that it is available for recognition and valuation within that system, and at the same time generates the

52 Landes WM and Posner RA (2003) *The Economic Structure of Intellectual Property Law*, Cambridge MA, Harvard UP: 64.

53 Certain marks, if deemed to be well known marks, are protected under Art 6 *bis* of the Paris Convention for the Protection of Industrial Property, without requiring registration. At the same time, however, fame may lead to loss of protection through the mark becoming generic.

54 Landes WM and Posner RA (2003) *The Economic Structure of Intellectual Property Law*, Cambridge MA, Harvard UP: 64.

55 Lury C (1993) *Cultural Rights: Technology, Legality and Personality*, London, Routledge: 58.

mythology of "creativity" engaged in other examples of reliance upon the notion of the "genuine author." Again, as seen elsewhere, the "risk" of creativity is countered by greater certainty conferred upon the market (and those investing directly in that creativity). But of particular interest in the present discussion is the more overt relationship between celebrity and fan, in the instantaneity of contact and expression, in the nature of investment, such that the connections seemingly obscured in other areas are more difficult to contain within this model.

The Public Interest: Authenticity and Myth

> It's time for their secret identity to become their only identity.[56]

When it comes to the product of celebrity, the authenticity of the "image" (broadly speaking) is of particular interest, and may provide some insight into the product about which the public is apparently being deceived or misled. Larry Gross suggests that there is a kind of "rhetoric of authenticity" about the celebrity, and an intimation that in uncovering the "life" of the celebrity or star, "what is below the surface", the story of the celebrity will uncover the truth.[57] Paul MacDonald makes similar observations in his explanation of scandal discourse and its possibly paradoxical support for the myth of celebrity: "Scandal discourse had a special status, for it appeared to tell the ultimate truth which the fabrications of film narratives and promotional campaigns could not hide."[58] It is as though their "secret identity" is their "only identity", as though the original is the only copy. Indeed, is the "secret" or private identity of the celebrity becoming more and more part of the "only" identity of the celebrity, in that the private lives of stars are as much subject to the manufacturing and generation of publicity as the contrived identities of films and public appearances? It appears that the surrounding publications and representations of celebrity, the public "speech", are indeed instrumental in the creation of value.

Roland Barthes asks: "What is a myth, today? I shall give at the outset a first, very simple answer, which is perfectly consistent with etymology: *myth is a type of speech*."[59] Barthes makes this assertion in the text, *Mythologies*, and his early insight into the construction of celebrity in the essay, "The Face of Garbo".[60] This understanding of the operation of myth provides a unique perspective on the construction of celebrity today in the context of publicity rights. Barthes suggests that myth, as a kind of speech, is not an idea but a "mode of signification, a form".[61]

56 *The Incredibles* (2004) Bird B (dir. and scr.). Character of Helen Parr/Elastigirl.

57 Gross L (2003) "Privacy and Spectacle: The Reversible Panopticon and Media-Saturated Society", in Gross L et al (eds) *Image Ethics in the Digital Age*, Minneapolis, U of Minnesota P: 95 at 97-98.

58 MacDonald P (1998) "Reconceptualising Stardom", supplementary chapter in Dyer R ([1979]1998) *Stars*, New ed, London, BFI Publishing: 175 at 178.

59 Barthes R ([1957]1990) *Mythologies*, Lavers A (trans), New York, Noonday P: 109.

60 Barthes R ([1957]1990) *Mythologies*, Lavers A (trans), New York, Noonday P: 56-57.

61 Barthes R ([1957]1990) *Mythologies*, Lavers A (trans), New York, Noonday P: 109.

In other words, myth (or indeed celebrity) is not the idea (the person perhaps) but the expression of that idea, the fixation that is protected in ways similar to or at least compatible with intellectual property perspectives upon ideas. Is the unauthorised photograph, therefore, a false attribution of the myth of celebrity? Indeed, Barthes goes on to explain myth in ways distinctly similar to the explanation of personality rights upon which this discussion has ventured, declaring "Myth is not defined by the object of its message, but by the way in which it utters this message."[62] The unauthorised photograph (the clandestine witness) copies the myth, doubles the original, and in doing so creates a "caricature", as it were – a copy that, as Barthes explains, lends itself to signification more than the original.[63] It might be suggested that the right not to be libelled[64] is, in effect, a right to protect the "real" – and this is the process of celebrity myth-making, where publicity rights are instrumental in the definition of the "real", the expression, that is the object of celebrity.

Of critical interest to the present concerns of this work is the relationship between the celebrity and the public that is, in this respect, instrumental in the speech of the celebrity's mythology. If the "creative" process of celebrity is understood to depend on the essential activity of the public and especially on fans, then the input of consumers and/or users must be recognised as integral to the "product" that is to be protected through publicity rights. In other words, then, what is the stake of consumers and, necessarily, does this justify a certain "return" to consumers? In the context of the present discussion, this is a critical concern for the possibility of articulating meaningfully the role of users within a functioning "intellectual property" system or other form of means by which to recognise the "right to benefit".

In the case of celebrity, the consumers are therefore "creators" of celebrity value, and thus "proprietors", intrinsically involved in the creative process of celebrity. This would justify an argument for positive rights of consumer access to "celebrity", without needing to rely upon arguments of waiver or necessary exceptions or limitations. This arguably is at play in the diversity of creativity recognised by intellectual property rights; however, that play in this system has been contained strategically, as we have seen. Therefore, in the broader expanse of intellectual property laws, what is necessary at this time is a mechanism by which to materialise the actions of users – their manifest creativity.

---

62 Barthes R ([1957]1990) *Mythologies*, Lavers A (trans), New York, Noonday P: 109.

63 Barthes R ([1957]1990) *Mythologies*, Lavers A (trans), New York, Noonday P: 110.

64 Compare the right not to be shown in a "false light", available in the United States as an element of privacy/publicity protection. The concept of "false light" is intriguingly resonant with the work's "aura" described by Walter Benjamin (see the discussion in Chapter 2) and suggests ways in which publicity might be related to a kind of authenticity of the subject. For further discussion of "false light", see Prosser WL (1960) "Privacy", 48 *California Law Review* 383. See also Tugendhat M and Christie I (eds) (2002) *The Law of Privacy and the Media*, Oxford, Oxford UP: 99-100.

Creative Communities

The collective and community are ostensibly about symbolic story-telling, through beliefs, the expression of culture, and the production of knowledge. The collective is thus instrumental in the building of community through networked narration – whether that is the network of software communities or of traditional communities. The way in which this process of story-telling is related to the legitimacy that is bestowed upon that community by the "official culture" is of express concern in the present work. In particular, the collective confounds the discrete concepts of "original", "imitation/copy", and "access" at work in the dominant narrative of intellectual property. A very specific and critical case of the way in which these concepts are re-phrased is found in traditional and indigenous communities.

The ideology of the "public domain" and the way in which it is authored within intellectual property discourse has critical consequences for the cultural and community integrity of indigenous and traditional peoples. At the same time, however, proposals for restrictions upon the access to traditional knowledge are interpreted as equally destructive to the broader creativity of a genuinely networked collective. Paradoxically, it is precisely the logic of the "public domain" as it is constructed within the narrative of intellectual property that at once discredits traditional knowledge from protection and mobilises its commodification as knowledge to be accessed. Thus, the relationship between traditional knowledge and the public domain, and notions of "access", present a complex intersection of the diverse issues at play in the ambition of "access to knowledge", and a critical articulation between the dominant conventions of "self" and the strategic negotiations of that "self", examined in the following chapter. In other words, "knowledge" and its effective access will be necessarily something broader than the mere exchange of information without attending duties or obligations towards the surrounding knowledge, culture, and value of that information.

Creative Territories, Public Domains

> There is no public domain in traditional knowledge … Even knowledge shared and used widely does not fall into the public domain. When knowledge is shared, it is shared among those who are trusted to know their roles and responsibilities in using the knowledge … Misuse, even when used by others outside of the tribe, or by tribal members who are outside of the control of customary authority, can cause severe physical or spiritual harm to the individual caretakers of the knowledge or their entire tribe from their failure to ensure that the Creator's gifts are properly used. For this reason, misappropriation and misuse is not simply a violation of "moral rights" leading to a collective offense, but a matter of cultural survival for many Indigenous peoples.[65]

---

65 Tulalip Tribes (2003) Statement by the Tulalip Tribes of Washington on Folklore, Indigenous Knowledge, and the Public Domain. 9 July. WIPO Intergovernmental Committee on Intellectual Property and Genetic Resources, Traditional Knowledge and Folklore. Fifth Session. Geneva, 5-17 July.

Indigenous and traditional knowledge has emerged as critical subject matter in international trade and development.[66] While presenting significant commercial and research potential in various areas of knowledge and technology – including medicine, agriculture, and creative industries – such cultural resources are also intrinsic to the integrity and identity specific to local and traditional communities. Historically, the appropriation of that knowledge was "justified" in the taking of territory; that is, as legitimate spoils of colonial, scientific, and anthropological endeavour. In this way, the knowledge (like any other aspect of the environment "discovered" through colonial exploration) was itself deemed "natural", part of humanity's global heritage, and for the benefit of all. Indeed, the subjugation of the knowledge and cultures of colonised peoples to the "superior" knowledge of the coloniser can be identified as a critical and violent aspect of imperialist process.

Similarly, within current concerns over expanding intellectual property rights, access to knowledge, and the vitality of the "public domain", the debate over traditional knowledge seems to be dominated by the prior and governing concerns of a global knowledge of a global public, as considered in earlier discussions. In other words, traditional knowledge was, and to an extent continues to be, interpreted within the dominant legal and social discourse as common heritage rather than creative or personal knowledge.[67] Thus, the same presumptions of the creative process and genuine creativity that are used to dispossess the user may be similarly deployed to disinherit traditional and indigenous peoples of their cultural resources. The knowledge of traditional and indigenous communities is presented as a nostalgic and archaic object, created for the benefit and sharing of all.[68] The question of access to

---

66 For a more detailed examination of the protection of traditional knowledge, international trade and intellectual property, see Gibson J (2005) *Community Resources: Intellectual Property, International Trade and Protection of Traditional Knowledge*, Aldershot, Ashgate.

67 Gray S (1996) "Squatting in Red Dust: Non-Aboriginal Law's Construction of the 'Traditional' Aboriginal Artist", 14(2) *Law in Context*: 29 at 30. Note also the rejection of this management of traditional knowledge as public domain goods, with respect to crop genetic resources, particularly in the context of the International Treaty on Plant Genetic Resources for Food and Agriculture in Brush SB (2003) "The Demise of 'Common Heritage' and Protection for Traditional Agricultural Knowledge". Conference Paper. Biodiversity, Biotechnology and the Protection of Traditional Knowledge. St Louis MO, 4-5 April. See also the discussion of this Treaty and the potential impact on traditional knowledge in genetic resources in IISD (2003) "Traditional Knowledge and Patentability". IISD Trade and Development Brief. No 7. Summer.

68 Chander and Sunder discuss this romanticisation of traditional knowledge and identify the polarisation (and as such, hierarchisation) of knowledge from the north and south as private (commercial, useful) and public (archaic, natural) respectively. See Chander A and Sunder M (2004) "The Romance of the Public Domain", 92 *California Law Review* 1331. See also the discussion in Nwokeabia H (2001) "Why Industrial Revolution Missed Africa: A 'Traditional Knowledge' Perspective". Economic Commission for Africa. ECA/ESPD/WPS/01/02, which identifies a similar polarisation of useful (commercial) private knowledge and insignificant (non-commercial) traditional or public knowledge: "Because of the insignificance of African traditional knowledge on the livelihood of the owners, comparative to the European

those resources is legitimated and prioritised over the question of cultural integrity, rather than recognised as being perhaps just one aspect of the interests at stake.

Public Knowledge – No Space for Tradition

The notion of the "public domain" as defined, understood, and applied within intellectual property frameworks[69] continues to legitimate ongoing appropriation of traditional knowledge as "archaic", public goods. Constructing traditional knowledge as public goods in this way, it is sometimes argued to be legally (and morally) impossible to exclude access. In this way, arguments for access to traditional knowledge are seemingly ethically privileged over arguments for recognition of the importance of traditional knowledge as cultural resources, by virtue of the construction of the public domain around the "good" of traditional knowledge rather than the diversity and internal governance of community.[70]

Somewhat supporting this presumption with respect to traditional knowledge (of public access and public goods), international standardisation of intellectual property protection has been criticised as a potentially unjust generalisation of protection, almost inevitably in conflict with the needs of traditional knowledge holders.[71] First,

---

counterparts in the Western perception and intellectual property laws, African TK is regarded as information in the 'public domain,' static and freely available for use by anyone" (15). Graham Dutfield also notes a cultural bias in the way in which the public domain is applied to traditional knowledge. See Dutfield G (2002) "Protecting Traditional Knowledge and Folklore: A Review of Progress in Diplomacy and Policy Formulation". UNCTAD/ICTSD Capacity Building Project on Intellectual Property Rights and Sustainable Development. October: 47, n 90.

69 Tauli-Corpuz notes that the development of the concept of the public domain is tied to the development of intellectual property rights. See Tauli-Corpuz V (2005) "Biodiversity, Traditional Knowledge and Rights of Indigenous Peoples". IPRs Series No 5. International Workshop on Traditional Knowledge. 21-23 September. UN Department of Economic and Social Affairs, Division for Social Policy and Development, Secretariat of the Permanent Forum on Indigenous Issues. PFII/2005/WS.TK/5: 11. Similar criticism of the universalising of the concept was raised in the concerns of the Tulalip Tribes of Washington in their Statement to the Fifth Session of the IGC. See Tulalip Tribes (2003) Statement by the Tulalip Tribes of Washington on Folklore, Indigenous Knowledge, and the Public Domain. 9 July. WIPO Intergovernmental Committee on Intellectual Property and Genetic Resources, Traditional Knowledge and Folklore. Fifth Session. Geneva, 5-17 July.

70 For further discussion on the notion of resources as a means of individual communities, as distinct from discrete products or goods to be identified through trading relationships, see Gibson J (2005) *Community Resources: Intellectual Property, International Trade and Protection of Traditional Knowledge*, Aldershot, Ashgate.

71 Graham Dutfield notes this conflict between intellectual property regimes in developing and developed countries, and capacity building in developing countries in Dutfield G (2003) *Intellectual Property Rights and the Life Science Industries: A Twentieth Century History*, Aldershot, Ashgate: 29.

there is an increasing emphasis on the economic analysis[72] and conceptualisation of the knowledge according to a Western norm of efficiency and certainty in international trade,[73] as disengaged from the personal understanding and investment of the community. This is similar to what has been identified throughout this work, in that the "efficiency" of the market has ensured the framework for the development of rights to be that of investment, as indeed an indication of the underlying structure for creativity itself. The assimilation of traditional knowledge within intellectual property models suggests, therefore, an (implicit) deference to international trade relationships. Secondly, the interests of communities in preserving and managing resources on a cohesive local basis, while respecting the global diversity of communities and their self-governance, is at best compromised and at worst rendered impossible under this generalising economy of commodities.

Indeed, the very construction of traditional knowledge as "public" common knowledge within the public domain is built upon essentially commercial concerns for that public. The public domain is, in and of itself, a question of commercial construction, comprised as it is of those goods for which the monopoly (as an assessment of the value in time required to recover the "costs" in the risks of creativity and innovation) has expired. It is therefore implied that the commercial utility of anything within the public domain has passed, while the value and priority continues to attach to knowledge that is protected by intellectual property rights.[74] Traditional knowledge recognised and governed as resources of and by the community, and acknowledgement and application of the specific "public domains" that operate within specific communities, are thus rejected, as it were, by both the commercial interests seeking access to the creation of intellectual property rights and by certain aspects of campaigns for greater public access. Rightly or wrongly, the focus created by the "public domain" debate is defined by "commercial" reasons in the broader sense, because of the way in which the public domain is itself constructed, interpreted, and applied. Thus, the public domain is a strategic factor not only in arguments for access but also in industry rhetoric, to support commercial interests seeking access to traditional knowledge and genetic resources as public resources.

There appears to be an uneasy conflict between traditional knowledge and access debates, despite the concerns regarding expanding intellectual property rights, almost uniformly shared by both interests. Paradoxically, the traditional knowledge holders

---

72 The globalisation of intellectual property rights has been identified as emphasising the economic analysis of rights, in which a Western perspective dominates the international standards. For a discussion of this emphasis in the context of the TRIPS negotiations, see Gervais D (2003) *The TRIPS Agreement: Drafting History and Analysis*, 2nd ed, London, Sweet & Maxwell.

73 The drive towards greater efficiency is coupled with notions of increased certainty and risk-management. The notion of "risk" and international regulation of knowledge and information is considered in more detail in Gibson J (2005) *Community Resources: Intellectual Property, International Trade and Protection of Traditional Knowledge*, Aldershot, Ashgate.

74 Nwokeabia H (2001) "Why Industrial Revolution Missed Africa: A 'Traditional Knowledge' Perspective". Economic Commission for Africa. ECA/ESPD/WPS/01/02: 15.

are sometimes vilified by access groups as seeking an expansion of intellectual property rights, a construction which arguably misreads and misrepresents the fundamental terms of the debate. In creating the universal public domain, therefore, and in situating traditional knowledge within that fictive space, the relevance of local or traditional cultural identity and understanding is dis-organised. That is, the application of the label of public domain to traditional knowledge assists in the organisation of all knowledge without reference to indigenous or local tradition. In other words, a "public" of users is created without any reference to conflicting (historically and otherwise) cultural and ideological circumstances for the production of that knowledge. In particular, in territories where there is ongoing conflict between indigenous peoples and invaders (including, for example, Australia, Canada, the United States, New Zealand) this interpretation of traditional knowledge as public domain knowledge conjures a uniform public of both colonisers and colonised in what is arguably an ongoing imperialist process of the assimilation of the diversity of traditional cultural knowledge. The circumstances for knowledge production, the cultural and political identity attaching to that knowledge, and the practices associated with that knowledge, are "forgotten" in this process,[75] which depends upon the extraction of traditional knowledge as "products".

The Public Domain as Protection

International discussion towards the resolution of these apparently competing interests has been placed formally under the administration of WIPO's Intergovernmental Committee on Intellectual Property and Genetic Resources, Traditional Knowledge and Folklore (IGC).[76] To date most applications of protection have been merely defensive, through exclusions from the creation of intellectual property and the documentation and delivery of traditional knowledge in the public domain.[77] In this

75 In this construction of the public the figure of the "global" user becomes clear and one which almost depends upon an obscuring of the cultural diversity otherwise at work in the production of knowledge.

76 The WIPO Intergovernmental Committee on Intellectual Property and Genetic Resources, Traditional Knowledge and Folklore (IGC) was established in the 26th (12th Extraordinary Session) of the WIPO General Assembly, held in Geneva, 25 September to 3 October 2000, to consider and advise on appropriate actions concerning the economic and cultural significance of tradition-based creations, and the issues of conservation, management, sustainable use, and sharing of the benefits from the use of genetic resources and traditional knowledge, as well as the enforcement of rights to traditional knowledge and folklore. For a review of the progress of the IGC, see Gibson J (2004) "Intellectual Property Systems, Traditional Knowledge, and the Legal Authority of Community", 26(7) *European Intellectual Property Review* 280; and Gibson J (2005) *Community Resources: Intellectual Property, International Trade and Protection of Traditional Knowledge*, Aldershot, Ashgate: Chapter 4.

77 Examples of defensive mechanisms include moves towards the documentation of traditional knowledge, for example, to assist its recognition as prior art (see the extensive report on registers and databases in Alexander M et al (2003) *The Role of Registers and*

way, mechanisms to ensure the status of traditional knowledge as knowledge in the public domain (such as prior art databases,[78] digital libraries,[79] and the concept of *domaine public payant*[80]) have been presumed to be logical and relevant means of protection.[81] However, such approaches prioritise a certain user public without

Databases in the Protection of Traditional Knowledge: A Comparative Analysis. Report. Tokyo, UNU-IAS. See also the discussion in Gibson J (2004) "Intellectual Property Systems, Traditional Knowledge, and the Legal Authority of Community", 26(7) *European Intellectual Property Review* 280; and Gibson J (2005) *Community Resources: Intellectual Property, International Trade and Protection of Traditional Knowledge*, Aldershot, Ashgate: Chapter 4, on the developments in international patent classification tools for traditional knowledge. Similarly, the 2004 United Nations Development Programme (UNDP) Human Development Report also unreservedly recommends documentation, maintaining that it is frequently essential to achieve protection and "does not prejudice rights". See UNDP (2004) *Cultural Liberty in Today's Diverse World*. Human Development Report. New York: 95. However, documentation is not unproblematic in its application.

78 For example, note the Traditional Ecological Knowledge Prior Art Database of AAAS which has met much criticism. See also the discussion of traditional knowledge as prior art in Ruiz M (2002) *The International Debate on Traditional Knowledge as Prior Art in the Patent System: Issues and Options for Developing Countries*. Trade-Related Agenda, Development and Equity (TRADE) Occasional Papers. Paper No 9. Geneva, South Centre.

79 For example, the Traditional Knowledge Digital Library (TKDL) for Indian systems of medicine has met both positive (see Sen N (2002) "TKDL: A Safeguard for Indian Traditional Knowledge", 82(9) *Current Science* 1070) and negative receptions (see Sharma D (2002) "Digital Library Another Tool for Biopiracy", *Mindfully.org*. 29 May and Jayaraman KS (2002) "Biopiracy Fears Cloud Indian Database", *Science and Development Network*. 5 December). For more on the TKDL, see CIPR (2002) Commission on Intellectual Property Rights. *Integrating Intellectual Property Rights and Development Policy*, London: 81. See the extensive report on databases and registers undertaken for the UNU-IAS in Alexander M et al (2003) *The Role of Registers and Databases in the Protection of Traditional Knowledge: A Comparative Analysis*. Report. Tokyo, UNU-IAS. See also the concerns regarding documentation and misappropriation in Tauli-Corpuz V (2005) "Biodiversity, Traditional Knowledge and Rights of Indigenous Peoples". IPRs Series No 5. International Workshop on Traditional Knowledge. 21-23 September. UN Department of Economic and Social Affairs, Division for Social Policy and Development, Secretariat of the Permanent Forum on Indigenous Issues. PFII/2005/WS.TK/5.

80 The *domaine public payant* (a paying public domain) involves the collection of funds from those seeking access to the knowledge within. Such funds would ordinarily be used towards programmes within the communities of the traditional knowledge holders involved. See the discussion in Gervais D (2001) "Traditional Knowledge: A Challenge to the International Intellectual Property System". Fordham University Conference on International Intellectual Property Law & Policy. New York City, 20 April: 13. See also Dutfield G (2002) "Protecting Traditional Knowledge and Folklore: A Review of Progress in Diplomacy and Policy Formulation". UNCTAD/ICTSD Capacity Building Project on Intellectual Property Rights and Sustainable Development. October: 34.

81 Downes D (1997) "Using Intellectual Property as a Tool to Protect Traditional Knowledge: Recommendations for Next Steps". CIEL Discussion Paper. November; See also

giving effect to customary systems of governance and maintenance of cultural integrity with respect to that knowledge.[82] Thus, in many cases, it is accepted that traditional knowledge can nevertheless be understood as "public knowledge", as it were, without recognising community authority with respect to the way in which that knowledge is accessed, disseminated, and used.

Indigenous and traditional groups have made strong arguments against this rendition of their knowledge, throughout the international discussions and in various arenas. In a recent Joint Statement to the 23rd session of the Working Group on Indigenous Populations,[83] the Indigenous World Association and Indigenous Media Network raised several concerns about the concept of the public domain and about the articulation of protection through the application of public and private databases:

> [W]e stress that there are striking similarities between seizing our territories and the taking of our knowledge by defining it as part of the public domain. Both are based on the notion that they constitute *res nullius*, the property of no one, and can be treated as such. Placing our knowledge into the public domain turns it into a freely available resource for commercial utilization. Thus, it also creates the pre-condition for using non-indigenous Intellectual Property Rights (IPR) regimes to patent "inventions" based upon our knowledge ...We therefore strongly reject the application of the public domain concept to any aspect related to our cultures and identities, including human and other genetic information originating from our lands and waters.[84]

Significantly, this Joint Statement likens the construction of traditional knowledge as public to the imperialist conquering of territory during colonisation, as suggested earlier. Knowledge is a critical tool not only historically in forces of colonisation but also in a contemporary context through the prioritisation of particular economic constructions of innovation, models of knowledge production, and presumptions of

---

the discussion in Chapman AR (2001) "Approaching Intellectual Property as a Human Right", 35(3) *Copyright Bulletin* 4.

82 Tauli-Corpuz explains: "We have developed nuanced systems and mechanisms which enable us to safeguard and protect our knowledge and to define how, when and to whom it can be shared with. The public domain concept has not taken these into consideration." See Tauli-Corpuz V (2005) "Biodiversity, Traditional Knowledge and Rights of Indigenous Peoples". IPRs Series No 5. International Workshop on Traditional Knowledge. 21-23 September. UN Department of Economic and Social Affairs, Division for Social Policy and Development, Secretariat of the Permanent Forum on Indigenous Issues. PFII/2005/WS.TK/5: 11.

83 Commission on Human Rights, Sub-Commission on the Promotion and Protection of Human Rights, Working Group on Indigenous Populations.

84 Indigenous World Association and Indigenous Media Network (2005) Joint Statement. Commission on Human Rights, Sub-Commission on the Promotion and Protection of Human Rights, Working Group on Indigenous Populations. 23rd Session, 18-22 July 2005. Review of Developments Pertaining to the Promotion and Protection of the Rights of Indigenous Peoples, Including Their Human Rights and Fundamental Freedoms: Principal Theme, "Indigenous Peoples and the International and Domestic Protection of Traditional Knowledge". Item 4(b) of the provisional agenda. 13 July 2005. E/CN.4/Sub.2/AC.4/2005/CRP. 3.

how and why we create. These concerns are supported in the reports and studies of non-governmental organisations (NGOs). For instance, the policy discussion paper of the United Nations Commission on Trade and Development (UNCTAD) and International Centre for Trade and Sustainable Development (ICTSD) Joint Project on IPRs and Sustainable Development identifies the following:

> [F]or many traditional peoples and groups, certain expressions and works are central to their cultural identity and should therefore never be fully released into the public domain, at least not to the extent that others would be free to do whatever they like with them. This is not to say that copyright protection should therefore be permanent for culturally significant expressions and works, but that copyright law should not be seen as the appropriate approach for each and every kind of cultural work.[85]

Evident in these discussions is the key concern that while traditional knowledge is presumed to be sacred and cultural knowledge, for which certain "exclusions" from intellectual property protection would be adequate,[86] this kind of defensive archiving and "safeguarding" continues the historical and classical anthropological effect[87] upon indigenous and traditional communities, documenting knowledge as a kind of "ethnographic present".[88] While defensive approaches are an aspect of mechanisms of protection, they risk an ongoing paternalism and persistent historicising of the value of knowledge.

Furthermore, this conceptualisation of protection maintains the underlying presumption with respect to the processes of innovation and creativity within indigenous and traditional communities, that such processes are processes of the "global" public, rather than creativity of the community. As such, the innovation is not recognised for the purposes of the "self" of intellectual property, and so the knowledge is not recognised as personal to the community. Rather, the knowledge is distanced as an end in and of itself and as a right of the public domain.

---

85 UNCTAD/ICTSD (2003) "Intellectual Property Rights: Implications for Development". Policy Discussion Paper. UNCTAD/ICTSD Capacity Building Project on Intellectual Property Rights and Sustainable Development. August: 120.

86 The basis of this approach is the argument that cultural symbols would be appropriately protected through recognition as "national" emblems or royal insignia, and thus excluded from trade mark registration. See the discussion of the Zia Indians of New Mexico in Lopez R (1999) "Tribes seek trademark protection for sacred symbols", *Revista Magazine*, 9 July.

87 This is of course with reference, in particular, to classical 19th-century anthropology and the perceived relationship with colonial efforts, as distinct from contemporary critical anthropology which seeks to problematise and dismantle dominant relationships between the privileged anthropological eye and the natural, organic, anthropological object. For instance, see the concerns with the relationship between imperialist endeavour and anthropology in Africa, in Masolo DA (1994) *African Philosophy in Search of Identity*, Bloomington, Indiana UP; and Mudimbe VY (1988) *The Invention of Africa*, Bloomington, Indiana UP.

88 Note James Clifford's comments on the tendency of early anthropology to presume and idealise an "ethnographic present" as "a static, pre-contact, traditional culture". See Clifford J (2003) *On the Edges of Anthropology: Interviews*, Chicago, Prickly Paradigm P: 9.

Repeatedly implied in this approach, and in the construction of traditional knowledge as public domain knowledge, is an informal distinction between the validation of conventional knowledge production and the invalidation of traditional forms of innovation.[89] Discussions in earlier chapters have considered the way in which such institutionalised legitimation of the production of knowledge and the circumstances of that production create a higher social class of genuine creators.[90] In the case of traditional knowledge, as seen in the examples of earlier discussions, the result is that innovation in that context and by traditional methods and "institutions" is not recognised for the purposes of the "personality" of intellectual property. Furthermore, if categorised within the public domain, communities are denied full governance with respect to that knowledge. In other words, "traditional knowledge" is "historical" not only for the purposes of anthropological record and in the context of a kind of knowledge imperialism, as it were, but also for the purposes of contemporary governance of knowledge resources within the community itself. For protection to be relevant, the community must begin to realise "authority" over that knowledge other than as an anthropological object itself. Thus, defensive forms of protection that rely upon situating traditional knowledge within the public domain are limited. Indeed, such protection constructs the community in question as merely another anonymous individual within a greater public, for which access is thus facilitated through the public domain. In other words, the very "protection" offered by the public domain relies upon the legitimation of the appropriation of traditional knowledge as its starting point.

Where traditional knowledge is deemed "unoriginal", and thus in the public domain, conventional standards of intellectual property cannot protect the personal attachment of the community to that knowledge, the incremental creativity of multiple selves. Rather, intellectual property laws facilitate the disengagement of the community, its distancing from the knowledge, and its anonymity within a global audience seeking access to that knowledge. Access and appropriation is legitimated under these systems, notwithstanding that such appropriation may constitute an offensive use, taking from the community in question through the inappropriate application and dissemination of knowledge (for instance, cultural symbols, dress, and artistic methods).[91]

---

89 Note the earlier discussion on the polarisation of valuable (commercial) knowledge and expired (traditional) knowledge through the operation of the public domain.

90 For instance, see the discussion in Chapter 2 of the distinctions drawn between the genuine composer and the "user" accessing Creative Commons material.

91 Owen Morgan provides a useful analysis of the relevance of offence in his discussion of the taking of Māori words and the legislative response in the New Zealand Trade Marks Act 2002: Morgan O (2003) "The New Zealand Trade Marks Act: No Place for Offence", Occasional Paper No 2/03. Intellectual Property Institute of Australia, University of Melbourne. See the discussion of cultural offence in WIPO/GRTKF/IC/6/6 (30 November 2003): 24. See also the references to offence caused by the patenting of traditional knowledge in the final report of the United Kingdom Commission on Intellectual Property Rights, *Integrating Intellectual*

Even current trends[92] towards requiring the disclosure of origins in traditional knowledge somewhat simplify the critical relationship between the community and its knowledge resources, and the offence and harm caused by the assumption that such taking is fundamentally just.[93] Protection offered by geographical indications, trade marks, and so on, is not readily available other than through efforts to "exclude" certain material from trade mark registration[94] or to anonymise communities within national publics (as in the use of geographical indications). Any efforts within these models (including disclosure of origin, certification and authenticity marks, and so on) depend upon a presumption of the importance of safeguarding the knowledge as cultural artefact, rather than recognising community and respecting and giving effect to customary law.

The Public in the Domain

The process by which traditional knowledge is rendered part of the public domain raises questions beyond the mere criteria by which intellectual property is recognised. Recalling the discussion of the public domain at the outset of this chapter, the construction of a "global" and singular public is equally strategic in this context. As in that earlier discussion, traditional knowledge communities are also assimilated within what is articulated as a culturally and socially uniform public, indeed, a uniform and international culture – the "official culture". In that the right to benefit from one's contribution to "official culture" is administered at present by the intellectual property system, the same system thereby becomes the guardian of culture and its use. The noise of the collective, the literally dysfunctional[95] and asocial "rabble",[96] is quietened.

Property Rights and Development Policy. See Commission on Intellectual Property Rights (2002) *Integrating Intellectual Property Rights and Development Policy*. London: 81-83.

92 In particular, see the development of protection on an international level in the documents of the WIPO IGC. All documents of the WIPO IGC are available at http://www.wipo.int/ tk/en/igc/documents/index.html.

93 In other words, the taking will occur in the context of scientific progress and the advance of civilisation, and so on, making it appear to be inherently just. Thus, discussions are invariably towards a way to facilitate cooperation with that taking, in the form of traditional knowledge protection. Bruno Latour challenges the way in which scientific discourse draws upon this revolutionary difference between tradition and modern science in Latour B (1987) *Science in Action: How to Follow Scientists and Engineers Through Society*, Cambridge MA, Harvard UP: Chapter 6.

94 Problems persist in relying on exclusions of emblems and symbols, in that these must be fixed and repeatable for protection. Such defensive mechanisms cannot capture methods in cultural expressions (such as dot painting).

95 Hannay A (2005) *On the Public*, London, Routledge: 7.

96 Hegel GWF ([1821]1991) *Elements of the Philosophy of Right*, Wood AW (ed), Nisbet HB (trans), Cambridge, Cambridge UP: 453.

The anonymous public, as described earlier, is a strategic construction in which the active user and the singularity of its creative activity will be obscured by the mythic control of the "creator". Nevertheless, a simple dismantling of regulation and the notion of a completely "free" network of access does not re-instate the user. Indeed, certain limits upon the abstraction and construction of knowledge would suggest limits upon the abstraction of cultures implied by this same process. More critically, perhaps, it is necessary to unsettle the dynamics of the dominant rhetoric of intellectual property, and the delimiting polarity of the public domain/private knowledge paradigm, such that other relations and connections are indeed imaginable and materialised.

The Public Frame

> It's true that frames are nice for showing: gilded, white, carved, baroque, aluminium, etc. but have you ever met a painter who began his masterpiece by first choosing the frame? That would be a bit odd, wouldn't it?[97]

The preoccupation with the public, and with the preservation of the public domain, both frames and constrains the consideration of access. Indeed, it is in the very concept of the public domain that use is articulated as coming after the creation of property, after the exhaustion of value. Thus, that use will always be outside the creative economy, and users will always be "outsiders" of the system. Thus, it is a mere spectacle of access, but potentially nothing more.

It becomes increasingly clear that the articulation of the relations in the intellectual property system depends upon an objectification of the user: that is, a disregard for the user and a suspension of them as mere objects. However, the selected strategic negotiations of the system examined in the following chapter will reveal the disingenuousness of this description. What remains is the need to identify the way in which that very disregard is indeed perhaps the best evidence of the critical action of users.

It remains that it is no longer adequate simply to frame the user with a version of the "public"; it is necessary to enact the user as stakeholder in every singular event of creativity. It is now necessary to move from the ideology of the public domain to the capabilities of the user.

97 Latour B (2005) *Reassembling the Social*, Oxford, Oxford UP: 143.

Chapter 4

Negotiating Self

> Write, form a rhizome, increase your territory by deterritorialization, extend the line of flight to the point where it becomes an abstract machine covering the entire plane of consistency.[1]

Introduction

> *Socrates*: Let us suppose the existence of two objects: one of them shall be Cratylus and the other the image of Cratylus, and we will suppose, further, that some god makes not only a representation such that a painter would make of your outward form and colour, but also creates an inward organisation like yours, having the same warmth and softness; and into this infuses motion and soul and mind, such as you have, and in a word copies all your qualities, and places them by you in another form. Would you say that this was Cratylus and the image of Cratylus, or that there were two Cratyluses?
>
> *Cratylus*: I should say that there were two Cratyluses.[2]

As the discussion thus far has followed, creativity has become inextricably bound up in the institution of intellectual property. As a cultural value, creativity has tremendous import, fuelling diverse sets of interests in the present discussions, and operating as a kind of moral and social justification for often opposed positions. As discussed, a reliance upon "creativity" has come to work in operation with the institution of intellectual property (and copyright) in ways that seemingly facilitate the objections and obstacles to strategic responses, such as those imagined and practised by the Creative Commons movement and embodied in the free and open source software and open science models of innovation. Notably, these responses are occurring within intellectual property systems and are indeed dependent upon intellectual property rights for their operation. They are not alternative systems as such, but their construction of creativity may well be, leading to their seeming illogicality according to the grand narrative and "official culture" of intellectual property and the "genuine creator".

This chapter will begin with a consideration of the nature of these "alternatives" and, in particular, the potential revision of the concept of creativity offered by these models. The critical concern of this chapter will be strategies in use and consumption,

---

1 Deleuze G and Guattari F ([1980]1987) *A Thousand Plateaus: Capitalism and Schizophrenia*, Massumi B (trans), Minneapolis, U of Minnesota P: 11.

2 Plato (1875) "Cratylus", *The Dialogues of Plato*, Vol II. Oxford, Clarendon P, 257.

read through the accountability and action of consumers. The intersection of creative use and indeed creative alternatives (such as free software and Creative Commons) can be materialised, arguably, in the brand.

Use – Secondary Creativity

> The social and technical functioning of contemporary culture hierarchizes these two activities. To write is to produce the text; to read is to receive it from someone else without putting one's mark on it, without remaking it … What has to be put in question is unfortunately not this division of labor (it is only too real), but the assimilation of reading to passivity.[3]

The negotiation of self is to negotiate this division of labour, this dispossession from the creative work, and this relegation of the user to passivity. Indeed, the dynamics of intellectual properties and their exchanges suggest that this "only too real" division of labour is striking in its constructedness with respect to subject matter (for example, the work in software) and with respect to expanding rights (for example, in webcasting). The critical nexus, the means by which to materialise the activity of the reader/the user, is to be found not necessarily in the functional "work" with which intellectual property purports to deal, but rather, in the indication of the work – the brand – where the value of the good and the activity of the user is precipitated, is real.[4]

Indeed, the very nature of the current developments in intellectual property rights and subject matter suggest that the "work" is a mere fiction, an obfuscation of the critical value at stake – the market. Webcasting, discussed in the previous chapter, is an important example of the way in which the traditions of intellectual property and copyright – the "author", the "work" – are deployed in a tragi-comedy of disingenuousness. What is really at stake is the transmission, the communication, the use. But what the user might make of all this noise is, as Michel de Certeau suggests, "The enigma of the consumer-sphinx".[5] It is thus no longer adequate merely to read models of use, including the model provided by intellectual property law itself. Such circumstances seem to distance the value and quality of "use", rather than generate its genuine centrality to the system. It is critical therefore to recognise the artificial distance created between the "originality" of the "work" recognised in intellectual property law (and indeed, this permeates throughout its manifestations – inventions and patents; broadcasts and copyright; and so on) and its use. The relationships described by the law disguise the activity and co-creation of the user: "Use must thus

---

3 De Certeau M (1984) *The Practice of Everyday Life*, Rendall S (trans), Berkeley, U of California P: 169.

4 On the relationship between value (in goods) and the brand, see the collection Hart S and Murphy J (eds) (1998) *Brands: The New Wealth Creators*, Basingstoke, Palgrave.

5 De Certeau M (1984) *The Practice of Everyday Life*, Rendall S (trans), Berkeley, U of California P: 31.

be analyzed in itself."[6] In this respect, intellectual property products are not "what" is used, but rather are mere "effects" of the activity of users.[7] That is, it is the capacity and contribution of the user that inscribes the value, and thus the singularity, of the object of intellectual property protection.

Nevertheless, the language that frames this inquiry is indeed pre-emptive of the indoctrination of the original. The very language of consumption appears to maintain a hierarchy that must be resisted – that between production and consumption – as though these are mutually exclusive and not necessarily interdependent activities. But at the same time, consumption suggests a bodily process that fundamentally changes the material to create the resources for indeed more consumption, more use. It is not waste, it is indeed what unlocks the value in that material. It is thus necessary to revitalise "use" and, in the process, understand how inadequate the term is for the activities at stake.

Open Cities and Genuine Creators

> The author is the principle of thrift in the proliferation of meaning … [H]e is a certain functional principle by which, in our culture, one limits, excludes, and chooses; in short, by which one impedes the free circulation, the free manipulation, the free composition, decomposition, and recomposition of fiction. In fact, if we are accustomed to presenting the author as genius, as a perpetual surging of invention, it is because, in reality, we make him function in exactly the opposite fashion.[8]

The emergence and operation of critical networks of creativity is of particular significance to this work. Such communities, largely articulated through international online communities – including Creative Commons and the Free Software Foundation – are strengthened by the interconnections with personal and civil society web logs, online publishing, and various informal and unanticipated expressions.[9] The presence of such negotiations and networks provides a particular insight into the resilience or otherwise of the seemingly coherent concepts of "originality", "authorship", and "creativity". Indeed, the very nature of these networks has been contradictory to the conventional stabilities of these concepts, especially in the unsettling of the supposed originality and creativity of the "genuine creator" and the "copying" of original works. The nature of this virtual "conflict" highlights further the identity

---

6 De Certeau M (1984) *The Practice of Everyday Life*, Rendall S (trans), Berkeley, U of California P: 32.

7 De Certeau M (1984) *The Practice of Everyday Life*, Rendall S (trans), Berkeley, U of California P: 35.

8 Foucault M (1979) "What is an Author?", in Harari JV (ed) *Textual Strategies: Perspectives in Post-Structuralist Criticism*, Ithaca, Cornell UP: 141 at 159.

9 For a useful review of the Creative Commons system and its interaction with the mainstream music industry, see Fox M et al (2005) "Creative Commons: An Alternative, Web-Based Copyright System", 16(5) *Entertainment Law Review* 111.

and personality that is attached to creativity in conventional (economic) Western approaches.

The challenges presented by open source and free software (FLOSS),[10] as well as other developments such as Creative Commons, have been criticised as relying on the seemingly contrary assumption that creativity is copying, and thereby upon an assumption that making material available to copy will encourage more creativity. In other words, the conflict is constructed as being between the private, individual creator (rewarded and socially respectable) and the anonymous imitator (for whom the tools of imitation are provided by "open" approaches to innovation), between "high" creativity and "low" applications.[11] As systems of knowledge development, these various initiatives "protect", as it were, the process of collaboration. As distinct from an emphasis on the products or commodities of creativity, the rights of intellectual property laws are harnessed in order to direct them towards the protection of the process of creativity.

Copying Copyright

In the preceding chapters, discussions have traced the way in which intellectual property laws and the supporting industries have been established as in and of themselves incentives to create, and indeed the prerequisite for creativity. In this way, the intellectual property system is held out to be part of the fabric of a civilised society, in its protection and sustenance of culture, and in its social and economic development. Thus, Creative Commons has emerged in a context in which copyright is put forward as contributing to the circumstances necessary for economic, social, and intellectual development of a civilised society, through the facilitation of the market necessary for creativity. Intellectual property has become, rather crudely, a social value. As discussed earlier, copyright is thereby the means by which the originality and novelty of culture and creativity becomes sensible. Copyright makes good cultural sense.

Thus, in the case of Creative Commons, the conflicts between this simplification of the creative process and the implications for diverse approaches to creativity are of significant interest, as seen in earlier chapters. More subtle, perhaps, is the operation of these notions in software development. While intellectual property rights are seemingly part of the infrastructure of civilised values of creativity towards which all legitimate citizens will strive, free software communities and, to a lesser extent, open source communities, are disregarded as unpredictable, "primitive", and

---

10 The term FLOSS comes from free, *libre*, open source software. For a useful background to open source and free software, see Taylor M (2005) "'Open Source' and 'Free' Software", 11(3) *Computer and Telecommunications Law Review* 97; and Guadamuz González A (2004) "Viral Contracts or Unenforceable Documents? Contractual Validity of Copyleft Licences", 26(8) *European Intellectual Property Review* 331.

11 See the discussion of the "high" and "low" categorisation introduced in Chapter 1 and developed throughout.

dystopic. Not only do such communities confound the conventional processes of assigning creativity, but also the seemingly commonsense model of creativity that underpins the discursive power of intellectual property protection is unsettled by the kind of knowledge governance suggested in open source and the free software models (FLOSS). In the context of this work, it is clear that these models may not be characterised merely by an opposition between individual and collaborative models of innovation. Rather, the debate surrounding these technologies and their innovation is instructive in bringing to the surface the way in which the institution of intellectual property is implicated in the social recognition of "creativity" and "genuine" creative output and thus, the way negotiations of intellectual property through efforts such as FLOSS are de-legitimated. What will be considered in more detail in this chapter is the way in which this notion of "creativity" might operate, at least informally, in the institution of intellectual property, and how it might relate to the justifications for protection and therefore the objections to initiatives such as Creative Commons, Free Software Foundation, open source, and other strategies of negotiating intellectual property frameworks.

A Financial Incentive

Recalling the way in which the link between creativity has come to be defined primarily within the economic circumstances for that creativity, the notion of "incentive" has become firmly tied to the supporting industries, as well as individual creators. This aspect of the economic analysis of copyright protection[12] suggests a presumption of an underlying efficiency in the model,[13] which in turn proposes to justify the projected harmonisation of copyright (and other categories of international intellectual property laws) for the purposes of the efficiency and certainty of international trade.[14] The creation of value and the certainty of markets are presented as rendering efficient an otherwise inefficient process – in other words, without adequate mitigation through the regulation of the use of creative products (regulation which, in itself, has in mind the production of value in that product) innovative activity within this model becomes fundamentally inefficient. Within this economic model, the act of being creative suddenly appears fraught with danger and thus inextricable from the supporting industries that are able to buffer that risk. Within this model, innovation is thus a development with economic impact, a change which can be quantified as innovative by virtue of this impact. In other words, creativity

12 Note that Landes and Posner argue that the economic analysis of intellectual property law is frequently and problematically simplified as one of incentive and access. See Landes WM and Posner RA (2003) *The Economic Structure of Intellectual Property Law*, Cambridge MA, Harvard UP.

13 See Cooter R and Ulen T (2004) *Law and Economics*, 4th ed, Boston MA, Addison Wesley, where the authors argue that information has a distinctive quality, making the creation of monopolies efficient as well as providing important incentives to continue creation.

14 Dutfield G (2003) *Intellectual Property Rights and the Life Science Industries: A Twentieth Century History*, Aldershot, Ashgate: particularly 195-205.

can be found where value is added, where economic activity is enhanced – thus, the supporting industries are rendered "creative".

In the software model, the supposed risk of creativity (financial, labour, and otherwise) may be countered by the perceived certainty that copyright protection promises through these rewards and conferral of control upon the "corporate author" of that material. But further, the conferral of control in the case of these particular industries produces a kind of "creative accountability", as it were, through the construction of an "author" in what is otherwise an industry of distributed, collaborative, and incremental development.[15] Artificial scarcity is therefore created by copyright protection and is seemingly necessary to create the markets in what is essentially an inexhaustible good, thus "correcting" the inefficiencies otherwise posed by unregulated and uncontrolled innovation. This interaction between incentive mechanisms (including the mitigation of risk and conferral of control through the calculation of monopolies in return for investment) and the creation of markets for information goods can be traced through the increasing corporatisation of research and intellectual output in various areas of creative and innovative activity.[16] As discussed earlier, the cultural institution of intellectual property becomes both a condition for creativity as well as the evidence that it occurs.

A significant example of this comes from the music industry, where the International Federation of Phonographic Industry (IFPI) has described the industry-wide culture of research and development models of creativity, where profits are re-invested in the economic bases for creativity, in what it refers to as "artists and repertoire". Thus, a "surplus" is not connected to the particular artist potentially responsible for that profit, but rather to the industry itself, and the maximisation and maintenance of the market, an investment in the "future". In the way in which rights are being created and extended to the recognition of protection for various supporting industries in diverse areas of innovation, the link between the economic infrastructure and individual creators seems well established: "[W]e know that where there's no effective copyright protection, there are no creative enterprises."[17]

The calculation of regulatory mechanisms by which to manage the attending risk, such as the creation of specific terms of monopoly in copyright protection,

---

15 Notably, Biggs and Leach identify a certain expectation or trust between reader and author, which they suggest is upset in the case of auto-generated texts, for which meaning is not readily formed upon authorial intent within the dominant systems for identifying and ascribing sense and value to a work. See Biggs S and Leach J (2004) *Autopoeisis: Novelty, Meaning and Value*, London, Artswords P.

16 Dutfield G (2003) *Intellectual Property Rights and the Life Science Industries: A Twentieth Century History*, Aldershot, Ashgate. See also Sell SK (2003) *Private Power, Public Law: The Globalization of Intellectual Property Rights*, Cambridge, Cambridge UP; Drahos P and Braithwaite J (2002) *Information Feudalism: Who Owns the Knowledge Economy?* London, Earthscan.

17 Parsons RD (2001) Statement. Online Entertainment and Copyright Law: Coming Soon to a Digital Device Near You. Senate Hearing 107-283, 3 April. http://gopher.quux.org:70/ Government/USA/Law/IP/napster-hearing.txt.

corresponds to decisions not only on the risks inherent in innovation, but also on the "value" of those risks and indeed the "culture" produced: "To one extent or another, all risk assessments involve the calculation not just of odds, but of the value of those odds … Cost, however, is a subjective matter."[18] Thus, risk is not merely uncertainty, as suggested by the self-legitimating narrative of intellectual property law, but is partly constructed through the processes of evaluating and hierarchising innovation in Western culture. In other words, the public discourse of risk[19] has been appropriated as a universalising rhetoric of regulation.[20] The individual has become collectively responsible for collaborative innovation and for militating against copying and imitation.

Risk of Infection

The incentive justification presumes (contrary to the open networks of collaboration and creative connections possible through, for example, Creative Commons and FLOSS) simplistic models of innovation and creativity, for which the source of innovation is singular, the development intentional, and the control personal. This purposeful and personal control that operates in intellectual property models of creativity and innovation maintains a kind of logical and predictable narrative of authorial intent and originality that is entirely compatible with Western or capitalist models of progress and innovation as economic activities. The "risk" posed by open models of innovation and collaboration is seemingly incomparable within this paradigm, impossible to quantify.

Indeed, the "literary" history underpinning copyright is similarly concerned with infection, with contamination. Indeed the Roman *fabula palliata* (produced by Andronicus and others) is usually referred to as contamination, because of its production through a practice of "sampling" and re-combination of Greek New Comedy.[21] This notion of contamination ensures the persistence of the "original", the purity of the original work, as a trace within any subsequent revision. Thus, contamination is more frankly a requisite for originality – the original is made known precisely through its capacity to be copied. In other words, the original is manifest by

18 Steele J (2004) *Risks and Legal Theory*, Oxford, Hart Publishing: 24.

19 See, for instance, Beck U (1992) *Risk Society: Towards a New Modernity*, Ritter M (trans), London, SAGE; Beck U (1999) *World Risk Society*, Camiller P (trans), Cambridge, Polity; Beck U (2000) *What is Globalization?* Camiller P (trans), Cambridge, Polity.

20 This is particularly apparent in environmental and intellectual property laws applied to emerging technologies, particularly gene technology, where the uncertainty of the scientific paradigm is responded to by the certainty conferred by legal regulation as to release and so on. For a comprehensive account of legislation and common law in this area, see Cain B (2003) *Legal Aspects of Gene Technology*, London, Sweet & Maxwell.

21 Cuddon JA (1999) *Dictionary of Literary Terms and Literary Theory*, London, Penguin: 177.

virtue of the copy: "the mark, the warrant, the certification of the original."[22] Indeed, revisiting de Certeau, to use is perhaps to put one's mark on the creative work.

In the context of software developments and the incremental "contamination", of Creative Commons, anxieties attaching to these developments nevertheless persevere with the adherence to the original form and the mythology of the creator. However, it is arguable that something quite different is at work in the extension of copyright to such systems as software – and indeed, it is this incomparability and incongruity that is richly demonstrated, with respect to more "traditional" works of copyright, in the cultural and social context of Creative Commons. Software is seemingly inconceivable in the parameters of conventional copyright in that the limits of the work are difficult to perceive. What is occurring, as seen in the earlier discussion of broadcasts and webcasting, is that increasingly copyright is extended not to works, but to communication. Communications are therefore "embodied" by their conceptual value, their limits within the market. The work has become the "value" – the consumption. Therefore, intellectual property protection (especially the acute example of copyright in software, databases, and broadcasts) can be understood as being about the market for production for consumption (directed towards an economic market motivated by "ownership") – an economic model of creativity as market value. Innovation becomes known as literally a development with economic impact, consistent with this economic model of creativity. The grand narrative of intellectual property and economic progress is always already rational, and the suggestion of alternative conceptualisations of knowledge and value, such as the collaborative, "imitative" models offered by FLOSS and Creative Commons, are therefore *a priori* uncivilised, unprogressive,[23] and "superstitious"[24] – an unacceptable risk of infection.

Intellectual Property Inoculation

> The virus of the new idea is there, and sooner or later it will break out not merely in one focus but in many places.[25]

On the other hand, these models of development are not necessarily compatible with or relevant to free and open source software communities, for which innovation is suspect as otherwise random or indeed viral creativity, an unpredictable autopoeitic,[26]

22 Krauss RE (1986) *The Originality of the Avant-Garde and Other Modernist Myths*, Cambridge MA, MIT P: 162.

23 Dutfield G (2003) *Intellectual Property Rights and the Life Science Industries: A Twentieth Century History*, Aldershot, Ashgate: 208-209.

24 Kaplinsky J (2003) "Protecting Superstition", *Spiked*, 20 May.

25 Wiener N ([1954]1993) *Invention: The Care and Feeding of Ideas*, Cambridge MA, MIT P.

26 Deleuze G and Guattari F ([1980]1987) *A Thousand Plateaus: Capitalism and Schizophrenia*, Massumi B (trans), Minneapolis, U of Minnesota P. See also Biggs S and Leach J (2004) *Autopoeisis: Novelty, Meaning and Value*, London, Artswords P.

and accidental event,[27] beyond narration.[28] Such concerns are raised not only by the incremental and participatory development of software communities, but also by distributed and fan-based development of online games, and the random generation in computer music and auto-generated text.[29] Further, strikingly similar objections are made when it comes to the recognition of creativity and innovation in traditional knowledge, in that traditional and mimetic systems of knowledge production are incompatible within intellectual property models of innovation.

It is intriguing that James George Frazer describes the process of mimesis in traditional societies, in his text, *The Golden Bough*, as the Law of Contact or Contagion.[30] In other words, the process by which knowledge is transferred and developed in traditional societies is, indeed, viral. If the viral metaphor may be pursued a moment further, intellectual property laws are part of a kind of immunity of modern society, an immunity which allows us to recognise "copies" and mount the necessary antibodies against them, while forgetting the very constructed nature of originality itself. Intellectual property laws inoculate against the virus of incremental innovation and imitation, against difference, and against the possibility of the creativity and agency of the user. Thus, the "other" of the user is recognisable and separable from the singular creator, a simple object in the background.

> [U]sing self-generative grammars, textual innovation occurs for its own sake, generating endless new texts. When reading such texts it becomes apparent that the appearance of meaning is only that; an illusion, as in the absence of the author there is no authorial intent to invest an original meaning. Any meaning found "in" the texts is thus established as the projection of the reader.[31]

Within the dominant copyright model of creativity, therefore, activities of imitation and sharing (even though they may well be creative) are suppressed as threatening creativity and meaning (or at least, the construction of creativity that we are offered by the cultural institution of intellectual property), or indeed threatening to the supporting industry. The agency of the reader is dismissed as mere "projection" and denied any subjectivity in the construction of meaning within the object of intellectual property. As considered throughout this work, what unifies and controls

27 See, for instance, the work of Paul Virilio on accident and artistic expression, in particular his collaborative work with Sylvère Lotringer. See Lotringer S and Virilio P (2005) *The Accident of Art*, Taormina M (trans), New York, Semiotext(e).

28 Lyotard J-F ([1979]1984) *The Postmodern Condition: A Report on Knowledge*, Bennington G and Massumi B (trans), Minneapolis, U of Minnesota P.

29 On the removal of authorial intent and the illusion of meaning in auto-generated text, see Biggs S and Leach J (2004) *Autopoeisis: Novelty, Meaning and Value*, London, Artswords P.

30 Frazer J ([1922]1993) *The Golden Bough: A Study of Magic and Religion*, Ware Hertfordshire, Wordsworth Editions: 11.

31 Biggs S and Leach J (2004) *Autopoeisis: Novelty, Meaning and Value*, London, Artswords P: 3.

the proliferation of meaning is necessarily the "author-function"[32] of the creator in intellectual property laws, in service of the civilising value of creativity.

Brands: the Authors of Software

In an industry notable for its incremental innovation, distributed and collaborative creativity, software development presents unusual insight, as a network, into the connected flows of innovation. However, it appears entirely contrary to the "author" model of copyright that is imposed. Nevertheless, the constructed nature of the original is somewhat concealed by the operation of copyright in concert with the mythology of the genuine author and the "circumstances" and "incentives" for creativity, located within the figure of the supporting "corporate" patron. In this way, it is possible to forget completely about the copy.

> Now the strange thing about this silly if not desperate place between the real and the really made-up is that it appears to be where most of us spend most of our time as epistemically correct, socially created, and occasionally creative beings ... our practice of practices is one of actively forgetting such mischief each time we open our mouths to ask for something or to make a statement.[33]

Arguably, the authorship of software, within an increasingly corporatised conceptualisation of creativity, is achieved through branding. Indeed, proprietary software development is similarly distributed, evolutionary, and incremental, but is assimilated within intellectual property models of "creativity" by virtue of the corporate identity. In this way, the proliferative and seemingly chaotic meaning of collaborative and incremental knowledge development, as in the development of software and online games, is simplified and contained, thus achieving the singularity of the source of meaning, so essential to intellectual property frameworks. At the same time, a certain accountability[34] is suggested by the language and culture of branding, and the ability to identify the "owner" as the source.[35] This is quite distinct from the suspicion of the "chaos" or perceived instability that is created by the input of multiple creators. This is precisely the mythology of the corporate entity in the free software and open source debates. In such debates, corporations (such as Microsoft) suggest a simplification of this proliferation while at the same

---

32 Foucault M (1979) "What is an Author", in Harari JV (ed) *Textual Strategies: Perspectives in Post-Structuralist Criticism*, Ithaca, Cornell UP: 141.

33 Taussig M (1993) *Mimesis and Alterity: A Particular History of the Senses*, New York, Routledge: xvii-xviii.

34 Notably, Biggs and Leach identify a certain expectation or trust between reader and author, which they suggest is upset in the case of auto-generated texts, for which meaning is not readily formed upon authorial intent within the dominant systems for identifying and ascribing sense and value to a work. See Biggs S and Leach J (2004) *Autopoeisis: Novelty, Meaning and Value*, London, Artswords P.

35 On the unifying capacity of branding, see Twitchell JB (2004) *Branded Nation: The Marketing of Megachurch, College, Inc., and Museumworld*, New York, Simon & Schuster.

time protesting against the "unreliability" and "instability" of the creative network. As discussed earlier, the nature of the creative process (as an incremental activity) is in itself de-valued in the dominant model, ultimately leading to a similar de-valuation (and suspicion) of the products arising from that process.[36] The model of the apparently single and accountable entity suggests an ongoing adherence to the concepts of "genuine creator" and authenticity that have been considered throughout this work. Furthermore, this modelling of a classical narrative of creativity also proposes a human intervention and control of a process that might otherwise be a genuine network of subjects and objects (as considered in the following chapter) – indeed, a genuine cause for technophobic concern. Open source and free software models of innovation are de-valued in this system. And indeed, particularly in the context of the economic model of "true innovation", free software is "suspect" because it involves a less "valuable" process in terms of the investment and effort that is seen to "evaluate" the kind of human intervention necessary to find intellectual property which may be rewarded.[37] The value, the creativity, cannot be calculated in the conventional ways, except in terms of what it is not. The authorial power of the corporate identity, as brand, therefore inserts the originality and the creativity by which intention is implied, meaning is inferred, innovation is recorded, and value is ascribed. The brand is the sensibility of the text, as it were.

Indeed, such is the power of branding, with respect to the construction of the authorship and creativity of software, that monopolies created through statute may of course be "extended"[38] by the effects and security of branding. In this regard, it has been noted that trade mark protection has evolved within this narrative of creativity offered by intellectual property ideologies. In the increasing emphasis on origin within trade mark law,[39] the definition of a trade mark has become more

36 For instance, see in Chapter 2 the discussion of similar kinds of criticisms of Wikipedia, the online encyclopedia, based upon arguments against the quality possible in such a genuinely proliferative network, based mainly upon notions of lost control and the lack of an organising authority.

37 See the discussion of the initial relationship between the corporatisation of software brands and their likely uptake by large clients: Selby N (2004) "Easy-To-Use Linux Distributions Make European Businesses Switch", 22 August. http://www.nickselby.com/articles/technology/easy-linux.htm.

38 Similarly, pharmaceutical patents may informally extend beyond the monopoly period (including any protection conferred by a Supplementary Protection Certificate or the like), by virtue of branding and trade marks, and the influence on consumer trust and confidence. Indeed, branding suggests a significant means by which to secure commercial return to powerful industry without necessarily denying access to generics through long patents. Thus, branding, as an indication of the user investment in the product, could support reforms in patent law and/or a shortening of the monopoly period.

39 Comments made by Steven Jennings, trade mark practitioner from the firm Lewis Silkin, on the move away from solely the function of a description of quality, to one of designation of origin. See Jennings S (2005) "The Corporation". Seminar. QMIPRI, 16 June.

consistent with the concept of the corporatised author underlying other categories in modern intellectual property law.

Brand of the Free

> I fear that perhaps you do not quite understand what I mean by "way out." I use the expression in its fullest and most popular sense. I deliberately do not use the word "freedom." ... In passing: may I say that all too often men are betrayed by the word freedom. And as freedom is counted among the most sublime feelings, so the corresponding disillusionment can be also sublime. In variety theatres I have often watched, before my turn came on, a couple of acrobats performing on trapezes high in the roof. They swung themselves, they rocked to and fro, they sprang into the air, they floated into each other's arms, one hung by the hair from the teeth of the other. "And that too is human freedom," I thought, "self-controlled movement." What a mockery of holy Mother Nature! Were the apes to see such a spectacle, no theater walls could stand the shock of their laughter.[40]

While open models may not necessarily be beyond intellectual property models, they appear to defy the "branding" which is becoming increasingly necessary to the establishment of the "product". Nevertheless, branding may be appropriated by these movements, in the very fact of being identified as a movement, such that consumers may make decisions in favour of the product. Indeed, Creative Commons is an extremely successful example of the importance of branding, in models other than purely economic, so as to materialise the actions, contributions, and creativity of users within the system. Thus, the nature of "branding" in these examples offers much to unsettle the increasingly corporatised model of creativity as something which can be measured by investment, secured by branding, and rewarded by monopolies.

What these initiatives demonstrate is that creativity cannot be simply summarised and secured to the singular authorial source. Rather, the system must account in some way for the activities of users as creators, modifiers, copyists, and revisionists. Indeed, there is insight to be found in the distinction thus drawn between users as experts (modifiers of online games, free software communities, and so on) and the users as "public". Certainly, in the case of the evolutionary modifications seen within online gaming communities and within free software and open source communities, the copy brings the original into being. The act of imitating, appropriating, and modifying re-affirms the original in the knowledge and understanding (the source code) necessary to achieve the developments, but at the same time renders undeniable the agency and creativity of the user.

The free software and open source communities are arguably about knowledge development for the community itself (that is, motivated by the user, as participant, as expert). The dissemination, use, and regulation of knowledge are all subject to the internal governance of that community – a communal or collaborative model

40 Kafka F ([1933-1954]1992) "A Report to an Academy", *The Complete Short Stories of Franz Kafka*, Glatzer NN (ed), London, Minerva: 250 at 253.

of creativity as a valuable process rather than a finite value. In this context, it is useful to recognise that these various initiatives all depend upon a certain internal governance in order to regulate the conditions of access and the sustainability of that sharing.[41] The FLOSS and Creative Commons models of knowledge development depend not merely upon open sharing (as they are sometimes over-simplified by their critics) but upon the regulation of access to the knowledge that is shared, such that the sharing is sustainable and ongoing, in the form of continuing dissemination (such as the source code and modifications, in the case of software).

This departs markedly from the predominant economic context for creativity. In this way, the various initiatives operating within the framework of intellectual property offer important examples of the opportunity for users to be identified and recognised within the system itself. Furthermore, what becomes clear is the way in which branding might be relevant both in terms of the articulation of such models within the dominant system and as means by which to register the activity and capabilities of users. Indeed, the creative consumption of users is a way in which the users' actions may indeed count within the terms set by intellectual property.

Creative Consumption

Following the discussion of value in innovation, it may be suggested that, in cooperation with this model, value is also being added by the trade marks and branding authored by the corporation. Indeed, in the "future-oriented" development of intellectual property rights, it is conceivable that almost any new technology or method that adds value to the economy could conceivably be constructed as creative for the purposes of falling within "intellectual property". Trade marks present a critically uncomfortable case when it comes to the value-driven concept of knowledge, and yet they remain relatively peripheral to the central debates. This is intriguing in that trade marks present quite an unusual case in which the concept of creativity has been appropriated in a strategically economic sense and, further, this economic construction and compartmentalisation may indeed have unintended and unexpected consequences for freedom of speech. The history of trade mark protection in the United Kingdom and United States is instructive in this regard. The 1878 US decision of *Leidersdorf v Flint*[42] expressly rejected the passage of legislation on trade marks on the basis of their non-creativity. As Sherman and Bently explain:

> While the rights granted by design, patents and copyright could be excused (and justified) because they were only granted for new creations (and as such nothing was therefore

41 See the earlier discussion of access in the context of traditional knowledge and the public domain, in Chapter 3.

42 (1878) (15 F Cas 260). Subsequent trade mark legislation in the United States was based, not on the copyright and patents clause, but on the commerce clause.

> being taken away from the public), this was not the case with trade marks which, in many cases dealt with pre-existing subject matter.[43]

Indeed, one of the major concerns, repeated throughout the historical literature, is the preoccupation of trade marks with materiality, with the material. Indeed, creativity appears to depend upon being in and of itself essentially non-material. What makes creativity property, as in intellectual property, is the rendering of that prior non-materiality into a later material effect (an effect arguably of commercial value, towards which the emphasis in intellectual property frameworks increasingly leans). In other words, intellectual property frameworks narrate the progression of creativity (the non-material) to commerce or business (the material). Engaging the trace of a well-known brand in this very discussion, the user is relegated to the role of listening to "his master's voice", as it were, in order to register creativity of value. But what of you, now, thinking of the mark, "using" the trade mark? What values are you creating?

On this question, the history of trade marks is instructive on another level, one which appears to be critical to their appropriation of "creative" production. In their comprehensive history of intellectual property law, Sherman and Bently note the second reason trade marks were considered to be outside the ambit of intellectual property systems, namely, "whereas copyright, patents and designs were primarily concerned with the creation and protection of property, trade marks were more concerned with forgery or fraud".[44] What is of interest here is the relationship between trade marks and the recognition of the authenticity of the object – that is, the recognition of its genuine nature as distinct from its forgery. Indeed, this emphasis continues today, with the vigorous pursuit of counterfeit products and the appropriation of luxury marks, applying them to inferior goods. Perhaps the concern may be less with the quality of the good (that is, more and more counterfeit goods are of increasingly high quality), and more with the authenticity of the good;. that is, the creative identity of the good, the authentic brand. But conversely, the counterfeit indeed contributes to the quality of the original, and re-invigorates its authenticity as the genuine article.

Thus, trade marks and branding somewhat confound the teleological model of creativity found elsewhere in intellectual property, in that trade mark law does not narrate the same story of creativity of the progression of the creative event. Yet, perhaps ironically, trade mark law is unbranded (and somewhat untested) when it comes to the current international discussions. Following the earlier discussion in the case of the branding of non-proprietary distributed enterprises, the question of the "author" nevertheless persists as a functioning principle in intellectual property ideology. This interaction between incentive mechanisms (including the mitigation of risk and conferral of control through the calculation of monopolies in return

43 Sherman B and Bently L (1999) *The Making of Modern Intellectual Property Law*, Cambridge, Cambridge UP.

44 Sherman B and Bently L (1999) *The Making of Modern Intellectual Property Law*, Cambridge, Cambridge UP: 171.

for investment) and the creation of markets for information goods can be traced through the increasing corporatisation of research and intellectual output.[45] It is this development in the concept that provides a critical perspective on the way in which seemingly economic industry is rendered creative in the case of trade mark protection.

The Incentive to Mark

In the context of trade marks, Bently and Sherman[46] suggest that the trade mark in itself is instrumental to the creativity of goodwill or the creativity of a new association (between the mark and the product). In the first instance then, the trade mark, as it were, is the means by which the goodwill is generated, rather than the expression of that goodwill.[47] The material (the mark) thus generates the immateriality of creativity (as distinct from the materialisation of the non-material creative idea that is suggested in conventional narratives provided by intellectual property law). The mark (signifier) creates a new association (signified).

When it comes to the discourse on trade marks, it would seem that the emphasis on the goods, on the products, somewhat obscures the potentially more significant consequences for the debates and developments in this area of the law. That is, the material, the conventional form of the narrative, distracts and diminishes the consumer; while the indeterminate nature of the creativity, the fluidity of the "products" of goodwill and brand loyalty, suggest an authoring by the consumer of "goods", as it were, of critical importance to the so-called creative economy. Contrary to the preoccupation with the material in conventional evidence of innovation, rather paradoxically, the immateriality of the creativity of the trade mark may introduce fresh insight into the creativity and consumption discussions.

In other words, what is of great significance here, in respect of current debates over the rights and interests of users to access material, is that the "authoring" of that goodwill, as it were, is in collaboration with the customer, the consumer, the user. This collaboration with the consumer, in such a way that the consumer is also instrumental in the creativity in the final product, is not beyond the dominant voices in the debate. Indeed, in emphasising creativity as the adding of value and the growth of the economy, then the construction of celebrity, of brand value, of goodwill is part of the "source" (the author) of that creativity. Bently and Sherman argue that this is what weakens the justification for protection of trade marks: "while the associations between the mark and a source or goodwill may be instigated and nurtured by the

---

45 Dutfield G (2003) *Intellectual Property Rights and the Life Science Industries: A Twentieth Century History*, Aldershot, Ashgate. See also Sell SK (2003) *Private Power, Public Law: The Globalization of Intellectual Property Rights*, Cambridge, Cambridge UP; Drahos P and Braithwaite J (2002) *Information Feudalism: Who Owns the Knowledge Economy?* London, Earthscan.

46 Bently L and Sherman B (2004) *Intellectual Property Law*, 2nd ed, Oxford, OUP.

47 Bently L and Sherman B (2004) *Intellectual Property Law*, 2nd ed, Oxford, OUP: 699.

trader, they are as much created by the customers and the public."[48] However, it is suggested that the rhetorical emphasis on the adding of value, together with the unanticipated intrusion of the customer in the authoring of creativity in trade marks, can be appropriated in such a way that users' interests and access rights would be positive aspects of intellectual property, in the creative industries, as distinct from mere exceptions and limitations.

The creativity ascribed to trade marks is arguably related to the construction of creativity in publicity or celebrity, discussed in the previous chapter. In that discussion, the way in which the law appears to respond to a considered risk to celebrity value, where consumption of celebrity or access to celebrity is unregulated, was identified. This is similar to the artificial scarcity imposed on what is arguably inexhaustible and intangible (information) by intellectual property regimes, discussed in earlier chapters. That is, the "value added", or value proposition, as it is described by governments and industry alike, of celebrity, of the brand, is the creativity aspect that justifies the creation of intellectual property protection:

> We live in a world where creativity is celebrated as the solution to problems as diverse as personal anomie and the state of our twenty-first century post-industrial economies. Innovation is central to current knowledge economies and thus is spoken of as a value rather than as a description of an activity. Yet it is clear that innovation is not enough for the inscription of value to be established. For creativity to have occurred, something must come into being that is recognised as valuable in some way.[49]

The economic value added (the growth) becomes confused, as it were, with the creativity that is to be encouraged and protected. Indeed, this elision between the incentive to create and the incentive to growth can be traced back much further than the present day:

> Brand names, then, are the keystone of a competitive economy, an economy where every man is encouraged to do the best he can, and the public is the judge of whether or not he succeeds, because by branding his goods people will know that they came from him.[50]

Thus, the consumption of the creative product can reduce the value of that creativity in that the market is compromised. Creativity has become an economic question. As seen earlier, "the trademark and right-of-publicity cases that recognize that intellectual property can be diminished by consumption".[51] This underlying assumption of the nature of creativity is betrayed by the argument that products of intellectual activity must be protected and secure in order to create more intellectual activity; that is, in order to provide the incentive for creativity. It would seem that

48 Bently L and Sherman B (2004) *Intellectual Property Law*, 2nd ed, Oxford, OUP: 699.

49 Biggs S and Leach J (2004) *Autopoeisis: Novelty, Meaning and Value*, London, Artswords P: 2.

50 Rogers E (1947) "The Social Value of Trade Marks and Brand", 37 *TM Rep* 249: 253.

51 Landes WM and Posner RA (2003) *The Economic Structure of Intellectual Property Law*, Cambridge MA, Harvard UP: 223-24.

publicity, by which branding is consolidated (and, as discussed in the previous chapter, "celebrity" is created), may be the very process by which the "value" in that creativity is depleted, the very limiting process of creativity, according to the value model. In other words, access to value must be restricted to an extent. Access to value must be regulated. So, the consumption of brands, and the development of brand loyalty, is regulated in order to maintain the value, the quality, the "author" of those brands. As the United Kingdom Stella Artois campaign claims, Stella is "reassuringly expensive". Lack of access is a value in itself.

The Author Brand

However, the collaboration of the consumer in the "value" that is created (or added) in the trade mark is in fact of immense value to challenges to the mythology of the valuable subject or creator of intellectual property. This challenge then raises important questions in respect of the earlier discussion in this chapter, and the innovation networks in open source and free software, Creative Commons, sampling, and other strategic responses. As we can see, recognition of the "authorship" and the creativity in trade marks may be assisted and summarised (within the legal applications) within the value model set out earlier that is facilitated by an increasingly corporatised conceptualisation of creativity. This is relevant for other areas of activity that are contained within intellectual property frameworks and almost limited by the dominant concept of creativity in operation. Similarly, the collaborative nature of the creativity in the trade mark, the brand, is hidden by the construct of the "corporate author", assimilating this complexity within intellectual property models of "creativity" by virtue of the corporate identity.

The User Pays

Taking into account the power of branding, and the assertions of creativity in trade marks, it is possible to appropriate what at first may seem to be a disconcerting narrative on commercial intrusions into systems designed to protect creativity. Apart from the obvious critical negotiation of brand identities that might be undertaken by consumers,[52] the role of the consumer is even more complex. In the simplest sense, of course, countercultural responses to particular corporate entities, as well as the increased interest in ethical branding[53] are particularly insightful. Recalling

---

52 See, for instance, Heath J and Potter A (2005) *The Rebel Sell: How the Counterculture Became Consumer Culture*, Chichester, Capstone.

53 See the discussion of ethical consumerism in the collection, Harrison R et al (ed) *The Ethical Consumer*, London, SAGE. Also related to this is the way in which consumers negotiate certain technologies, and where branding and corporate accountability might create value through consumer confidence. In relation to consumer acceptance of genetically modified foods, see Bonny S (2004) "Factors Explaining Opposition to GMOs in France and the Rest of Europe", in Evenson RE and Santaniello V (eds) *Consumer Acceptance of Genetically Modified Foods*, Wallingford, CABI: 169.

the McLibel litigation,[54] the corporate identity of McDonalds is a key example for the present work, because the very identity that McDonalds invested in producing was indeed the identity that the consumer defendants appropriated as negative, with tangible material effects on McDonalds.

Indeed, the countercultural activity of the user, and the safeguarding of that capacity through freedom of speech, is made clear in this case, particularly in the compulsion for accountability on the part of the corporate entity.[55] What is possible, arguably necessary, is the recognition of the consumer, the user, in the creativity that is recognised in this form of intellectual property. The potential for a rejuvenation of the user within other categories of intellectual property protection is attractive and strategic, particularly in the context of Creative Commons licensing, the open source and free software movements, and open systems of scientific research and publishing, which become sensible within the very system that frequently marginalises and alienates the users and consumers of the knowledge, the creativity, that is regulated by that system.

The thought that trade marks – one of the most commercial forms of intellectual property, as it were, in that their protection as creative products has been criticised as wholly constructed, dubious, and disingenuous – might be the key to acknowledging user access more positively within the intellectual property system more broadly, is of great appeal. In that creativity has increasingly become appropriated as an economic value by the dominant language of the debate, it is here that the potential is available to impact upon positive policy-making and legislative actions in respect of consumers and indeed users in other areas of intellectual property. This is especially so with regard to the dominant model of creativity and innovation as a teleological economic process, with the industry as the progressively most legitimate face or identity of the source of that creativity. The importance of trade marks as a way into the debate, in order to up-end the momentum of expanding protection and increasing obstacles to access through the use of the very arguments themselves, presents great potential and somewhat appealing irony.

Arguably the legal complexities of trade marks, in their justification, their perpetual protection, and their emphasis on the identity as the certain object of

---

54 The so-called *McLibel* litigation lasted for seven years (being the longest running civil case in modern English legal history) and culminated in a decision of the European Court of Human Rights (*Steel v UK* (2005) 41 EHRR 22), which held that parts of the case were in contravention of obligations under the European Convention on Human Rights. The court held that the parties' rights to a fair trial were undermined because they did not have adequate legal advice, legal aid being unavailable. The law has now changed in the United Kingdom, making legal aid available (discretionary) under special circumstances. Discussion of the first part of the case is available in Vidal J (1998) *McLibel: Burger Culture on Trial*, New York, New Press. See further the discussion in Lury C (2004) *Brands: The Logos of the Global Economy*, London, Routledge: 140-41.

55 On the relationship between branding and accountability, see the collection, Ind N (ed) (2005) *Beyond Branding: How the New Values of Transparency and Integrity are Changing the World of Brands*, London, Kogan Page.

creativity, introduce some valuable examination of the role of user throughout the various categories of intellectual property and throughout the current debates and developments. Indeed, in the immateriality of goodwill (rather than the "good" comprising intellectual property) the roles and connections of the publics materialise.

What strategic movements such as free software, open source, Creative Commons, and more have shown is that these are sophisticated models of knowledge development, far more complex than utopian fields of shared dreams. In this way, such strategies challenge the security of the corporatised narrative of creativity. Indeed, creativity is not contained by a brand or managed by investment; rather, creativity proliferates. Nevertheless, such networks are frequently dismissed as mere alternatives to the "official culture" of innovation, marginalised and inapplicable within the commercial context of the creative economy. However, the very commercial world of trade marks and celebrity shows us that the consumer is in fact instrumental, essential, and at the centre of the production of value in these industries.

It is necessary to account for the location of the user within the text, such that the law can reflect in real and applicable ways the creativity of the user and the value for society in harnessing and facilitating that creativity. The economic realities of trade mark protection and value-generation, as well as the emerging area of publicity and celebrity explored in the previous chapter, suggest the necessary territory or locality within which the user can be recognised for its creative input. The user dwells within that community of experts, of brand savvy, and not only occupies the text but also creates it.

Indeed, the very language of "user" or of "consumer" suggests the presence only at the end-point of the intellectual product, as a complete and finite object. But the immateriality of the creativity of trade marks confounds this interpretation. Indeed, the creativity of trade marks is impossible without the consumer. It is in that access to the mark that the creative associations, the signification, become meaningful. A more appropriate term would unsettle the hierarchy as well as acknowledge the action and capabilities of users. If intellectual property is the incentive for creativity which has emerged as the critical concern of the contemporary economy, a complete picture and an efficient economic picture of any such growth must address the dynamic exchange between creator, user, and industry.

Use. That is the fundamental measure of value in the creative economy.

Chapter 5

Creating Selves

"What happens when we throw a ball against a wall? The wall bounces it back. But the way we pick it up and throw it again can vary according to the rules of the game.
"We go from ease to strain, slack off after exertion, all without forethought.
"Dialogue is the same way," he said.[1]

Introduction

This, the final chapter, revisits the way in which creativity interacts with the intellectual property system, and the way in which it is understood and celebrated more generally and informally. Throughout this discussion in this work, a consideration of current international intellectual property developments has sought to characterise the cultural and economic priorities of intellectual property industries and the actions of users within these industries as key stakeholders and drivers of value. In the context of obligations to cultural diversity, education, and innovation, the role of the user is one of increasing significance and accountability. At this stage, it is necessary to articulate more fully the value of the way in which users negotiate and create, and thus to identify mechanisms to identify that value within a system of delivering the "right to benefit".

A Tradition of Use

How are we to account for the work of otherness at the heart of selfhood?[2]

Paul Ricoeur's hermeneutical ethics characterise selfhood through the dialectic of action with the other. Thus, it is through the dialogue of knowledge and relation to the other that genuine self-identity is achieved.[3] In other words, drawing upon the

1 Jabès E ([1984]1987) *The Book of Dialogue*, Waldrop R (trans), Middletown, Wesleyan UP: 21.

2 Ricoeur P ([1990]1992) *Oneself as Another*, Blamey K (trans), Chicago, U of Chicago P: 318.

3 See in particular Ricoeur P (1984) *Time and Narrative: Volume 1*, McLaughlin K and Pellauer D (trans), Chicago, U of Chicago P; Ricoeur P (1985) *Time and Narrative: Volume 2*, McLaughlin K and Pellauer D (trans), Chicago, U of Chicago P; Ricoeur P (1988) *Time and Narrative: Volume 3*, McLaughlin K and Pellauer D (trans), Chicago, U of Chicago P; Ricoeur P ([1990]1992) *Oneself as Another*, Blamey K (trans), Chicago, U of Chicago P.

earlier re-reading of *habitus*, Ricoeur similarly dismantles the common opposition between tradition and innovation, and revives tradition as something necessarily and importantly part of each individual's self-recognition and self-narration: "without myths that have been passed on there would be nothing to transform poetically."[4] Indeed, for Ricoeur, tradition is in itself constituted by such use and creative transformation: "In fact, a tradition is constituted by the interplay of innovation and sedimentation."[5]

Of particular interest to the present discussion is that this communication with the other does not depend upon closeness and proximity in the conventional sense. Thus, Ricoeur's analysis rejects the bounds of territory for such "connection" and instead understands a critical plurality (the I, the you, the third) in what he describes as a dialogical[6] philosophy. In this way, the network can be imagined within Ricoeur's method, and the connections between distributed actors are not devalued, but rather are crucial:

> It can be tempting for a dialogical philosophy to limit itself to relations with other individual people, which are usually placed under the heading of an I-thou dialogue. It is precisely these relations with other individuals that are held to be worthy of being qualified as interpersonal. But this face-to-face relation lacks the relation to a *third* party that seems just as primitive as the relation to an individual "you." This point is of the greatest importance if we want to account for the transition from the notion of the capable human being to that of the real subject of rights. Only the relation to the third, situated in the background of the use, gives us a basis for the institutional mediation required by the constitution of a real subject of rights – in other words, of a citizen.[7]

Thus, the methodology offered by Ricoeur seems especially relevant to the contemporary network and access to knowledge, in that knowledge maintains (and

---

4 Ricoeur P (1984) *Time and Narrative: Volume 1*, McLaughlin K and Pellauer D (trans), Chicago, U of Chicago P: 47.

5 Ricoeur P (1984) *Time and Narrative: Volume 1*, McLaughlin K and Pellauer D (trans), Chicago, U of Chicago P: 68. This notion of the "third" appears elsewhere (in psychoanalysis, for instance) and in the work of Michel Serres, where it becomes especially meaningful in his work on education and instruction, and thus for the discussion later in this chapter, on the practical implications of these ways of conceptualising the self and creativity as traced through education and teaching. On the nature of "thirdness", and the proliferation of new voices, new "thirds", Serres writes: "Teaching is this sowing." See Serres M (1991) *The Troubadour of Knowledge*, Glaser SF and Paulson W (trans), Ann Arbor, U of Michigan P.

6 The concept of dialogism or the dialogical will be considered in greater detail below, particularly in the context of the reading of users and creators as actors within the network. However, for the moment it is useful to note that the concept, generally attributed to Mikhail Bakhtin, understands various relations between the work and its readers, users, and other works. These various "discourses" (or heteroglossia or polyphony) open the use of texts and of knowledge in ways very critical to the understanding of the knowledge community as a network of actors and to question the hierarchy between users and creators in the context of contemporary networks and technologies of use.

7 Ricoeur P ([1995]2000) *The Just*, Pellauer D (trans), Chicago, U of Chicago P: 5.

indeed builds upon) its value through its free exchange. It is access to knowledge that is the basis for self and for participation. Thus, tradition is valuable, innovative, creative, in the way in which it is used and re-used in the present, ending, as Ricoeur explains, "epic distance that provides the definitive basis for opposing 'low' literature to all the rest of 'high' literature".[8] Ricoeur's thesis, therefore, maps well onto contemporary renditions of "high" culture (as developed through institutionally legitimated processes and sites and monitored through intellectual property) and the "low" aberrant expressions that resist conventional proprietary constraints. Further, the renewal of tradition, as it were, is of great assistance in identifying the collaboration of users as well as validating collaborative and incremental processes of innovation – whether in the context of the scientific laboratory or the traditional community. The connections, the ties, with tradition are intrinsic and critical to the flow of knowledge: "At this level, creating is translating."[9] Indeed, translation betrays the stability that is the very fiction of "tradition": "To translate is to betray: ambiguity is part of translation."[10]

Selves, the Work of Others

> Never has the artist been more in need of a people.[11]

The dialogic model of selfhood described by Ricoeur owes much to Mikhail Bakhtin, a Russian philosopher who wrote (in largely coded language) during Stalin's regime, but whose work was revived in the West during the 1960s and 1970s.[12] Bakhtin's understanding of selfhood identifies a problem of representation that recalls the earlier consideration of the story by Borges, "The Aleph". As Bakhtin explains:

> *Creative understanding* does not renounce itself, its own place in time, its own culture; and it forgets nothing. In order to understand, it is immensely important for the person who understands to be *located outside* the object of his or her creative understanding – in time, in space, in culture. For one cannot even really see one's own exterior and comprehend it as a whole, and no mirrors or photographs can help: our real exterior can

8 Ricoeur P (1985) *Time and Narrative: Volume 2*, McLaughlin K and Pellauer D (trans), Chicago, U of Chicago P: 155.

9 Ricoeur P (1985) *Time and Narrative: Volume 2*, McLaughlin K and Pellauer D (trans), Chicago, U of Chicago P: 145.

10 Latour B ([1993]1996) *Aramis, or The Love of Technology*, Porter C (trans), Cambridge MA, Harvard UP: 48.

11 Deleuze G and Guattari F ([1980]1987) *A Thousand Plateaus: Capitalism and Schizophrenia*, Massumi B (trans), Minneapolis, U of Minnesota P: 346.

12 Morson GS and Emerson C (1990) *Mikhail Bakhtin: Creation of a Prosaics*, Stanford, Stanford UP: 3.

> be seen and understood only by other people, because they are located outside us in space and because they are *others*.[13]

For Bakhtin, the many languages at work in a community work together towards understanding and diversity, in his concept of dialogism (or heteroglossia). Literally, these many voices interrupt the possibility of a major and dominant language becoming entrenched as the sole means of relations between individuals in that community. Bakhtin refers to this tension as that between the monoglossia of the dominant or "common language"[14] and the heteroglossia of the competing dissonance throughout the community: "Thus the speech of another is introduced into the author's (the story) in *concealed form*, that is, without any of the *formal* markers usually accompanying such speech, whether direct or indirect."[15]

This resonates with the earlier discussion of the "grand narrative"[16] of intellectual property law, whereby that language narrates and presupposes the relations to knowledge that are conceivable in that context. In the polarised monologic world that Bakhtin describes, "a thought is either affirmed or repudiated; otherwise it simply ceases to be a fully valid thought".[17] In this concept of monologism, Bakhtin provides a critique of the ideological containment of creativity seen elsewhere in the present discussion. In particular, the way in which the dominant institution for recognising creativity effectively constrains cultures as one uniform culture, and indeed, the way in which the diversity of the network, of communities, and of users situated "outside the system", is summarised within a uniform and universalising "public", can be described by the processes identified by Bakhtin in the centrality of the monological and authoritative voice:

> All that has the power to mean, all that has value, is everywhere concentrated around one center – the carrier. All ideological acts are conceived and perceived as possible expressions of a single consciousness: the spirit of a nation, the spirit of a people, the spirit of history, and so forth.[18]

Bakhtin thus describes a principle of ideological authoring and containment of a community's diversity and expression, through a process similar to that of the legitimation of the grand narrative. Indeed, the inadequacy (or selection) of the monologic narrative in its purported representation of totality is particularly instructive: "In the presence of the monologic principle, ideology – as a deduction,

---

13 Bakhtin MM (1986) *Speech Genres and Other Late Essays*, McGee VW (trans), Austin, U of Texas P: 7.

14 This can be understood as the language of the "official culture", as discussed below.

15 Bakhtin MM (1981) *The Dialogic Imagination*, Emerson C and Holquist M (trans), Austin, U of Texas P: 303.

16 Chapter 1.

17 Bakhtin MM (1984) *Problems of Dostoevsky's Poetics*, Emerson C (ed and trans), Booth WC (intro), Minneapolis, U of Minnesota P: 80.

18 Bakhtin MM (1984) *Problems of Dostoevsky's Poetics*, Emerson C (ed and trans), Booth WC (intro), Minneapolis, U of Minnesota P: 81-82.

as a semantic summation of representation – inevitably transforms the represented world into a *voiceless object of that deduction*."[19] However, as for the "grand narrative", the "minor narratives", or *petit récits*, fracture that dominance and de-legitimate the dominant voice. Similarly, Bakhtin's work is helpful in understanding not only the way in which communities may intervene and counter the dominance of a particular institution (including intellectual property law), but also the actions and collaborations of users in the generation, meaning, and heteroglossia of knowledge being exchanged. At the same time, the polyphony of languages, genres, new forms, and new meanings is assured.

These relationships are developed further in Bakhtin's concept of the carnival,[20] in ways with particular significance for a re-reading of creativity in the network. Indeed, the network offers the three distinct forms of carnival identified by Bakhtin: *ritual spectacles*; *comic verbal compositions*; *various genres of billingsgate*.[21] In the way in which the "folk culture"[22] of the carnival characterises connections within communities, it is meaningful in the present context for its interrogation of the public and private, performance and audience, actor and spectator. Indeed, the carnival, for its duration, subverts the very hierarchies that impose the kind of distinction seen in the classes of "official culture" and "unofficial culture",[23] "aristocracy" and "peasants", implied in the modern intellectual property system.[24] As Bakhtin explains, "during carnival there is a temporary suspension of all hierarchic distinctions and barriers among men and of certain norms and prohibitions of usual life". But in the contemporary carnival of the network, arguably that "temporary suspension" is reproduced and reiterated throughout the potentially enduring continuous flow of the network, upsetting "the principle of an immovable and unchanging hierarchy in which the higher and the lower never merge", upon which the "official culture" is founded.[25] The usual (and thus seemingly invisible) structures by which dominant

---

19 Bakhtin MM (1984) *Problems of Dostoevsky's Poetics*, Emerson C (ed and trans), Booth WC (intro), Minneapolis, U of Minnesota P: 83.

20 The carnival and the concept of the carnivalesque come from the carnivals of the Renaissance and the Middle Ages: "A boundless world of humorous forms and manifestations opposed the official and serious tone of medieval ecclesiastical and feudal culture." See Bakhtin MM ([1968]1984) *Rabelais and His World*, Iswolsky H (trans), Bloomington, Indiana UP: 4.

21 Bakhtin MM ([1968]1984) *Rabelais and His World*, Iswolsky H (trans), Bloomington, Indiana UP: 5.

22 Bakhtin MM ([1968]1984) *Rabelais and His World*, Iswolsky H (trans), Bloomington, Indiana UP.

23 Bakhtin MM ([1968]1984) *Rabelais and His World*, Iswolsky H (trans), Bloomington, Indiana UP. See, for instance, the disjunction between cultures in relation to language and expression: 166.

24 Bakhtin MM ([1968]1984) *Rabelais and His World*, Iswolsky H (trans), Bloomington, Indiana UP: 15.

25 Bakhtin MM ([1968]1984) *Rabelais and His World*, Iswolsky H (trans), Bloomington, Indiana UP: 166.

relations are organised and maintained are revealed, by the very dismantling of the institutional staging, and the discord of the carnival. The very "star" system of intellectual property is confounded by the carnival of the network, without footlights, without stage directions:

> In fact, carnival does not know footlights, in the sense that it does not acknowledge any distinction between actors and spectators. Footlights would destroy a carnival, as the absence of footlights would destroy a theatrical performance. Carnival is not a spectacle seen by the people; they live in it, and everyone participates because its very idea embraces all the people. While carnival lasts, there is no other life outside it. During carnival time life is subject only to its laws, that is, the laws of its own freedom.[26]

Indeed, the concept of the carnivalesque dismantles the very polarity required to maintain these distinctions as uniform and universalising categories, as meaningless and antagonistic abbreviations of the diversity of the community. Not only does the carnival confound conventional relations to authority, but also it disconcerts the dominant narrative, mobilising the polyphony of voices within the community. The carnival is, in a sense, a re-invigorated public sphere (a networked "public domain"):

> The main arena for carnival acts was the square and the streets adjoining it. To be sure, carnival also invaded the home; in essence it was limited in time only and not in space; carnival knows neither stage nor footlights. But the central arena could only be the square, for by its very idea carnival *belongs to the whole people,* it is *universal, everyone* must participate in its familiar contact. The public square was the symbol of communal performance. The carnival square – the square of carnival acts – acquired an additional symbolic overtone that broadened and deepened it. In carnivalized literature the square, as a setting for the action of the plot, becomes two-leveled and ambivalent: it is as if there glimmered through the actual square the carnival square of free familiar contact and communal performances of crowning and decrowning.[27]

The network is indeed a genuine phenomenon of contemporary carnival and an important means by which to understand the territory and materiality of the contemporary network space and its interconnections[28] – literally "grounding" the

---

26 Bakhtin MM ([1968]1984) *Rabelais and His World*, Iswolsky H (trans), Bloomington, Indiana UP: 7.

27 Bakhtin MM (1984) *Problems of Dostoevsky's Poetics*, Emerson C (ed and trans), Booth WC (intro), Minneapolis, U of Minnesota P: 128.

28 See further Henri Lefebvre's work on festivity and the production and politicisation of space in his concept of *la fête*: Lefebvre H (1996) *Writings on Cities*, Kofman E and Lebas E (trans and ed), Oxford, Blackwell. Arguably, Lefebvre's concept of unproductive consumption does not imagine the same kind of generative productive power (a kind of creative consumption, as it were) seen in Bakhtin's concept of the carnivalesque, that which is generated through the relations and forces of the carnival. See also Lefebvre H ([1974]1991) *The Production of Space*, Nicholson-Smith D (trans), Oxford, Blackwell.

experience, social life, and interrelations of participants.[29] This offers important insight into the materiality and territoriality of the otherwise distributed, disaggregated network – the sense of belonging and territory that confounds the dismissal and dispossession of the network by the dominant institutionalised "sites" for creative process.

In his work on Rabelais and the "philosophy of the word",[30] Bakhtin describes the grotesque body, recalling in the present work Deleuze and Guattari's concept of the body without organs (BwO). The organism of the grotesque body articulates prosaically the nature of the network and its interconnections:

> The grotesque body, as we have often stressed, is a body in the act of becoming. It is never finished, never completed; it is continually built, created, and builds and creates another body. Moreover, the body swallows the world and is itself swallowed by the world ... This is why the essential role belongs to those parts of the grotesque body in which it outgrows its own self, transgressing its own body, in which it conceives a new, second body.[31]

Like Deleuze and Guattari, Bakhtin rejects "the narrow and modified meaning which modern ideology, especially that of the nineteenth century, attributed to 'materiality' and to the 'body'".[32] Rather, the grotesque body is the materiality of the people – at once organic, but not organised; proliferating, but not whole; universal but not uniform:

> In grotesque realism, therefore, the bodily element is deeply positive. It is presented not in a private, egotistic form, severed from the other spheres of life, but as something universal, representing all the people. As such it is opposed to severance from the material and bodily roots of the world; it makes no pretense to renunciation of the earthy, or independence of the earth and the body. We repeat: the body and bodily life here have a cosmic and at the same time an all-people's character; this is not the body and its physiology in the modern sense of these words, because it is not individualized. The material bodily principle is contained not in the biological individual, not in the bourgeois ego, but in the people, a people who are continually growing and renewed. This is why all that is bodily becomes grandiose, exaggerated, immeasurable.[33]

---

29 Bakhtin describes, in the carnival presented in Goethe's work, the way in which the people's destiny is "indissolubly linked to earth". See Bakhtin MM ([1968]1984) *Rabelais and His World*, Iswolsky H (trans), Bloomington, Indiana UP: 252. This recalls the subterranean rhizomatic growth identified in Deleuze and Guattari's concepts of interconnecting communities and knowledge, considered more fully in Chapter 2.

30 Bakhtin MM (1981) *The Dialogic Imagination*, Emerson C and Holquist M (trans), Austin, U of Texas P: 309-10.

31 Bakhtin MM ([1968]1984) *Rabelais and His World*, Iswolsky H (trans), Bloomington, Indiana UP: 317.

32 Bakhtin MM ([1968]1984) *Rabelais and His World*, Iswolsky H (trans), Bloomington, Indiana UP: 18.

33 Bakhtin MM ([1968]1984) *Rabelais and His World*, Iswolsky H (trans), Bloomington, Indiana UP: 19.

The network is a carnival; a feast of abundance; "the true feast of time, the feast of becoming, change, and renewal";[34] the banquet of "increasing returns to scale".[35] We can recognise many at the table.

Creativity – A Catastrophic Refrain

> And what would *thinking* be if it did not constantly confront chaos?[36]

> The problem of catastrophe. Catastrophe is not finalization. It is the culmination, in collision and struggle, of points of view (of equally privileged consciousness, each with its own world). Catastrophe does not give these points of view resolution, but on the contrary reveals their incapability of resolution under earthly conditions; catastrophe sweeps them all away without having resolved them. Catastrophe is the opposite of triumph and apotheosis. By its very essence it is denied even elements of catharsis.[37]

> It is as if one were casting a net, but the fisherman always risks being swept away and finding himself in the open sea when he thought he had reached port. The three disciplines [philosophy, science, and art] advance by crises or shocks in different ways, and in each case it is their succession that makes it possible to speak of "progress." It is as if the *struggle against chaos* does not take place without an affinity with the enemy, because another struggle develops and takes on more importance – the struggle *against opinion*, which claims to protect us from chaos itself.[38]

For successive "improvements" to be recognised, the newness and novelty of previous works or products must be, as it were, undone. In other words, and by the same token, the newness and novelty of the subsequent product is later and utterly dependent upon the previous work for meaning and, indeed, for the recognition of creatorship. The law concretises the technology, the creativity, as a value, but not (despite the fictions) "what it has to become",[39] what it is to mean. Paradoxically, this might be otherwise the "shock" of innovation – not its newness and surprise, but its sheer expectedness. *Why did it take so long?*

This is the mythology of "innovation", and "creativity". By virtue of the imposition of discrete "moments" of newness, the recognition of new inventions, new works, indeed novelty and originality themselves, the language of the intellectual

---

34 Bakhtin MM ([1968]1984) *Rabelais and His World*, Iswolsky H (trans), Bloomington, Indiana UP: 11.

35 Chapter 1.

36 Deleuze G and Guattari F ([1991]1994) *What is Philosophy?* Burchell G and Tomlinson H (trans), London, Verso: 208.

37 Bakhtin MM (1984) *Problems of Dostoevsky's Poetics*, Emerson C (ed and trans), Booth WC (intro), Minneapolis, U of Minnesota P: 298.

38 Deleuze G and Guattari F ([1991]1994) *What is Philosophy?* Burchell G and Tomlinson H (trans), London, Verso: 203.

39 Latour B ([1993]1996) *Aramis, or The Love of Technology*, Porter C (trans), Cambridge MA, Harvard UP: 46.

property system conjugates what might otherwise be an unnarratable continuous flow of knowledge and incremental advances: "By definition, a technological project is a fiction, since at the outset it does not exist, and there is no way it can exist yet because it is in the project phase."[40]

The stability of the network, therefore, comes not from the objectification and spatialisation of knowledge, but from the capabilities of its actors and the connections thus made. It is necessary then to consider the ways in which the actions in the knowledge network can be recognised and indeed valued.

Co-Creativity

> To understand a given text as the author himself understood it. But our understanding can and should be better. Powerful and profound creativity is largely unconscious and polysemic. Through understanding it is supplemented by consciousness, and the multiplicity of its meanings is revealed. Thus, understanding supplements the text: it is active and also creative by nature. Creative understanding continues creativity, and multiplies the artistic wealth of humanity. The co-creativity of those who understand.[41]

Thus, the work is never finished, and so the proliferative and multiplicative potential of the network is necessarily without limit. Throughout, this work has considered the nature of completeness imposed upon "products" of creativity and innovation – through various mechanisms, not least the tropes of "authorship", "originality", and the accompanying attachment to the institutional legitimacy conferred by the supporting industries and "sites" (publishing industries, corporate research, the library, and so on). Such spatial rendition of the time of creativity and innovation has been necessary for the associated rendering of the transactions in creativity within the law. Paradoxically, however, it is this same process that limits the very creativity it is proposed to safeguard: "Only when the position is dogmatically inert is there nothing new revealed in the work."[42]

What Bakhtin's conceptualisation of creativity offers in the present debates in access to knowledge is an opportunity to re-articulate the relationships between individuals, users, producers, and knowledge otherwise than the current conceptualisation of knowledge as objects in which we can contract and transact, according to the dominant intellectual property system. In this way, the relationship of users to knowledge (and its products) must be valued and indeed nurtured, rather than denigrated in a process of the dispossession of users: "Co-experiencing with the author is a sharing of the actively creative position he has assumed in relation

---

40 Latour B ([1993]1996) *Aramis, or The Love of Technology*, Porter C (trans), Cambridge MA, Harvard UP: 23.

41 Bakhtin MM (1986) *Speech Genres and Other Late Essays*, McGee VW (trans), Austin, U of Texas P: 141-42.

42 Bakhtin MM (1986) *Speech Genres and Other Late Essays*, McGee VW (trans), Austin, U of Texas P: 142.

to what is presented, i.e., it is not co-experiencing any longer, but *co-creation*."[43] Arguably, the concept of co-creativity, re-read in the context of networks and actors, provides a genuine basis upon which to characterise the authentic and legitimate stakes of users, the "co-creativity of those who understand".[44]

The action of individuals is also critical to Jean-François Lyotard's consideration of legal and ethico-political capacity. Indeed, in so far as time is perceived by virtue of movement, of the orientation of its effects in space, then the actions of individuals are necessary components of the heterogeneity of the system. Lyotard's notion of capacity recognises selves as capable within an ethico-political network, recalling the earlier consideration of Ricoeur's hermeneutical strategy. As Ricoeur explains:

> By launching the idea of capacity by way of that of being able to say things, we confer on the notion of human action the extension that justifies the characterization of the self as the capable human being recognizing himself in his capacities. Acting will then be the most appropriate concept at the level of the philosophical anthropology that characterizes my approach.[45]

Thus, in this understanding of selfhood, it is not through private, individualised, and solitary notions of property that the self is actualised, but rather, through the dialogue with others, through the "selves" of others. All players within the international network of knowledge are thus capable of action, are thus contributing to the dialogue, are thus taking up space. But it is the discursive ordering of the "law", and of the institution of intellectual property law in the present discussion, that has been shown to be instrumental in the suspension of these relations, in the manifestation of seemingly fixed and stable structures, hierarchical and settled positions. The technology of innovation, the process of creativity, is thus subjected to the narrative necessarily imagined by the intellectual property system in order for it to operate. However, in contemporary networked relations of creativity and access to knowledge, that presupposed stability is open to question, indeed, to dialogue, and to action.

Actor-Network-Theory (ANT)

> The ants are of all the social insects the most successful and perhaps the most extraordinary.[46]

---

43 Bakhtin MM (1990) *Art and Answerability: Early Philosophical Essays by MM Bakhtin*, Holquist M and Liapunov V (eds), Liapunov V (trans), Austin, U of Texas P: 65-66.

44 Bakhtin MM (1986) *Speech Genres and Other Late Essays*, McGee VW (trans), Austin, U of Texas P: 142.

45 Ricoeur P (2005) *The Course of Recognition*, Pellauer D (trans), Cambridge MA, Harvard UP: 94.

46 Huxley J ([1930]1962) *Ants*, London, Grey Arrow: 19.

The dynamics of Actor-Network-Theory (ANT) were considered in the first chapter, but are necessarily re-visited at this stage of the user's re-entry into the system. ANT is useful in the current work of recuperating the user. This is precisely because of the user's alienation by the system and yet its undeniable cooperation as an object (the public) by which to articulate the value of the knowledge objects (through the duration of the market, the time *before* the public). Thus, ANT recovers and records the very action of the user within the system. The user is an actor. In other words, by the very process of dispossession in the current economic model of intellectual property, the user is in fact situated in such a way as to be indispensable to the calculation of the value of that system – albeit in a negative way. The subjectivity of the "creator", the individual unity of the object, the unity of the system – these characters of the model are all entirely reliant upon the action of the user. The dispossession of the user is in itself evidence of its indispensability to the system. But because the system has offered us an abbreviation of the "user", a stereotype of a uniform "public", at this time the concept of the user through intellectual property law is incomplete. Thus, the user must be recuperated by a description of its action: "the task of tracing connections has to be resumed and redirected towards all those objects they had thought reasonable to leave aside."[47]

In this way, the dynamics of the collective, the international "coalition" in its access to knowledge, generate authentic multiplicity, while at the same time, genuine autonomy of the many cultures cooperating in that network. As actors, within Latour's conceptualisation of ANT, the absolutism of the "official culture" that produces a sense of relativism in social interrogations of that officialdom is itself unseated by "the continuity and commensurability of what we call the associations"[48] in ANT. Indeed, this is why Latour favours the term "collective" as replacing that of "society".[49] ANT therefore articulates and describes, rather than merely suggests, the materiality of the connections between users:

> Using a slogan from ANT, you have "to follow the actors themselves," that is try to catch up with their often wild innovations in order to learn from them what the collective existence has become in their hands, which methods they have elaborated to make it fit together, which accounts could best define the new associations that they have been forced to establish. If the sociology of the social works fine with what has been already *assembled*, it does not work so well to connect anew the participants in what is not – *not yet* – a sort of social realm.[50]

Thus, ANT suggests a tool by which the governance and "society" of the collective, the knowledge and creativity network, might be adequately described. It is a sociology of the associations (of the collective) as distinct from an always

47 Latour B (2005) *Reassembling the Social*, Oxford, Oxford UP: 248.
48 Latour B (2005) *Reassembling the Social*, Oxford, Oxford UP: 117.
49 Latour B (2005) *Reassembling the Social*, Oxford, Oxford UP: 75.
50 Latour B (2005) *Reassembling the Social*, Oxford, Oxford UP: 12.

already social.[51] In this way, ANT can be used to describe the actions of users in the present intellectual property system (as in the creative use of trade marks and branding, but in other meaningful ways within the system) that would otherwise not be accountable in conventional assessments. This is precisely because the user, despite the genuine creativity use might generate, has to date not figured as an actor within the system, merely an object. Thus, in clarifying the capabilities of users, it might be possible to review current norms and to account for activity and generation of value in future reform and developments of intellectual property laws.

A System of Co-Actors

Reading this back through the dialogical model of understanding, it is proposed that the stakeholders in the system might more adequately be described as co-actors (users, creators, industry), for which individual actions and roles might be deciphered. In this way, interactions may change but the value to the system of the individual capabilities of the co-actors would be compatible and comparable. Thus, it is possible to draw upon the tools provided by ANT to describe a network system imagined through the dialogical understanding of co-creativity. The re-inscription of the user has, indeed, a scientific basis.

The "crisis" of intellectual property, the stakes of the new "culture wars", the surprises of the "network", cannot be dismissed. The inventiveness of the network and the politics of its connections materialise.

Learning Creatively

> We learn nothing from those who say: "Do as I do." Our only teachers are those who tell us to "do with me".[52]

The model of co-actors has special significance in an area of particular concern in the present debate. That is, learning occurs through the engagement and dialogue with the other: "Learning takes place not in the relation between a representation and an action (reproduction of the Same) but in the relation between a sign and a response (encounter with the Other)."[53] This is the passage to selfhood and is the way of the apprenticeship to knowledge. To learn is not a passive imitation; that would be merely dogmatism, and "the dogmatist gains nothing; he cannot be enriched".[54] Rather, creative understanding comes from an active cooperation and co-experience

---

51 Latour B (2005) *Reassembling the Social*, Oxford, Oxford UP: 68.

52 Deleuze G ([1968]1994) *Difference and Repetition*, Patton P (trans), New York, Columbia UP: 23.

53 Deleuze G ([1968]1994) *Difference and Repetition*, Patton P (trans), New York, Columbia UP: 22.

54 Bakhtin MM (1986) *Speech Genres and Other Late Essays*, McGee VW (trans), Austin, U of Texas P: 142.

with the text. Thus, it is only through the free (as in freedom) access to knowledge that "the co-creativity of those who understand"[55] can be generated in what would be a genuinely productive society, with the abundant profits of "increasing returns to scale". As an economic model, surely this is the most viable for the generation of cultural capital and wealth. Learning and teaching is an active co-creation: "We learn nothing from those who say: 'Do as I do.' Our only teachers are those who tell us to 'do with me,' and are able to emit signs to be developed in heterogeneity rather than propose gestures for us to reproduce."[56]

Recalling the "*do as I do*" in the history of art education, the dynamics of teaching in art (as considered in Chapter 2), the education of artists is through the imitation and thus affirmation of the original. On the surface, this teaching proposes to create nothing, sow nothing. By way of contrast, cultural expression through interconnected networks (whether digital or through the other "digital" means of networked interactions) proceeds by way of "*do with me*". In the specific example of digital technology, Castells explains:

> The Internet offers the possibility of collective, interactive, joint artistic creation, through groupware practices that allow people at a distance to paint, sculpt, design, compose, and produce together, in interaction, and often in contradiction. In most instances, these co-artists do not know each other, except in their art – and this is all that matters. Open source art is the new frontier of artistic creation.[57]

In this way, teaching and learning present a critical example of the dialogical relationship and of co-creativity as producing anew. Indeed, the "sowing" of teaching is arguably the invaluable germination of the network and the fundamental principle of full and meaningful participation in cultural life.

Conclusion

> There is neither a first nor a last word and there are no limits to the dialogic context.[58]

Throughout this work the communicative nature of meaning and cultural activity has been emphasised and the role of the user in the expression of culture has emerged as not merely incidental but arguably essential. Through the collective activity of creating, reviewing, and dealing with cultural resources, the sense of self-creation is no longer limited to the Romantic notion of the isolated and gifted

55 Bakhtin MM (1986) *Speech Genres and Other Late Essays*, McGee VW (trans), Austin, U of Texas P: 142.

56 Deleuze G ([1968]1994) *Difference and Repetition*, Patton P (trans), New York, Columbia UP: 23.

57 Castells M (2002) *The Internet Galaxy: Reflections on the Internet, Business, and Society*, Oxford, Oxford UP: 199.

58 Bakhtin MM (1986) *Speech Genres and Other Late Essays*, McGee VW (trans), Austin, U of Texas P: 170.

individual. In expressing ideas it is the very form of those ideas that is itself part of that communicative experience. In other words, the goods comprising intellectual property are not transacted in pure exchanges, but must be understood in terms of the political and ideological context of creativity, knowledge diversity, and the rich cultural and critical progress of a networked society. For intellectual property, the basic principle of the need to "express" the "idea" (whether through the copyright work, the patent specification, the registered trade mark, the design drawings, and so on) is built upon the notion that the idea cannot exist for the purposes of protection independently of that expression. Arguably, in a networked society, the expression can no longer exist independently of the cultural and ideological experience of knowledge creation. It is part of the cultural practice of the society. Therefore, the commercial system of intellectual property necessarily must come to grips with the networking of information and the critical nature of access to the means of communication and knowledge development for all citizens. In that the language for expression is shared, our individual subjectivity is built upon the collective subjectivity of that shared meaning. It is built on the creation of selves.

It is not just the idea. It is not just the form. It is the experience, the sensation, the creations of cultures.

After Word

> Even the story I am in the process of narrating reveals that any narrative whatsoever begins in the middle of things and that its so-called "end" is an arbitrary cut in the infinite sequence of data.[1]

In *Aramis, or The Love of Technology*, Bruno Latour renders clear much of what has been traced throughout the present work. Narrated by a polyphony of voices, no authorial source takes precedence in the story. Rather, what occurs is a performance of the collaborative and incremental progress of any technological innovation, situated as it is in a field of cultural production:

> Although this variability can never be eliminated, its scope can nevertheless be limited. Here is where law comes into its own. No technology without rules, without signatures, without bureaucracies and stamps. Law itself is no different from the world of technologies: it is the set of the modest technologies of writing, registering, verifying, authenticating that makes it possible to line up people and statements. It is a world of flexible technologies coming to the aid of even more flexible technologies of interest in order to allow slightly more solid technologies to harden a bit. A signature on a contract, an endorsement, an agreement stabilizes the relative size of the actors by lending to the provisional definition of alliances the assistance of the law, a law whose weight is enormous because it is entirely formal and because it applies equally to everyone.[2]

Latour continues, describing how the iterability of signatures lends permanence to the players, but "That will never be enough, for signed documents can turn back into scraps of paper".[3] Similarly while patents appear to stabilise the identity of the technology itself, an identity that is now "a plan protected by law", they say nothing of what the technology is to become,[4] suggesting the potential transformations through its use and re-use, and the "innovation" and collaboration of its users. Indeed, Latour cautions: "Woe betide those who trust the law alone to shelter their projects from random hazards."[5] Thus, the law pretends stability, and "a project becomes weightier, like a little sailboat whose hull has been ballasted with some heavy metal.

---

1 Lyotard J-F (1988) *Peregrinations: Law, Form, Event*, New York, Columbia UP: 2.

2 Latour B ([1993]1996) *Aramis, or The Love of Technology*, Porter C (trans), Cambridge MA, Harvard UP: 45.

3 Latour B ([1993]1996) *Aramis, or The Love of Technology*, Porter C (trans), Cambridge MA, Harvard UP: 45.

4 Latour B ([1993]1996) *Aramis, or The Love of Technology*, Porter C (trans), Cambridge MA, Harvard UP: 46.

5 Latour B ([1993]1996) *Aramis, or The Love of Technology*, Porter C (trans), Cambridge MA, Harvard UP: 46.

It can still be overturned, but one would have to work *a little harder* to prevent it from righting itself, from returning to its former position."[6]

It is time for us all to work *a little harder*.

6 Latour B ([1993]1996) *Aramis, or The Love of Technology*, Porter C (trans), Cambridge MA, Harvard UP: 45.

Resources

Aigrain P (2006) "Capabilities in the Information Era". Presentation. TACD Conference. The Politics and Ideology of Intellectual Property. Brussels. 20 March.

Alexander M et al (2003) *The Role of Registers and Databases in the Protection of Traditional Knowledge: A Comparative Analysis*. Report. Tokyo, UNU-IAS.

Ansell-Pearson K (1999) *Germinal Life: The Difference and Repetition of Deleuze*, London, Routledge.

Appadurai A (1996) *Modernity at Large: Cultural Dimensions of Globalization*, Minneapolis, U of Minnesota P.

Bacon-Smith C (1992) *Enterprising Women: Television Fandom and the Creation of Popular Myth*, Philadelphia, U of Pennsylvania P.

Bailey C (1996) "Virtual Skin: Articulating Race in Cyberspace", in Moser MA and MacLeod D (eds) *Immersed in Technology: Art and Virtual Environments*, Cambridge MA, MIT P.

Bakhtin MM ([1968]1984) *Rabelais and His World*, Iswolsky H (trans), Bloomington, Indiana UP.

Bakhtin MM (1981) *The Dialogic Imagination*, Emerson C and Holquist M (trans), Austin, U of Texas P.

Bakhtin MM (1984) *Problems of Dostoevsky's Poetics*, Emerson C (ed and trans), Booth WC (intro), Minneapolis, U of Minnesota P.

Bakhtin MM (1986) *Speech Genres and Other Late Essays*, McGee VW (trans), Austin, U of Texas P.

Bakhtin MM (1990) *Art and Answerability: Early Philosophical Essays by MM Bakhtin*, Holquist M and Liapunov V (eds), Liapunov V (trans), Austin, U of Texas P.

Barney D (2004) *The Network Society*, Cambridge, Polity.

Barry A (1995) "Reporting and Visualising", in Jenks C (ed), *Visual Culture*, London, Routledge.

Barthes R ([1957]1990) *Mythologies*, Lavers A (trans), New York, Noonday P.

Barthes R (1977) "The Photographic Message", in *Image Music Text*, Heath S (trans), London, Fontana.

Barthes R (1977) *Image Music Text*, Heath S (trans), London, Fontana.

BBC News, "Newsreader Loses Privacy Bid", 31 July 2001, http://news.bbc.co.uk/1/hi/ uk/1466459.stm.

Beck U (1992) *Risk Society: Towards a New Modernity*, Ritter M (trans), London, SAGE.

Beck U (1999) *World Risk Society*, Camiller P (trans), Cambridge, Polity.

Beck U (2000) *What is Globalization?* Camiller P (trans), Cambridge, Polity.

Benjamin W ([1955]1970) *Illuminations*, Arendt H (ed and intro), Zohn H (trans), London, Fontana.

Benkler Y (2006) *The Wealth of Networks: How Social Production Transforms Markets and Freedom*, New Haven, Yale UP.

Bently L and Sherman B (2004) *Intellectual Property Law*, 2nd ed, Oxford, Oxford UP.

Bergson H ([1888]2001) *Time and Free Will: An Essay on the Immediate Data of Consciousness*, Pogson FL (trans), 3rd ed (1913), Mineola NY, Dover.

Bergson H ([1911]1944) *Creative Evolution*, Mitchell A (trans), New York, Random House.

Bergson H ([1922]1999) *Duration and Simultaneity: Bergson and the Einsteinian Universe*, Lewis M and Durie R (trans), Manchester, Clinamen.

Beverley-Smith H (2002) *The Commercial Appropriation of Personality*, Cambridge, Cambridge UP.

Biggs S and Leach J (2004) *Autopoeisis: Novelty, Meaning and Value*, London, Artswords P.

Bohm D (1998) *On Creativity*, London, Routledge.

Bois Y-A (1997) "Very Slow", in Bois Y-A and Krauss R *Formless: A User's Guide*, New York, Zone.

Boltanski L and Chiapello E ([1999]2005) *The New Spirit of Capitalism*, Elliott G (trans), New York, WW Norton & Co.

Bolton R (ed) (1992) *Culture Wars: Documents from the Recent Controversies in the Arts*, New York, The New Press.

Bonny S (2004) "Factors Explaining Opposition to GMOs in France and the Rest of Europe", in Evenson RE and Santaniello V (eds) *Consumer Acceptance of Genetically Modified Foods*, Wallingford, CABI.

Borges JL (1967) "The Aleph", in *Jorge Luis Borges: A Personal Anthology*, Kerrigan A (ed), New York, Grove.

Bourdieu P ([1972]1977) *Outline of a Theory of Practice*, Nice R (trans) Cambridge, Cambridge UP.

Bourdieu P ([1979]1986) *Distinction: A Social Critique of the Judgement of Taste*, Nice R (trans), London, Routledge.

Bourdieu P ([1984]1993) *Sociology in Question*, Nice R (trans), London, SAGE.

Bourdieu P (1990) *In Other Words: Essays Towards a Reflexive Sociology*, Adamson M (trans), Stanford, Stanford UP.

Bourdieu P (1993) *The Field of Cultural Production: Essays on Art and Literature*, Johnson R (ed), Cambridge, Polity.

Boyle J (2005) "More Rights are Wrong For Webcasters", *Financial Times*, 26 September.

Boyle J (2005) Launch of the Adelphi Charter on Creativity, Innovation and Intellectual Property. Royal Society for the Encouragement of Arts, Manufactures and Commerce (RSA). London. 13 October.

Brush SB (2003) "The Demise of 'Common Heritage' and Protection for Traditional Agricultural Knowledge". Conference Paper. Biodiversity, Biotechnology and the Protection of Traditional Knowledge. St Louis MO, 4-5 April.

Burkhart G (2006) "Trade marks are 'possessions' – but applications are not (yet)", 1(4) *Journal of Intellectual Property Law and Practice* 240.

Butler J (1990) *Gender Trouble: Feminism and the Subversion of Identity*, New York, Routledge.

Butler J (1993) *Bodies that Matter: On the Discursive Limits of "Sex"*, New York, Routledge.

Butler J (2000) *Antigone's Claim: Kinship Between Life and Death*, New York, Columbia UP.

Cain B (2003) *Legal Aspects of Gene Technology*, London, Sweet & Maxwell.

Castells M (1997) *The Information Age: Economy, Society and Culture. Volume II: The Power of Identity*, Oxford, Blackwell.

Castells M (2000) *The Information Age: Economy, Society and Culture. Volume I: The Rise of the Network Society*, 2nd ed, Oxford, Blackwell.

Castells M (2000) *The Information Age: Economy, Society and Culture. Volume III: End of Millennium*. 2nd ed. Oxford, Blackwell.

Castells M (2002) *The Internet Galaxy: Reflections on the Internet, Business, and Society*, Oxford, Oxford UP.

Castells M and Ince M (2003) *Conversations with Manuel Castells*, Cambridge, Polity.

Chander A and Sunder M (2004) "The Romance of the Public Domain", 92 *California Law Review* 1331.

Chapman AR (2001) "Approaching Intellectual Property as a Human Right", 35(3) *Copyright Bulletin* 4.

CIPR (2002) Commission on Intellectual Property Rights. *Integrating Intellectual Property Rights and Development Policy*, London.

Clifford J (1988) *The Predicament of Culture: Twentieth-Century Ethnograph, Literature, and Art*, Cambridge MA, Harvard UP.

Clifford J (2003) *On the Edges of Anthropology: Interviews*, Chicago, Prickly Paradigm P.

Coombe R (1996) "Left Out on the Information Highway", 75 *Oregon Law Review* 237.

Coombe R (1998) *The Cultural Life of Intellectual Properties: Authorship, Appropriation, and the Law*, Durham, Duke UP.

Cooter R and Ulen T (2004) *Law and Economics*, 4th ed, Boston MA, Addison Wesley.

Cornish W (2002) "The Author as Risk-Sharer", 26 *Columbia (VLA) Journal of Law and the Arts* 1.

Cuddon JA (1999) *Dictionary of Literary Terms and Literary Theory*, London, Penguin.

Davis J (2000) "The King is Dead: Long Live the King", *Cambridge Law Journal* 33.

De Certeau M (1984) *The Practice of Everyday Life*, Rendall S (trans), Berkeley, U of California P.

De Landa M (2000) *A Thousand Years of Nonlinear History*, New York, Zone.

De Landa M (2002) *Intensive Science and Virtual Philosophy*, New York, Continuum.

Deleuze G ([1968]1994) *Difference and Repetition*, Patton P (trans), New York, Columbia UP.

Deleuze G and Guattari F ([1972]1983) *Anti-Oedipus: Capitalism and Schizophrenia*, Hurley R et al (trans), Minneapolis, U of Minnesota P.

Deleuze G and Guattari F ([1975]1986) *Kafka: Toward a Minor Literature*, Polan D (trans), Minneapolis, U of Minnesota P.

Deleuze G and Guattari F ([1980]1987) *A Thousand Plateaus: Capitalism and Schizophrenia*, Massumi B (trans), Minneapolis, U of Minnesota P.

Deleuze G and Guattari F ([1991]1994) *What is Philosophy?* Burchell G and Tomlinson H (trans), London, Verso.

Derrida J ([1972]1981) *Dissemination*, Johnson B (trans), Chicago, U of Chicago P.

Dienst R (1994) *Still Life in Real Time: Theory After Television*, Durham, Duke UP.

Downes D (1997) "Using Intellectual Property as a Tool to Protect Traditional Knowledge: Recommendations for Next Steps". CIEL Discussion Paper. November.

Drahos P (1996) *A Philosophy of Intellectual Property*, Aldershot, Dartmouth.

Drahos P and Braithwaite J (2002) *Information Feudalism: Who Owns the Knowledge Economy?* London, Earthscan.

Dutfield G (2002) "Protecting Traditional Knowledge and Folklore: A Review of Progress in Diplomacy and Policy Formulation". UNCTAD/ICTSD Capacity Building Project on Intellectual Property Rights and Sustainable Development. October.

Dutfield G (2003) *Intellectual Property Rights and the Life Science Industries: A Twentieth Century History*, Aldershot, Ashgate.

Eco U (1976) *A Theory of Semiotics*, Bloomington, Indiana UP.

Eco U (1989) *The Open Work*, A Cancogni (trans), London, Hutchinson Radius.

Esrock EJ (1994) *The Reader's Eye: Visual Imaging as Reader Response*, Baltimore, Johns Hopkins UP.

Fish S (1980) *Is There a Text in This Class? The Authority of Interpretive Communities*, London, Harvard UP.

Fish S (1989) *Doing What Comes Naturally: Change, Rhetoric, and the Practice of Theory in Literary and Legal Studies*, Oxford, Clarendon P.

Foster H (1985) *Recodings: Art, Spectacle, Cultural Politics*, Seattle, Bay P.

Foucault M (1979) "What is an Author?", in Harari JV (ed) *Textual Strategies: Perspectives in Post-Structuralist Criticism*, Ithaca, Cornell UP.

Fox M et al (2005) "Creative Commons: An Alternative, Web-Based Copyright System", 16(5) *Entertainment Law Review* 111.

Frazer J ([1922]1993) *The Golden Bough: A Study of Magic and Religion*, Ware, Hertfordshire, Wordsworth Editions.
Frosh P (2003) *The Image Factory: Consumer Culture, Photography and the Visual Content Industry*, Oxford, Berg.
Frow J (1995) *Cultural Studies and Cultural Value*, Oxford, Clarendon P.
Galloway AR (2004) *Protocol: How Control Exists After Decentralization*, Cambridge MA, MIT P.
Gervais D (2001) "Traditional Knowledge: A Challenge to the International Intellectual Property System". Fordham University Conference on International Intellectual Property Law & Policy. New York City, 20 April.
Gervais D (2003) *The TRIPS Agreement: Drafting History and Analysis*, 2nd ed, London, Sweet & Maxwell.
Gibson J (2004) "Intellectual Property Systems, Traditional Knowledge, and the Legal Authority of Community", 26(7) *European Intellectual Property Review* 280.
Gibson J (2005) *Community Resources: Intellectual Property, International Trade and Protection of Traditional Knowledge*, Aldershot, Ashgate.
Gibson J (forthcoming) "Audiences in Tradition: Traditional Knowledge and the Public Domain", in MacQueen H and Waelde C (eds) *Intellectual Property: The Many Faces of the Public Domain*, Cheltenham, Edward Elgar.
Ginsburg J (2000) "International Copyright: From a 'Bundle' of National Copyright Law to a Supranational Code?", 47 *Journal of the Copyright Society* 265.
Gray S (1996) "Squatting in Red Dust: Non-Aboriginal Law's Construction of the 'Traditional' Aboriginal Artist", 14(2) *Law in Context*.
Gross L (2003) "Privacy and Spectacle: The Reversible Panopticon and Media-Saturated Society", in Gross L et al (eds) *Image Ethics in the Digital Age*, Minneapolis, U of Minnesota P.
Gross L et al (eds) (2003) *Image Ethics in the Digital Age*, Minneapolis, U of Minnesota P.
Guadamuz González A (2004) "Viral Contracts or Unenforceable Documents? Contractual Validity of Copyleft Licences", 26(8) *European Intellectual Property Review* 331.
Habermas J ([1973]1975) *Legitimation Crisis*, McCarthy T (trans), Boston, Beacon P.
Haineault D-L and Roy J-Y ([1984]1993) *Unconscious for Sale: Advertising Psychoanalysis and the Public*, Lockhart K and Kerslake B (trans), Minneapolis, U of Minnesota P.
Halpern SW (2003) "Copyright Law and the Challenge of Digital Technology", in Gross L et al (eds) *Image Ethics in the Digital Age*, Minneapolis, U of Minnesota P.
Hannay A (2005) *On the Public*, London, Routledge.
Haraway D (1991) *Simians, Cyborgs, and Women: The Reinvention of Nature*, London, Free Association Books.

Haraway D (1992) "The Promises of Monsters: A Regenerative Politics for Inappropriate/d Others", in L Grossberg et al (eds) *Cultural Studies*, New York, Routledge.

Hardt M and Negri A (2000) *Empire*, Cambridge MA, Harvard UP.

Harrison R et al (ed) *The Ethical Consumer*, London, SAGE.

Hart S and Murphy J (eds) (1998) *Brands: The New Wealth Creators*, Basingstoke, Palgrave.

Heath J and Potter A (2005) *The Rebel Sell: How the Counterculture Became Consumer Culture*, Chichester, Capstone.

Heelas P (2002) "Work Ethics, Soft Capitalism and the 'Turn to Life'", in Du Gay P and Pryke M (eds), *Cultural Economy*, London, SAGE.

Hegel GWF ([1807]1977) *Phenomenology of Spirit*, Miller AV (trans), Oxford, Oxford UP.

Hegel GWF ([1821]1991) *Elements of the Philosophy of Right*, Wood AW (ed), Nisbet HB (trans), Cambridge, Cambridge UP.

Heidegger M (1971) *Poetry, Language, Thought*, Hofstadter A (trans), New York, Harper & Row.

Hold DB (2004) *How Brands Become Icons: The Principles of Cultural Branding*, Boston, Harvard Business School P.

Huxley J ([1930]1962) *Ants*, London, Grey Arrow.

IISD (2003) "Traditional Knowledge and Patentability". IISD Trade and Development Brief. No 7. Summer.

Ind N (ed) (2005) *Beyond Branding: How the New Values of Transparency and Integrity are Changing the World of Brands*, London, Kogan Page.

Indigenous World Association and Indigenous Media Network (2005) Joint Statement. Commission on Human Rights, Sub-Commission on the Promotion and Protection of Human Rights, Working Group on Indigenous Populations. 23rd Session, 18-22 July 2005. Review of Developments Pertaining to the Promotion and Protection of the Rights of Indigenous Peoples, Including Their Human Rights and Fundamental Freedoms: Principal Theme, "Indigenous Peoples and the International and Domestic Protection of Traditional Knowledge". Item 4(b) of the provisional agenda. 13 July 2005. E/CN.4/Sub.2/AC.4/2005/CRP.

Iser W (1974) *The Implied Reader: Patterns of Communication in Prose Fiction from Bunyan to Beckett*, Baltimore, Johns Hopkins UP.

Iser W (1989) *Prospecting: From Reader Response to Literary Anthropology*, Baltimore, Johns Hopkins UP.

Jabès E ([1984]1987) *The Book of Dialogue*, Waldrop R (trans), Middletown, Wesleyan UP.

Jameson F (1991) *Postmodernism, or, the Logic of Late Capitalism*, London, Verso.

Jauss HR (1982) *Toward an Aesthetic of Reception*, T Bahti (trans), De Man P (Intro), Minneapolis, U of Minnesota P.

Jauss HR ([1982]1989) *Question and Answer: Forms of Dialogic Understanding*, Hays M (trans and ed), Minneapolis, U of Minnesota P.

Jayaraman KS (2002) "Biopiracy Fears Cloud Indian Database", *Science and Development Network*. 5 December.

Jenkins H (1988) "Star Trek Rerun, Reread, Rewritten: Fan Writing as Textual Poaching", 5 *Critical Studies in Mass Communications* 85.

Jenkins H (1992) *Textual Poachers: Television Fans and Participatory Culture*, New York, Routledge.

Jenks C (2005) *Culture*, 2nd ed, London, Routledge.

Jennings S (2005) "The Corporation". Seminar. QMIPRI, 16 June.

Joas H ([1992]1996) *The Creativity of Action*, Gaines J and Keast P (trans), Cambridge, Polity.

Jones P (2003) "The GPL is a License, Not a Contract", *LWN.net*, 3 December.

Kafka F ([1933-1954]1992) "A Report to an Academy", *The Complete Short Stories of Franz Kafka*, Glatzer NN (ed), London, Minerva.

Kaplinsky J (2003) "Protecting Superstition", *Spiked*, 20 May.

Kaufman PB (2005) *Marketing Culture in the Digital Age: A Report on New Business Collaborations Between Libraries, Museums, Archives and Commercial Companies*. Report. Intelligent Television. 25 August.

Kelly K (1994) *Out of Control: The New Biology of Machines*, London, Fourth Estate.

Krauss RE (1986) *The Originality of the Avant-Garde and Other Modernist Myths*, Cambridge MA, MIT P.

Kretschmer M (2005) "Artists' earnings and copyright: A review of British and German music industry data in the context of digital technologies", *First Monday*, volume 10, number 1 (January).

Kwon M (2002) *One Place After Another: Site-Specific Art and Locational Identity*, Cambridge MA, MIT.

Landes WM and Posner RA (2003) "Indefinitely Renewable Copyright", 70 *University of Chicago Law Review* 471.

Landes WM and Posner RA (2003) *The Economic Structure of Intellectual Property Law*, Cambridge MA, Harvard UP.

Lash S (2002) *Critique of Information*, London, SAGE.

Latour B (1987) *Science in Action: How to Follow Scientists and Engineers Through Society*, Cambridge MA, Harvard UP.

Latour B ([1991]1993) *We Have Never Been Modern*, Porter C (trans), New York, Harvester Wheatsheaf.

Latour B ([1993]1996) *Aramis, or The Love of Technology*, Porter C (trans), Cambridge MA, Harvard UP.

Latour B (2004) *Politics of Nature: How to Bring the Sciences into Democracy*, Porter C (trans), Cambridge MA, Harvard UP.

Latour B (2005) *Reassembling the Social*, Oxford, Oxford UP.

Latour B and Woolgar S ([1979]1986) *Laboratory Life: The Construction of Scientific Facts*, Princeton, Princeton UP.

Lefebvre H ([1974]1991) *The Production of Space*, Nicholson-Smith D (trans), Oxford, Blackwell.

Lefebvre H (1996) *Writings on Cities*, Kofman E and Lebas E (trans and eds), Oxford, Blackwell.

Lessig L (1999) *Code and Other Laws of Cyberspace*, New York, Basic Books.

Levin DM (ed) (1993) *Modernity and the Hegemony of Vision*, Berkeley, U of California P.

Lewinski, S von (2001) "The WIPO Diplomatic Conference on Audio-Visual Performances: A First Resume", 23(7) *European Intellectual Property Review* 333.

Lopez R (1999) "Tribes seek trademark protection for sacred symbols", *Revista Magazine*, 9 July.

Lotringer S and Virilio P (2005) *The Accident of Art*, Taormina M (trans), New York, Semiotext(e).

Lury C (1993) *Cultural Rights: Technology, Legality and Personality*, London, Routledge.

Lury C (2002) "Portrait of the Artist as a Brand", in McClean D and Schubert K (eds) *Dear Images: Art, Copyright and Culture*, London, ICA.

Lury C (2004) *Brands: The Logos of the Global Economy*, London, Routledge.

Lyotard J-F ([1979]1984) *The Postmodern Condition: A Report on Knowledge*, Bennington G and Massumi B (trans), Minneapolis, U of Minnesota P.

Lyotard J-F ([1986]1992) *The Postmodern Explained to Children: Correspondence 1982-1985*, Pefanis J and Thomas M (eds), Barry D et al (trans), Sydney, Power Publications.

Lyotard J-F (1988) *Peregrinations: Law, Form, Event*, New York, Columbia UP.

MacDonald P (1998) "Reconceptualising Stardom", supplementary chapter in Dyer R ([1979]1998) *Stars*, New ed, London, BFI Publishing.

Macherey P ([1966]1978) *A Theory of Literary Production*, Wall G (trans), London, Routledge.

Macmillan F (2002) "The Cruel ©: Copyright and Film", 24(10) *European Intellectual Property Review* 483.

Macmillan F (2003) "Copyright's Commodification of Creativity", 2 *ICFAI Journal of Intellectual Property Rights* 53.

Maniatis S (2002) "Trade Mark Rights – A Justification Based on Property", *Intellectual Property Quarterly* 123.

Marchant R (2005) Interview with Barbara Cookson. QMIPRI. London. 28 November.

Masolo DA (1994) *African Philosophy in Search of Identity*, Bloomington, Indiana UP.

May C (2002) *The Information Society: A Sceptical View*, Cambridge, Polity.

Monod J ([1970]1972) *Chance and Necessity: An Essay on the Natural Philosophy of Modern Biology*, Wainhouse A (trans), London, Collins.

Morgan O (2003) "The New Zealand Trade Marks Act: No Place for Offence", Occasional Paper No 2/03. Intellectual Property Institute of Australia, University of Melbourne.

Morson GS and Emerson C (1990) *Mikhail Bakhtin: Creation of a Prosaics*, Stanford, Stanford UP.

Mouffe C (2000) *The Democratic Paradox*, London, Verso.

Mudimbe VY (1988) *The Invention of Africa*, Bloomington, Indiana UP.

Negri A (2004) *The Politics of Subversion: A Manifesto for the Twenty-First Century*, New ed, Cambridge, Polity.

Negus K and Pickering M (2004) *Creativity, Communication and Cultural Value*, London, SAGE.

New W (2005) "Nations Clash on Future of WIPO Development Agenda", *IP-Watch*, 11 April.

Nwokeabia H (2001) "Why Industrial Revolution Missed Africa: A 'Traditional Knowledge' Perspective". Economic Commission for Africa. ECA/ESPD/WPS/01/02.

Orchard R (2006) "The trade in fakes is linked to terrorism and gun-running". Letter. *Financial Times*. 27 January: 10.

Parsons RD (2001) Statement. Online Entertainment and Copyright Law: Coming Soon to a Digital Device Near You. Senate Hearing 107-283, 3 April. http://gopher.quux.org: 70/Government/USA/Law/IP/napster-hearing.txt.

Patton P (1996) "Introduction", in Patton P (ed) *Deleuze: A Critical Reader*, Oxford, Blackwell.

Peat FD (2000) *The Blackwinged Night: Creativity in Nature and Mind*, Cambridge MA, Perseus.

Plant A (1934) "The Economic Theory Concerning Patents for Invention", 1 *Economica* 30.

Plato (1875) "Cratylus", *The Dialogues of Plato: Vol II*, Oxford, Clarendon P.

Pollock R (2006) "IP and the Knowledge Commons: Political Parties". Panel 4. The Politics and Ideology of Intellectual Property. Trans Atlantic Consumer Dialogue (TACD) Conference. 20 March.

Pope R (2005) *Creativity: Theory, History, Practice*, London, Routledge.

Prosser WL (1960) "Privacy", 48 *California Law Review* 383.

Quah D (2006) Panel Presentation – Patents. Gowers Review of Intellectual Property. London. Department of Trade and Industry Conference Centre. 2 March.

RAIN (2003) *Shifting Map: Artists' Platforms and Strategies for Cultural Diversity*, Rotterdam, NAi Publications 23.

Ricoeur P (1984) *Time and Narrative: Volume 1*, McLaughlin K and Pellauer D (trans), Chicago, U of Chicago P.

Ricoeur P (1985) *Time and Narrative: Volume 2*, McLaughlin K and Pellauer D (trans), Chicago, U of Chicago P.

Ricoeur P (1988) *Time and Narrative: Volume 3*, McLaughlin K and Pellauer D (trans), Chicago, U of Chicago P.

Ricoeur P ([1990]1992) *Oneself as Another*, Blamey K (trans), Chicago, U of Chicago P.

Ricoeur P ([1995]1998) *Critique and Conviction: Conversations with François Azouvi and Marc de Launay*, Blamey K (trans), Cambridge, Polity.

Ricoeur P ([1995]2000) *The Just*, Pellauer D (trans), Chicago, U of Chicago P.
Ricoeur (2005) *The Course of Recognition*, Pellauer D (trans), Cambridge MA, Harvard UP.
Ringer B (1968) "The Role of the United States in International Copyright – Past, Present, and Future", 56 *Georgetown Law Journal* 1050.
Robertson G and Nicol A (2002) *Media Law*, 4th ed, London, Sweet & Maxwell.
Rogers E (1947) "The Social Value of Trade Marks and Brand", 37 *TM Rep* 249.
Roughton A et al (eds) (2005) *The Modern Law of Patents*, London, LexisNexis.
Ruiz M (2002) *The International Debate on Traditional Knowledge as Prior Art in the Patent System: Issues and Options for Developing Countries*. Trade-Related Agenda, Development and Equity (TRADE) Occasional Papers. Paper No 9. Geneva, South Centre.
Rushdie S (1991) *Imaginary Homelands*, London, Penguin.
Sainsbury of Turville, Lord (2005) Speech. Creative Economy Conference. London. 7 October.
Schechter F (1926) "The Rational Basis of Trademark Protection", 40 *Harvard Law Review* 813.
Schwartz H (1996) *The Culture of the Copy: Striking Likenesses, Unreasonable Facsimiles*, New York, Zone.
Seeger A (2004) "The Selective Protection of Musical Ideas: The 'Creations' and the Dispossessed", in Verdery K and Humphrey C (eds), *Property in Question: Value Transformation in the Global Economy*, Oxford, Berg.
Selby N (2004) "Easy-To-Use Linux Distributions Make European Businesses Switch", 22 August. http://www.nickselby.com/articles/technology/easy-linux.htm.
Sell SK (1999) "Multinational corporations as agents of change: the globalization of intellectual property rights", in Cutler AC et al (eds), *Private Authority and International Affairs*, Albany, SUNY P.
Sell SK (2003) *Private Power, Public Law: The Globalization of Intellectual Property Rights*, Cambridge, Cambridge UP.
Sen N (2002) "TKDL: A Safeguard for Indian Traditional Knowledge", 82(9) *Current Science* 1070.
Serres M (1991) *The Troubadour of Knowledge*, Glaser SF and Paulson W (trans), Ann Arbor, U of Michigan P.
Sharma D (2002) "Digital Library Another Tool for Biopiracy", *Mindfully.org*. 29 May.
Sherman B and Bently L (1999) *The Making of Modern Intellectual Property Law*, Cambridge, Cambridge UP.
Simpson T (1997) *Indigenous Heritage and Self-Determination: The Cultural and Intellectual Property Rights of Indigenous Peoples*, Copenhagen, IWGIA.
Spigel L (1992) *Make Room for TV: Television and the Family Ideal in Postwar America*, Chicago, Chicago UP.
Staiger J (ed) (1995) *The Studio System*, New Brunswick, Rutgers UP.

Stallabrass J (2003) *Internet Art: The Online Clash of Culture and Commerce*, London, Tate.

Stallman R ([1996]2006) "Confusing Words and Phrases that are Worth Avoiding". http://www.gnu.org/philosophy/words-to-avoid.html#IntellectualProperty.

Steele J (2004) *Risks and Legal Theory*, Oxford, Hart Publishing.

Sterling JAL (2004) "Space Law". British Literary and Artistic Copyright Association (BLACA). Presentation. 11 November.

Strathern M (1999) *Property, Substance and Effect: Anthropological Essays on Persons and Things*, London, The Athlone P.

Sulston, Sir J (2005) Launch of the Adelphi Charter. Royal Society for the Encouragement of Arts, Manufactures and Commerce (RSA). London. 13 October.

Tauber A (1997) *The Immune Self: Theory or Metaphor?* Cambridge, Cambridge UP.

Tauli-Corpuz V (2005) "Biodiversity, Traditional Knowledge and Rights of Indigenous Peoples". IPRs Series No 5. International Workshop on Traditional Knowledge. 21-23 September.

Taussig M (1993) *Mimesis and Alterity: A Particular History of the Senses*, New York, Routledge.

Taylor M (2005) "'Open Source' and 'Free' Software", 11(3) *Computer and Telecommunications Law Review* 97.

Tugendhat M and Christie I (eds) (2002) *The Law of Privacy and the Media*, Oxford, Oxford UP.

Tulalip Tribes (2003) Statement by the Tulalip Tribes of Washington on Folklore, Indigenous Knowledge, and the Public Domain. 9 July. WIPO Intergovernmental Committee on Intellectual Property and Genetic Resources, Traditional Knowledge and Folklore. Fifth Session. Geneva, 5-17 July.

Tuomi I (2002) *Networks of Innovation: Change and Meaning in the Age of the Internet*, Oxford, Oxford UP.

Twitchell JB (2004) *Branded Nation: The Marketing of Megachurch, College, Inc., and Museumworld*, New York, Simon & Schuster.

UNCTAD/ICTSD (2003) "Intellectual Property Rights: Implications for Development". Policy Discussion Paper. UNCTAD/ICTSD Capacity Building Project on Intellectual Property Rights and Sustainable Development. August.

UNDP (2004) *Cultural Liberty in Today's Diverse World*. Human Development Report. New York.

Urry J (2000) *Sociology Beyond Societies: Mobilities for the Twenty-First Century*, London, Routledge.

Urry J (2003) *Global Complexity*, Cambridge, Polity.

Vaver D (1997) *Intellectual Property Law: Copyright, Patents, Trademarks*, Toronto, Irwin Law.

Vidal J (1998) *McLibel: Burger Culture on Trial*, New York, New Press.

Virilio P ([1977]1986) *Speed and Politics: An Essay on Dromology*, Polizzotti M (trans), New York, Semiotext(e).

Virilio P (1994) *The Vision Machine*, London, BFI.

Wagner R (1981) *The Invention of Culture*, Rev ed, Chicago, U of Chicago P.

Waldrop M (1994) *Complexity*, London, Penguin.

Wallace AFC ([1982]2003) *The Social Context of Innovation: Bureaucrats, Families, and Heroes in the Early Industrial Revolution, As Foreseen in Bacon's New Atlantis*, Lincoln, U of Nebraska P.

Warner M (2005) *Publics and Counterpublics*, New York, Zone.

Weber M ([1904-5]2002) *The Protestant Ethic and the Spirit of Capitalism*, Kalberg S (trans), Oxford, Blackwell.

Westkamp G (forthcoming) "Information Access, *Lex Digitalis* and Fundamental Rights in Modern Copyright Law", in Macmillan F (ed) *New Directions in Copyright: Volume IV*, Cheltenham, Edward Elgar.

Wiener N ([1954]1993) *Invention: The Care and Feeding of Ideas*, Cambridge MA, MIT P.

Williams R (1974) *Television: Technology and Cultural Form*, London, Fontana.

Williams R (1981) *Culture*, London, Fontana.

WIPO Magazine (2006) January-February.

Wright S (2001) *International Human Rights, Decolonisation and Globalisation: Becoming Human*, London, Routledge.

Yúdice G (2003) *The Expediency of Culture: Uses of Culture in the Global Era*, Durham, Duke UP.

Zuck J (2006) "IP and the Knowledge Commons: Lobbying and Advocacy II". Panel. The Politics and Ideology of Intellectual Property. Trans Atlantic Consumer Dialogue (TACD) Conference. 20 March.

Index

Note: numbers in brackets preceded by n are footnote numbers.